5 STEPS TO A 5

500

AP English Language Questions

to know by test day

Also in the 5 Steps Series:

5 Steps to a 5: AP English Language 2021
5 Steps to a 5: AP English Language 2021, Cross-Platform Prep Course

Also in the 500 AP Questions to Know by Test Day series:

5 Steps to a 5: 500 AP Biology Questions to Know by Test Day, Third Edition
5 Steps to a 5: 500 AP Calculus AB/BC Questions to Know by Test Day, Third Edition
5 Steps to a 5: 500 AP Chemistry Questions to Know by Test Day, Third Edition
5 Steps to a 5: 500 AP English Literature Questions to Know by Test Day, Third Edition
5 Steps to a 5: 500 AP Environmental Science Questions to Know by Test Day, Third Edition
5 Steps to a 5: 500 AP European History Questions to Know by Test Day, Third Edition
5 Steps to a 5: 500 AP Human Geography to Know by Test Day, Third Edition
5 Steps to a 5: 500 AP Microeconomics Questions to Know by Test Day, Third Edition
5 Steps to a 5: 500 AP Macroeconomics Questions to Know by Test Day, Third Edition
5 Steps to a 5: 500 AP Physics 1 Questions to Know by Test Day, Third Edition
5 Steps to a 5: 500 AP Physics C Questions to Know by Test Day
5 Steps to a 5: 500 AP Psychology Questions to Know by Test Day, Third Edition
5 Steps to a 5: 500 AP Statistics Questions to Know by Test Day, Third Edition
5 Steps to a 5: 500 AP U.S. Government & Politics Questions to Know by Test Day, Second Edition
5 Steps to a 5: 500 AP U.S. History Questions to Know by Test Day, Third Edition
5 Steps to a 5: 500 AP World History Questions to Know by Test Day, Third Edition

5 STEPS TO A 5

500
AP English Language
Questions

to know by test day

THIRD EDITION

Allyson Ambrose

New York   Chicago   San Francisco   Athens   London   Madrid
Mexico City   Milan   New Delhi   Singapore   Sydney   Toronto

1 2 3 4 5 6 7 8 9   LCR   26 25 24 23 22 21

ISBN   978-1-260-47476-3
MHID   1-260-47476-3

e-ISBN   978-1-260-47475-6
e-MHID   1-260-47475-5

CONTENTS

PREFACE

The goal of this book is to provide passages and multiple-choice questions for you to become a skilled close reader who will have success on the AP English Language and Composition exam. By practicing your close-reading skills, you can become the type of reader who is able to think like a writer, one who understands that writers make many choices that depend on the purposes of their texts. The questions in this book will help you put yourself in the mind of a writer who thoughtfully chooses which words to use, what sentence types, what rhetorical techniques, what structure, what tone, etc. If you work through these passages and questions, I am confident you will do well on the exam.

Throughout my years of teaching AP English Language, I have asked my students what was most difficult about the exam and with what they would have liked more practice. Without fail, each year the answer is older texts and more multiple-choice questions. Because of their feedback, that is what this book provides—older texts (some from as early as the 1500s) and lots of multiple-choice questions—five hundred, to be exact! You can use this book as extra practice before the exam, perhaps in those last weeks or months, to feel and be well prepared.

This book is organized into ten chapters, six based on genre and four based on time period. Each chapter is set up like one multiple-choice section of the exam, with five passages and a total of fifty questions. Give yourself one hour to do one chapter, and you can practice your timing along with your close-reading skills.

The wonderful thing about practicing your close-reading skills is that these skills also translate to improved writing skills. Working through these chapters will help you analyze passages for their purposes and the techniques that achieve those purposes. This is the same process that you will need to follow for the rhetorical analysis essay on the exam. Working through these chapters will also help you to think like a writer and to understand the choices writers make. This understanding of writers' choices also will bring you success on the essay portion, which requires you to make choices and to think about your purpose and the best ways to achieve it. These skills are also crucial to your success in college.

I wish you success on the exam and beyond, and I'm confident that by working through this book you will be ready to meet the challenges of the AP English Language and Composition exam.

This newest edition of the book includes twenty writing passages in which you'll be asked to think like a writer and ask yourself how best to improve a draft. These composition questions mirror the types of questions now being asked on the exam. Each chapter will still function as a full multiple-choice section of the exam, with a combination of reading and writing questions to be completed in one hour.

Thank you to Dan Ambrose, whose continued love and support helped me to write this book. And thank you to my colleagues, whose professional support and faith in me have been invaluable. I'd also like to thank all of my past and current students; they make my work a joy and constantly delight me with their insight, diligence, and humor. Lastly, thank you to John Ambrose III, Dr. John Ambrose, Dan Ambrose, Julie Leventhal, and Christine Kingsley for their sharing of original writings for the composition questions, and thanks to Joan Sklover for the spinach quiche recipe!

ABOUT THE AUTHOR

Allyson L. Ambrose has taught AP English Language and Composition for more than a decade. She is a National Board certified teacher and a teacher of English language arts. A teacher leader, Allyson has written curricula, facilitated professional development workshops, and mentored teachers of AP English Language and Composition. Due in large part to Allyson's instructional leadership, more than 90 percent of students at her school taking the AP English Language and Composition exam over the past three years have earned at least a 3 on the exam, and more than 50 percent have earned at least a 4. Allyson has also been a College Board SAT essay reader. Allyson has now been teaching AP English Language and Composition for more than 15 years and serves as an assistant principal of English at a large New York City high school where she continues to teach the course while training others to teach it. Her passion for scholarship and commitment to education make her a leading pedagogue in the field of English language arts education.

INTRODUCTION

Congratulations! You've taken a big step toward AP success by purchasing *5 Steps to a 5: 500 AP English Language Questions to Know by Test Day*. We are here to help you take the next step and score high on your AP exam so you can earn college credits and get into the college or university of your choice.

This book gives you 500 AP-style multiple-choice questions that cover all the most essential course material. Each question has a detailed answer explanation. These questions will give you valuable independent practice to supplement your regular textbook and the groundwork you are already doing in your AP classroom.

This and the other books in this series were written by expert AP teachers who know your exam inside out and can identify the crucial exam information as well as questions that are most likely to appear on the exam.

You might be the kind of student who takes several AP courses and needs to study extra questions a few weeks before the exam for a final review. Or you might be the kind of student who puts off preparing until the last weeks before the exam. No matter what your preparation style is, you will surely benefit from reviewing these 500 questions, which closely parallel the content, format, and degree of difficulty of the questions on the actual AP exam. These questions and their answer explanations are the ideal last-minute study tool for those final few weeks before the test.

Remember the old saying "Practice makes perfect." If you practice with all the questions and answers in this book, we are certain you will build the skills and confidence needed to do great on the exam. Good luck!

—Editors of McGraw-Hill Education

Diagnostic Quiz

GETTING STARTED: THE DIAGNOSTIC QUIZ

The following passages and questions are like those you will encounter in this book. These questions will help you test your understanding of the concepts presented on the AP exam and give you an idea of where you need to focus your attention as you prepare. Unlike the AP exam, this quiz only has multiple-choice questions. For each question, simply circle the letter of your choice. Once you are done with the exam, check your work against the given answers, which will suggest similar passages in this book that you can use for additional practice.

Good luck!

DIAGNOSTIC QUIZ QUESTIONS

Passage A: Susan B. Anthony, *On Women's Right to Vote*

Friends and fellow citizens: I stand before you tonight under indictment for the alleged crime of having voted at the last presidential election, without having a lawful right to vote. It shall be my work this evening to prove to you that in thus voting, I not only committed no crime, but, instead, simply exercised my citizen's rights, guaranteed to me and all United States citizens   5
by the National Constitution, beyond the power of any state to deny.

The preamble of the Federal Constitution says:

"We, the people of the United States, in order to form a more perfect union, establish justice, insure domestic tranquillity, provide for the common defense, promote the general welfare, and secure the bless-   10
ings of liberty to ourselves and our posterity, do ordain and establish this Constitution for the United States of America."

It was we, the people; not we, the white male citizens; nor yet we, the male citizens; but we, the whole people, who formed the Union. And we formed it, not to give the blessings of liberty, but to secure them; not to the   15
half of ourselves and the half of our posterity, but to the whole people—women as well as men. And it is a downright mockery to talk to women of their enjoyment of the blessings of liberty while they are denied the use of the only means of securing them provided by this democratic-republican government—the ballot.   20

For any state to make sex a qualification that must ever result in the disfranchisement of one entire half of the people, is to pass a bill of attainder[1] or an ex post facto law,[2] and is therefore a violation of the supreme law of the land. By it the blessings of liberty are forever withheld from women and their female posterity.   25

To them this government has no just powers derived from the consent of the governed. To them this government is not a democracy. It is not a republic. It is an odious aristocracy; a hateful oligarchy of sex; the most hateful aristocracy ever established on the face of the globe; an oligarchy of wealth, where the rich govern the poor. An oligarchy of learning, where   30

---

1. This is an act of a legislature declaring a person or group of persons guilty of some crime and punishing them, often without a trial.

2. This is a law that retroactively changes the legal consequences of actions that were committed, or relationships that existed, before the enactment of the law.

the educated govern the ignorant, or even an oligarchy of race, where the Saxon rules the African, might be endured; but this oligarchy of sex, which makes father, brothers, husband, sons, the oligarchs over the mother and sisters, the wife and daughters, of every household—which ordains all men sovereigns, all women subjects, carries dissension, discord, and rebellion 35 into every home of the nation.

Webster,[3] Worcester,[4] and Bouvier[5] all define a citizen to be a person in the United States, entitled to vote and hold office.

The only question left to be settled now is: Are women persons? And I hardly believe any of our opponents will have the hardihood to say they 40 are not. Being persons, then, women are citizens; and no state has a right to make any law, or to enforce any old law, that shall abridge their privileges or immunities. Hence, every discrimination against women in the constitutions and laws of the several states is today null and void, precisely as is every one against Negroes.   45

3. Noah Webster, Jr. (1758–1843) was an American lexicographer, textbook pioneer, English-language spelling reformer, political writer, editor, and prolific author.

4. Joseph Emerson Worcester (1784–1865) was an American lexicographer who was the chief competitor to Noah Webster of *Webster's Dictionary* in the mid-nineteenth century. Worcester's dictionaries focused on traditional pronunciation and spelling, unlike Noah Webster's attempts to Americanize words.

5. John Bouvier (1787–1851) was an American jurist and legal lexicographer. He was recorder of Philadelphia in 1836, and from 1838 until his death was an associate justice of the court of criminal sessions in that city. He was best known, however, for his able legal writings.

1. The overall purpose of the passage is to:
   (A) defend the speaker's right to vote
   (B) defend the speaker after breaking the law by voting illegally
   (C) defend the speaker's definition of citizen
   (D) defend all disenfranchised people
   (E) defend women's right to vote

2. Most of the argument depends on the definition of the word:
   (A) rights
   (B) lawful
   (C) liberty
   (D) citizen
   (E) discrimination

3. The speaker quotes the Constitution in lines 8 to 12 in order to:
   (A) define "we" to include all people to make her argument for women's right to vote
   (B) refute the Founding Fathers' claim of establishing justice
   (C) prove that the Constitution is outdated and must be revised to include all people
   (D) assert that the government is incapable of securing the blessings of liberty
   (E) argue that government has no place in domestic issues

4. The tone of the sentence that begins, "And it is a downright mockery . . ." (lines 17–20) can best be described as:
   (A) confused disbelief
   (B) righteous indignation
   (C) mock surprise
   (D) aloof detachment
   (E) casual concern

5. The word "posterity," as used in line 25, most nearly means:
   (A) citizens
   (B) family members
   (C) community
   (D) future generations
   (E) peers

6. In lines 28–32, the speaker argues that the American government privileges people based on all of the following *except*:
   (A) sex
   (B) citizenship
   (C) wealth
   (D) education
   (E) race

7. According to lines 32–36, what makes women not having the right to vote so horrible is that:
   (A) it allows fathers and mothers to rule cruelly over their children
   (B) it privileges the young over the old
   (C) it forces women into stereotypical gender roles
   (D) it brings divisiveness into the home
   (E) it applies only to nuclear families

8. The final paragraph (lines 39–45) uses syllogism, or deductive reasoning, to make the claim that:
   (A) since women are people, they are citizens, and they should have the right to vote
   (B) states retain the right to make their own laws
   (C) African Americans and women do not suffer the same types of injustices
   (D) old laws must be reviewed periodically and revised as necessary
   (E) some opponents to women's suffrage have a hard time with the issue

9. Footnotes 1 and 2 provide:
   (A) translations
   (B) examples of legal precedence
   (C) citations for evidence provided
   (D) definitions of legal terms
   (E) refutations for claims made in the quoted material

10. Footnotes 3 through 5 show Webster, Worcester, and Bouvier to be all of the following *except*:
    (A) American
    (B) living in the 18th and 19th centuries
    (C) lexicographers
    (D) writers
    (E) politicians

Passage B: *The Importance of Gettysburg Draft*

(1) The Confederacy's Army of Northern Virginia pushed into Northern territory. (2) The army's commander, General Robert E. Lee, believed an invasion of the North—which had been largely exempt from the ravages of war on an up-close and personal scale—would turn the tide of Northern public opinion against continuation of the war. (3) General George Meade, commanding the Union's Army of the Potomac, moved to intercept Lee.

(4) Lee appeared to have the upper hand at first because Meade retreated throughout the first day of the confrontation, but the Union wisely fell back onto easily defended higher ground. (5) On the second day of the battle, Lee threw attack after attack at various points on the Union line, only to be thwarted each time. (6) On the third and final day, Lee ignored the advice of his most trusted advisor, General James Longstreet, who believed the Union positions were too strong to be overridden. (7) Instead, Lee concentrated a massive strike on the center of the Union line. (8) As Longstreet predicted, the assault was a costly failure.

(9) For several reasons, historians consider the Battle of Gettysburg to be the most important clash of the American Civil War. (10) First, prior to Gettysburg, the Confederacy was ascendant, winning virtually all major battles in the eastern theater of the war. (11) The Battle of Gettysburg was the true turning point of the war. (12) Next, the decisive Union victory chased a badly wounded Army of Northern Virginia back into Southern territory for good. (13) This Confederate battlefield fiasco splintered the "aura of invincibility" surrounding the bold and audacious Lee.

11. The writer wants to add an introductory phrase to the first sentence that orients the audience by providing contextual information. Which of the following phrases best accomplishes this goal if added at the beginning of sentence 1?

(A) <u>In the early summer of 1863,</u> the Confederacy's Army of Northern Virginia pushed into Northern territory.

(B) <u>Sometime during the Civil War,</u> the Confederacy's Army of Northern Virginia pushed into Northern territory.

(C) <u>In the 19th century,</u> the Confederacy's Army of Northern Virginia pushed into Northern territory.

(D) <u>In the second half of the 1800s,</u> the Confederacy's Army of Northern Virginia pushed into Northern territory.

(E) <u>Before the famous Battle of Gettysburg,</u> the Confederacy's Army of Northern Virginia pushed into Northern territory.

12. The writer would like to add the following sentence to paragraph 1:

    The two armies met at Gettysburg, Pennsylvania, resulting in a three-day engagement that remains the largest battle ever fought in the Western Hemisphere.

    What would be the most effective placement for this sentence?
    (A) Before sentence 1
    (B) Before sentence 2
    (C) Before sentence 3
    (D) After sentence 3
    (E) Left out completely

13. The author would like a transition that shows the sequencing of events at the beginning of sentence 5 (reproduced below):

    <u>*On the second day of the battle*</u>*, Lee threw attack after attack at various points on the Union line, only to be thwarted each time.*

    Which of the following transitions would work best for the underlined portion of this sentence?
    (A) as it is now
    (B) First
    (C) Secondly
    (D) Then
    (E) Next

14. The author would like a transition that shows the sequencing of events at the beginning of sentence 6 (reproduced below):

    <u>*On the third and final day*</u>*, Lee ignored the advice of his most trusted advisor, General James Longstreet, who believed the Union positions were too strong to be overridden.*

    Which of the following transitions would work best for the underlined portion of this sentence?
    (A) as it is now
    (B) After some time passed,
    (C) Despite knowing better,
    (D) As a result,
    (E) Surprisingly,

15. The writer would like to begin sentence 7 (reproduced below) by showing readers that Lee did not listen to his most trusted advisor when deciding to launch a massive strike on the center of the Union line.

> *Instead, Lee concentrated a massive strike on the center of the Union line.*

Which version of the underlined portion of the sentence best meets the writer's needs while avoiding redundancy and repetition?

(A) as it is now

(B) Instead of listening to his most trusted advisor,

(C) Instead of listening to General James Longstreet,

(D) Ignoring those who believed the Union positions were too strong to be overridden,

(E) Instead of listening to wise advice and choosing to do as he pleased,

16. The writer is considering adding the following underlined information into sentence 7.

> *Instead, Lee concentrated a massive strike—the famous "Pickett's Charge"—on the center of the Union line.*

Should the writer make this addition to sentence 7?

(A) No, because it makes the sentence incorrect and wordy.

(B) No, because only historians would need to know that specific information.

(C) No, because it interrupts the flow of the sentence and the paragraph.

(D) Yes, because it offers information that may be interesting, known, or useful to readers.

(E) Yes, because it would be difficult to understand this passage without knowing the correct term for this strike.

17. Which of the following sentences in the passage can best be described as the writer's thesis statement?

    (A) The Army's commander, General Robert E. Lee, believed an invasion of the North—which had been largely exempt from the ravages of war on an up-close and personal scale—would turn the tide of Northern public opinion against continuation of the war.

    (B) General George Meade, commanding the Union's Army of the Potomac, moved to intercept Lee.

    (C) Lee appeared to have the upper hand at first because Meade retreated throughout the first day of the confrontation, but the Union wisely fell back onto easily defended higher ground.

    (D) As Longstreet predicted, the assault was a costly failure.

    (E) For several reasons, historians consider the Battle of Gettysburg to be the most important clash of the American Civil War.

18. The writer is hoping to include a transition that will connect sentences 10 and 11 at the beginning of sentence 11 by showing a cause-and-effect relationship. Which version of the underlined portion of sentence 11 will best meet the writer's needs?

    (A) However, the Battle of Gettysburg was the true turning point of the war.

    (B) Nevertheless, the Battle of Gettysburg was the true turning point of the war.

    (C) Therefore, the Battle of Gettysburg was the true turning point of the war.

    (D) Secondly, the Battle of Gettysburg was the true turning point of the war.

    (E) Then, the Battle of Gettysburg was the true turning point of the war.

19. The writer is considering adding the following sentence after sentence 12 in order to provide more support for the claim that the Battle of Gettysburg was a major turning point:

    In addition, the verdict dashed Southern hopes for formal recognition of the Confederacy by European powers, many of whom had valuable trade relationships with the South.

    Should the writer make this addition after sentence 12?
    (A) No, because it makes the focus on the global, not national, impact.
    (B) No, because only historians would be interested in that level of detail.
    (C) Yes, because it offers more evidence of how decisive this battle was by providing information of another major impact.
    (D) Yes, because it would be impossible to understand how the Battle of Gettysburg unfolded without it.
    (E) Yes, because this text is only suitable for historians and scholars of the Civil War.

20. The writer is hoping to include a concluding transition at the beginning of sentence 13 that will end the paragraph and passage. Which version of the underlined portion of sentence 13 will best meet the writer's needs?
    (A) <u>Conclusively,</u> this Confederate battlefield fiasco splintered the "aura of invincibility" surrounding the bold and audacious Lee.
    (B) <u>Finally,</u> this Confederate battlefield fiasco splintered the "aura of invincibility" surrounding the bold and audacious Lee.
    (C) <u>Without further hesitation,</u> this Confederate battlefield fiasco splintered the "aura of invincibility" surrounding the bold and audacious Lee.
    (D) <u>At last,</u> this Confederate battlefield fiasco splintered the "aura of invincibility" surrounding the bold and audacious Lee.
    (E) <u>As hoped,</u> this Confederate battlefield fiasco splintered the "aura of invincibility" surrounding the bold and audacious Lee.

DIAGNOSTIC QUIZ ANSWERS

Passage A

1. (E) While the speaker does defend her own right to vote, defend herself for voting illegally, and define "citizen" to include all American people, none of those purposes cover the whole passage, which is a speech to defend women's right to vote. While she does speak about African Americans, defining the purpose as to defend all disenfranchised people is too broad for the scope of this passage.

2. (D) Most of the argument for women's right to vote is based on defining "citizens" to include women, who are also people, and which should guarantee them the right to vote.

3. (A) The purpose of quoting the Constitution is to define "we" as all people, so that she can go on to argue that of course women are people and should therefore be given the right to vote as US citizens.

4. (B) The speaker's use of the words "downright mockery" to describe the discussion of women's liberty while disallowing them the right to vote shows her righteous indignation or justified anger over injustice.

5. (D) "Posterity" most nearly means future generations. The statement is that liberty is withheld from women and their future female generations through their not being allowed to vote.

6. (B) The speaker calls the American government an oligarchy, or a small group of people who together govern a nation, based on sex, wealth, education, and race. While she discusses the meaning of a citizen in other places in the speech, citizenship is not discussed in these lines.

7. (D) She argues that this privileging of men over women brings "dissension, discord, and rebellion" into home since it pits men versus women under the same roof, which is worse than other differences.

8. (A) The deductive reasoning moves from arguing that people have the right to vote, to women are people, and therefore women have the right to vote. The movement is from a major premise to a minor premise and then to a conclusion.

9. (D) Both a bill of attainder and an ex post facto law are legal terms for which the footnotes provide definitions. While the footnote for ex post facto provides a translation, the first does not.

10. (E) While Webster is described as a political writer and Bouvier as an associate justice of the court, Worcester is only described as an American lexicographer who wrote a dictionary. The men are not all politicians.

Passage B

11. **(A)** The best introductory phrase for providing contextual information is "In the early summer of 1863," because it provides the most specific details about the timing of the battle and, as a result, provides the most useful information about the timing of the battle.

12. **(D)** The best place for the sentence is after sentence 3 because the two armies have been introduced, and it can serve as a unifying sentence for the rest of the passage.

13. **(A)** The phrase "On the second day of the battle" is the most effective sequencing transition because it not only counts the elements in the sentence, but it adds the more specific information that it is the second day of the battle.

14. **(A)** The phrase "On the third and final day" is the most effective sequencing transition because it provides the needed details that this day is both the third and last day of the battle. The other options are either too general or provide information that is related to cause and effect, not timing.

15. **(A)** The single word "instead" is most effective in showing that Lee did not listen to the advice of Longstreet. The other options repeat much of what is said in the sentence before and add extra, unnecessary information to the sentence and paragraph.

16. **(D)** The author should include this information because readers may have heard the term used before, and it could add to their understanding of the material. The information may be of interest or use, and its inclusion does not detract from the paragraph.

17. **(E)** The sentence, "For several reasons, historians consider the Battle of Gettysburg to be the most important clash of the American Civil War" can best be described as the writer's thesis statement because this sentence provides an arguable claim that the Battle of Gettysburg is considered the most important of the Civil War. In addition, the details of the passage can all be linked to supporting this major claim.

18. **(C)** The inclusion of "therefore" at the beginning of sentence 11 is useful in making clear that because the Confederacy had been winning the major battles, this decisive victory by the Union Army resulted in a major change, marking it as a "true turning point." "However" and "nevertheless" show a change in direction, while "secondly" and "then" are used to communicate sequence rather than causation.

19. **(C)** The addition of the sentence offers more evidence to support that claim that the Battle of Gettysburg was a major turning point of the Civil War by illustrating that Europe would not be recognizing the Confederacy after this loss, which adds another level to its importance.

20. **(B)** The choice of "finally" is the best choice of transition for this last sentence, communicating this as the concluding idea of both the paragraph and passage. The choices of "at last" and "as hoped" communicate a wish on the part of the writer that is not suited to the writer's needs to wrap up the objective narration of the Battle of Gettysburg and to support the claim that this battle was a major turning point in the Civil War.

The diagnostic quiz is equivalent to a 19th-century reading with draft passage. Similar passage questions can be found in Chapter 9: 19th Century with Draft Passages.

CHAPTER 1

Autobiographers and Diarists with Draft Passages

Passage 1a: Thomas De Quincey, *Confessions of an English Opium-Eater*

I here present you, courteous reader, with the record of a remarkable period in my life: according to my application of it, I trust that it will prove not merely an interesting record, but in a considerable degree useful and instructive. In that hope it is that I have drawn it up; and that must be my apology for breaking through that delicate and honourable reserve which, for the 5 most part, restrains us from the public exposure of our own errors and infirmities. Nothing, indeed, is more revolting to English feelings than the spectacle of a human being obtruding on our notice his moral ulcers or scars, and tearing away that "decent drapery" which time or indulgence to human frailty may have drawn over them; accordingly, the greater part of 10 our confessions (that is, spontaneous and extra-judicial confessions) proceed from demireps, adventurers, or swindlers: and for any such acts of gratuitous self-humiliation from those who can be supposed in sympathy with the decent and self-respecting part of society, we must look to French literature, or to that part of the German which is tainted with the spurious 15 and defective sensibility of the French. All this I feel so forcibly, and so nervously am I alive to reproach of this tendency, that I have for many months hesitated about the propriety of allowing this or any part of my narrative to come before the public eye until after my death (when, for many reasons, the whole will be published); and it is not without an anxious review of the 20 reasons for and against this step that I have at last concluded on taking it.

Guilt and misery shrink, by a natural instinct, from public notice: they court privacy and solitude: and even in their choice of a grave will sometimes sequester themselves from the general population of the churchyard,

as if declining to claim fellowship with the great family of man, and wishing   25
(in the affecting language of Mr. Wordsworth):

> Humbly to express
> A penitential loneliness.

It is well, upon the whole, and for the interest of us all, that it should
be so: nor would I willingly in my own person manifest a disregard of such   30
salutary feelings, nor in act or word do anything to weaken them; but, on
the one hand, as my self-accusation does not amount to a confession of
guilt, so, on the other, it is possible that, if it did, the benefit resulting to
others from the record of an experience purchased at so heavy a price might
compensate, by a vast overbalance, for any violence done to the feelings I   35
have noticed, and justify a breach of the general rule. Infirmity and misery
do not of necessity imply guilt. They approach or recede from shades of that
dark alliance, in proportion to the probable motives and prospects of the
offender, and the palliations, known or secret, of the offence; in proportion
as the temptations to it were potent from the first, and the resistance to it,   40
in act or in effort, was earnest to the last. For my own part, without breach
of truth or modesty, I may affirm that my life has been, on the whole, the
life of a philosopher: from my birth I was made an intellectual creature, and
intellectual in the highest sense my pursuits and pleasures have been, even
from my schoolboy days. If opium-eating be a sensual pleasure, and if I am   45
bound to confess that I have indulged in it to an excess not yet recorded of
any other man, it is no less true that I have struggled against this fascinating
enthrallment with a religious zeal, and have at length accomplished what
I never yet heard attributed to any other man—have untwisted, almost to
its final links, the accursed chain which fettered me. Such a self-conquest   50
may reasonably be set off in counterbalance to any kind or degree of
self-indulgence. Not to insist that in my case the self-conquest was unques-
tionable, the self-indulgence open to doubts of casuistry, according as that
name shall be extended to acts aiming at the bare relief of pain, or shall be
restricted to such as aim at the excitement of positive pleasure.   55

1. According to the writer, the purpose of his autobiography is to:
   (A) teach
   (B) inform
   (C) persuade
   (D) entertain
   (E) refute

2. The first paragraph of the passage (lines 1–21) serves as:
   (A) a reasoned introduction to an argument
   (B) an explanation of the author's reservations about breaking English decorum
   (C) a scathing critique of French literature
   (D) an anecdote that helps the author exemplify his main idea
   (E) an apology to readers who have criticized his work

3. In the first paragraph (lines 1–21), the writer uses the diction of illness to describe moral failings, with all of the following terms *except*:
   (A) infirmities
   (B) ulcers
   (C) scars
   (D) indulgence
   (E) frailty

4. In the sentence "Nothing, indeed, is more revolting to English feelings than the spectacle of a human being obtruding on our notice his moral ulcers or scars, and tearing away that 'decent drapery' which time or indulgence to human frailty may have drawn over them . . . ", (lines 7–10) the metaphor of "decent drapery" serves to:
   (A) compare the hiding of "moral ulcers or scars" to the use of drapery to block the vision of outsiders with a thick fabric
   (B) offer sensory images of thick drapery
   (C) personify time as something that reveals our faults
   (D) make an indirect comparison between drapery and human frailty
   (E) symbolize the disgust of the English

5. In line 11, the pronoun "our" refers to:
   (A) demireps
   (B) adventurers
   (C) swindlers
   (D) human beings
   (E) the English

6. In context, the word "propriety" in line 18 most nearly means:
   (A) immorality
   (B) decency
   (C) popularity
   (D) benefit
   (E) profitability

7. In paragraph two (lines 22–26), guilt and misery are personified, through all of the terms *except*:
   (A) shrink
   (B) instinct
   (C) notice
   (D) court
   (E) sequester

8. The primary rhetorical function of the sentence "Infirmity and misery do not of necessity imply guilt" (lines 36–37) is to:
   (A) refute the conditional claim made in the line before
   (B) present the major claim of the last paragraph
   (C) introduce a claim to be defended with evidence in the following lines
   (D) elucidate the underlying assumption of the paragraph
   (E) provide evidence to support the first sentence of the paragraph

9. The second half of the last paragraph, beginning with the sentence "If opium-eating be a sensual pleasure, and if I am bound to confess that I have indulged in it to an excess not yet recorded of any other man, it is no less true that I have struggled against this fascinating enthrallment with a religious zeal . . ." (lines 45–55) contributes to the sense that the writer looks on his own past with:
   (A) guilt
   (B) ambivalence
   (C) paranoia
   (D) fascination
   (E) shame

10. The writer's tone in this passage can best be described as:

(A) apologetic

(B) forthright

(C) indifferent

(D) wry

(E) effusive

Passage 1b: *Perfume Classification Draft*

(1) All together, there are five perfume concentrations, which range from approximately 1–40 percent of perfume oil per bottle. (2) Perfume, or fragrance, oils can be naturally or synthetically derived and are added to water and/or alcohol to make the bottle of perfume that can then be sprayed and enjoyed.

(3) The lightest concentration of perfume oil is present in "eau fraiche" formulations, which have between 1 and 2 percent of perfume oil per bottle. (4) These formulations are meant to be a light scent and generally don't last more than an hour or so. (5) Eau fraiche formulations are often marketed as "body mists" and are diluted with mostly water. (6) Next, "eau de cologne," often referred to as just "cologne," has approximately 2–4 percent perfume oil. (7) A cologne will last perhaps two hours or so on the skin.

(8) "Eau de toilette" has a fragrance concentration between 5 and 15 percent. (9) An eau de toilette can last between two and three hours and is a popular choice for many people looking for a medium-strength scent with average longevity. (10) Those seeking a stronger scent will opt for an "eau de parfum," or EDP, consisting of 15–20 percent fragrance oils per bottle. (11) An EDP can last four to five hours on the skin, and this formulation is often referred to as just "perfume." (12) In conclusion, "parfum," or "extrait," is the strongest of the scent types, with 20–40 percent fragrance oils and a longevity of six to eight hours.

(13) The types of scents available are more varied than just a choice between cologne and perfume, and fragrances don't have to be classified by genders. (14) Many men wear perfume, and many women wear cologne.

11. Which of the following sentences, if placed before sentence 1, would both capture the audience's interest and provide the most effective introduction to the topic of the passage?

    (A) Perfume has been used by women for centuries and is a traditional form of feminine expression.

    (B) Although most people believe "cologne" is for men and "perfume" is for women, these terms are actually used to describe the amount of perfume oil present in each bottle of fragrance.

    (C) Walking around your local department store, it is easy to get overwhelmed by all of the fragrance options available to consumers.

    (D) The most popular types of fragrance for women include floral and aromatic scents.

    (E) Most men prefer citrus scents that are refreshing and best enjoyed during warmer months.

12. Should the writer keep this sentence after sentence 1?

    Perfume, or fragrance, oils can be naturally or synthetically derived and are added to water and/or alcohol to make the bottle of perfume that can then be sprayed and enjoyed.

    (A) No, because it changes the topic from natural to synthetic ingredients

    (B) No, because it does not include relevant information for the topic

    (C) No, because it makes the first paragraph longer than necessary

    (D) Yes, because it offers information that is important to understanding the classification that follows

    (E) Yes, because it adds a personal opinion that develops the writer's voice

13. Which of the following sentences in the passage can best be described as the writer's thesis statement?

(A) All together, there are five perfume concentrations, which range from approximately 1–40 percent of perfume oil per bottle.

(B) Perfume, or fragrance, oils can be naturally or synthetically derived and are added to water and/or alcohol to make the bottle of perfume that can then be sprayed and enjoyed.

(C) The lightest concentration of perfume oil is present in "eau fraiche" formulations, which have between 1 and 2 percent of perfume oil per bottle.

(D) Next, the "eau de cologne," often referred to as just "cologne," has approximately 2–4 percent perfume oil.

(E) Finally, "parfum," or "extrait," is the strongest of the scent types, with 20–40 percent fragrance oils and a longevity of six to eight hours.

14. The writer would like to change the transition at the beginning of sentence 6 (reproduced below):

> *Next*, *"eau de cologne," often referred to as just "cologne," has approximately 2–4 percent perfume oil.*

Which of the following words best serves as a transition between the ideas expressed in sentences 5 and 6 and should replace the underlined portion above?

(A) However

(B) Nevertheless

(C) Ironically

(D) Additionally

(E) Surprisingly

15. Which of the following versions of sentence 8 (reproduced below) best previews the information provided in paragraph 3?

    "Eau de toilette" has a fragrance concentration between 5 and 15 percent.

    (A) as it is now
    (B) "Eau de toilette," the middle point in terms of strength and longevity and the least potent of the next three types of perfume described, has a fragrance concentration between 5 and 15 percent.
    (C) The best of all the fragrance types described, "eau de toilette" has a fragrance concentration between 5 and 15 percent.
    (D) Much superior to eau fraiche and eau de cologne, "eau de toilette" has a fragrance concentration between 5 and 15 percent.
    (E) Often preferred over its less potent counterparts, "eau de toilette" has a fragrance concentration between 5 and 15 percent.

16. In the underlined portion of sentence 9 (reproduced below), the writer wants to use a neutral tone when describing the fragrance concentration levels present in an eau de toilette.

    An eau de toilette can last between two and three hours and is a popular choice for many people looking for a medium-strength scent with average longevity.

    Which of the following choices best accomplishes this goal?

    (A) as it is now
    (B) the best
    (C) an ill-informed
    (D) the only
    (E) a superior

17. The writer would like to change the transition at the beginning of sentence 12 (reproduced below):

    In conclusion, "parfum," or "extrait," is the strongest of the scent types, with 20–40 percent fragrance oils and a longevity of six to eight hours.

    Which of the following words best serves as a transition between the ideas expressed in the earlier sentences and this sentence and should replace the underlined portion above?
    (A) Fifthly
    (B) Finally
    (C) Furthermore
    (D) Moreover
    (E) Therefore

18. In the fourth paragraph (sentences 13–14), the writer wants to provide further evidence to rebut the claim that nowadays men only wear cologne, and women only wear perfume. Which of the following pieces of evidence from fragrance expert Sue Phillips would best achieve this purpose?
    (A) "The trend over the past few years was [that everyone was making perfumes; first] it was the designers, then the celebrities, and suddenly every celebrity had a fragrance."
    (B) "Men started to get grooming essentials, so they had aftershave, cologne, deodorant, and so on."
    (C) "So the word 'perfume' is now becoming more generic. It doesn't apply to feminine anymore."
    (D) "It wasn't called 'perfume' for men, it was 'cologne.'"
    (E) "American men were always seen slapping on cologne as an aftershave."

19. The writer wants to provide descriptive details that appeal to the audience's emotions and experiences by adding one of the following sentences after sentence 13. Which version would best fit the writer's desired effect?

    (A) I, personally, long ago abandoned the idea that I can only wear floral, sweet, or fruity perfume as a woman.

    (B) I remember my grandmother's beautiful perfume collection catching the evening light on her dresser.

    (C) My father had a lovely cologne collection that he kept next to his shaving cream and old-fashioned, wooden-handled shaving brush.

    (D) Perfume is a deeply personal choice that should transport you to your own vivid memories of who you were or wildest imaginings of who you'd like to be.

    (E) It's important to honor the tradition of artistry that perfume has offered us through the ages.

20. The writer would like a sentence after sentence 14 that concludes the passage on classifying fragrance concentrations and keeps with the explanatory rather than evaluative purpose of categorizing scents. Which sentence is best suited to the purpose described?

    (A) It is clearly better to opt for the parfum, or extrait, because that formulation has both the highest concentration of fragrance and the best lasting power.

    (B) While there are many options, it is clear that men should choose traditional colognes, and women should stick with strong and appealing perfumes.

    (C) It goes without saying that the higher concentrations are superior to the too-light eau fraiche formulations.

    (D) While perhaps more expensive, always choose extrait when available in your desired scent.

    (E) People's choice of scent type depends on the strength, or projection, they're seeking and how long they want that scent to last on the skin.

Passage 1c: Benjamin Franklin, *The Autobiography of Benjamin Franklin*

It was about this time I conceiv'd the bold and arduous project of arriving at moral perfection. I wish'd to live without committing any fault at any time; I would conquer all that either natural inclination, custom, or company might lead me into. As I knew, or thought I knew, what was right and wrong, I did not see why I might not always do the one and avoid the 5 other. But I soon found I had undertaken a task of more difficulty than I had imagined. While my care was employ'd in guarding against one fault, I was often surprised by another; habit took the advantage of inattention; inclination was sometimes too strong for reason. I concluded, at length, that the mere speculative conviction that it was our interest to be completely 10 virtuous, was not sufficient to prevent our slipping; and that the contrary habits must be broken, and good ones acquired and established, before we can have any dependence on a steady, uniform rectitude of conduct. For this purpose I therefore contrived the following method.

In the various enumerations of the moral virtues I had met with in my 15 reading, I found the catalogue more or less numerous, as different writers included more or fewer ideas under the same name. Temperance, for example, was by some confined to eating and drinking, while by others it was extended to mean the moderating of every other pleasure, appetite, inclination, or passion, bodily or mental, even to our avarice and ambition. 20 I propos'd to myself, for the sake of clearness, to use rather more names, with fewer ideas annex'd to each, than a few names with more ideas; and I included under thirteen names of virtues all that at that time occurr'd to me as necessary or desirable, and annexed to each a short precept, which fully express'd the extent I gave to its meaning. 25

These names of virtues, with their precepts, were:

1. TEMPERANCE. Eat not to dullness; drink not to elevation.
2. SILENCE. Speak not but what may benefit others or yourself; avoid trifling conversation.
3. ORDER. Let all your things have their places; let each part of 30 your business have its time.
4. RESOLUTION. Resolve to perform what you ought; perform without fail what you resolve.
5. FRUGALITY. Make no expense but to do good to others or yourself; i.e., waste nothing. 35
6. INDUSTRY. Lose no time; be always employ'd in something useful; cut off all unnecessary actions.
7. SINCERITY. Use no hurtful deceit; think innocently and justly, and, if you speak, speak accordingly.
8. JUSTICE. Wrong none by doing injuries, or omitting the benefits 40 that are your duty.
9. MODERATION. Avoid extremes; forbear resenting injuries so much as you think they deserve.
10. CLEANLINESS. Tolerate no uncleanliness in body, cloaths, or habitation. 45

11. TRANQUILLITY. Be not disturbed at trifles, or at accidents common or unavoidable.
12. CHASTITY. Rarely use venery but for health or offspring, never to dullness, weakness, or the injury of your own or another's peace or reputation. 50
13. HUMILITY. Imitate Jesus and Socrates.

My intention being to acquire the habitude of all these virtues, I judg'd it would be well not to distract my attention by attempting the whole at once, but to fix it on one of them at a time; and, when I should be master of that, then to proceed to another, and so on, till I should have gone thro' 55 the thirteen; and, as the previous acquisition of some might facilitate the acquisition of certain others, I arrang'd them with that view, as they stand above. Temperance first, as it tends to procure that coolness and clearness of head, which is so necessary where constant vigilance was to be kept up, and guard maintained against the unremitting attraction of ancient habits, 60 and the force of perpetual temptations. This being acquir'd and establish'd, Silence would be more easy; and my desire being to gain knowledge at the same time that I improv'd in virtue, and considering that in conversation it was obtain'd rather by the use of the ears than of the tongue, and therefore wishing to break a habit I was getting into of prattling, punning, and jok- 65 ing, which only made me acceptable to trifling company, I gave Silence the second place. This and the next, Order, I expected would allow me more time for attending to my project and my studies. Resolution, once become habitual, would keep me firm in my endeavors to obtain all the subsequent virtues; Frugality and Industry freeing me from my remaining debt, and 70 producing affluence and independence, would make more easy the practice of Sincerity and Justice, etc., etc. Conceiving then, that, agreeably to the advice of Pythagoras in his Golden Verses[1], daily examination would be necessary, I contrived the following method for conducting that examination.

21. The main purpose of this passage is to:
    (A) argue for the impossibility of "arriving at moral perfection"
    (B) describe the writer's planned process of "arriving at moral perfection"
    (C) define the concept of "arriving at moral perfection"
    (D) analyze the effects of "arriving at moral perfection"
    (E) classify the ways of "arriving at moral perfection"

---

1. a collection of 71 moral exhortations, or lines addressed to urge someone to do something

22. In context, the word "rectitude" in line 13 most nearly means:
   (A) Consistent pattern
   (B) Continuous action
   (C) Morally correct behavior
   (D) Positive outlook
   (E) Ingrained custom

23. The lines "Temperance, for example, was by some confined to eating and drinking, while by others it was extended to mean the moderating of every other pleasure, appetite, inclination, or passion, bodily or mental, even to our avarice and ambition" (lines 17–20) serve all of the following functions *except*:
   (A) To illustrate the varied ways the virtues are defined by other writers
   (B) To define temperance in its many different meanings
   (C) To show Franklin's process of composing his list
   (D) To argue against the definition of temperance proposed by other writers
   (E) To make clear to the reader the reasons behind Franklin's decision making

24. In context, the word "precept" in line 24 most nearly means:
   (A) a definition of the virtue
   (B) an example of the virtue in action
   (C) an exception to the rules of the virtues
   (D) a particular course of action to follow the virtues
   (E) a preconceived notion about the virtue

25. The function of listing the virtues can best be described as:
   (A) Ranking them in importance
   (B) Comparing and contrasting them
   (C) Presenting them in their most logical order
   (D) Showing how many virtues must be followed
   (E) Disproving claims that there are fewer than thirteen virtues

26. The author would most likely agree with the following statements:
    (A) To remove faults, positive virtues must replace them
    (B) The listed virtues should come easily to people in civilized society
    (C) Religion must guide people in practicing each of the virtues
    (D) We must work with other people to practice the virtues
    (E) The sort of moral perfection described in the passage is infeasible

27. The speaker of the passage can best be characterized as someone who is:
    (A) disapproving
    (B) methodical
    (C) disinterested
    (D) unrealistic
    (E) judgmental

28. Franklin refers to The Golden Verses of Pythagoras as a model of:
    (A) Honesty
    (B) Productivity
    (C) Prudence
    (D) Reflection
    (E) Generosity

29. The style and organization of the passage can best be described as:
    (A) Allusive
    (B) Figurative
    (C) Systematic
    (D) Impressionistic
    (E) Circuitous

30. The tone of the passage as a whole can best be described as:
    (A) self-deprecating
    (B) resolved
    (C) bemused
    (D) reticent
    (E) irreverent

Passage 1d: *John Carpenter Draft*

(1) John Carpenter is widely considered to be one of the greatest horror-movie directors of all time. (2) He is best known for the landmark slasher film *Halloween*, which established the horror-movie blueprint for a generation. (3) Carpenter's directing credits also include such enduring chillers—spine-tingling and terrifying stories—as *The Thing*, *The Fog*, *Prince of Darkness*, and *In the Mouth of Madness*. (4) From the mid-1970s to the mid-1990s, Carpenter created one hit after another. (5) His films were derived from a wide range of sources—original stories, remakes of classic horror films, movie versions of horror novels, sequels to his own films, and so on.

(6) Initially, Carpenter's cinematic accomplishments extended beyond simply being a "slasher movie director." (7) First, he composed and performed most of his film's soundtracks, including the haunting and instantly recognizable score for *Halloween*. (8) Next, Carpenter's filmography contains highly regarded features in a variety of genres, including action (*Assault on Precinct 13* and *Escape from New York*), science fiction (*They Live* and *Starman*), and biography (the made-for-TV movie *Elvis*). (9) In addition, Carpenter appeared in front of the camera many times, working as an "extra" in many of his movies, and even taking a starring role in the horror/comedy anthology *Body Bags*.

(10) Now that Carpenter is retired from making the world's best horror movies, he continues to compose music (the *Lost Themes* albums), and he performs his pieces with a touring band.

31. Which of the following sentences can best be described as a thesis for the passage?

(A) John Carpenter is widely considered to be one of the greatest horror-movie directors of all time.

(B) He is best known for the landmark slasher film *Halloween*, which established the horror-movie blueprint for a generation.

(C) Carpenter's directing credits also include such enduring chillers—spine-tingling and terrifying stories—as *The Thing*, *The Fog*, *Prince of Darkness*, and *In the Mouth of Madness*.

(D) From the mid-1970s to the mid-1990s, Carpenter created one hit after another.

(E) His films were derived from a wide range of sources—original stories, remakes of classic horror films, movie versions of horror novels, sequels to his own films, and so on.

32. The writer wants to combine sentences 1 and 2 (reproduced below) into a single sentence.

> John Carpenter *is widely considered to be one of the greatest horror-movie directors of all time. He is best known for the landmark slasher film* Halloween, *which established the horror-movie blue-print for a generation.*

Which of the following revisions to the underlined portion of sentences 1 and 2 most effectively accomplishes this goal?

(A) is widely considered to be one of the greatest horror-movie directors of all time; he is best known for the landmark slasher film *Halloween*

(B) is widely considered to be one of the greatest horror-movie directors of all time, and he is best known for the landmark slasher film *Halloween*

(C) is widely considered to be one of the greatest horror-movie directors of all time, best known for the landmark slasher film *Halloween*

(D) is widely considered to be one of the greatest horror-movie directors of all time, is best known for the landmark slasher film *Halloween*

(E) is widely considered to be one of the greatest horror-movie directors of all time, who is best known for the landmark slasher film *Halloween*

33. In sentence 3 (reproduced below), the writer is considering deleting the underlined portion, adjusting the punctuation as necessary:

> Carpenter's directing credits also include such enduring chillers—spine-tingling and terrifying stories—as The Thing, The Fog, Prince of Darkness, and In the Mouth of Madness.

Should the writer keep or delete the underlined text?

(A) Keep it because it provides a necessary definition for the phrase "enduring chillers"

(B) Keep it because it adds to the writer's passionate tone about the subject

(C) Keep it because it helps specify the types of stories that will be listed

(D) Delete it because scary stories are not relevant to the topic or of interest to the reader

(E) Delete it because a definition of the phrases "enduring chillers" is not needed and it interrupts the flow of the sentence

34. The writer is considering adding the following sentence before sentence 5:

> For approximately two decades, Carpenter continued to release a series of highly successful movies.

Should the writer make this addition?

(A) Yes, because it emphasizes how long-lasting Carpenter's career has been

(B) Yes, because it clarifies how popular Carpenter's films have been to the reader

(C) No, because it contains inaccurate information that contradicts what came before it

(D) No, because it provides technical information that is not useful to those outside the film industry

(E) No, because it repeats what was stated in the sentence before and does not offer any new information

35. In sentence 5 (reproduced below), the writer wants to include relevant details to specify the types of sources used by Carpenter.

> *His films were derived from a wide range of sources—<u>original stories, remakes of classic horror films, movie versions of horror novels, sequels to his own films, and so on.</u>*

Which of the following versions of the underlined portion of sentence 5 best accomplishes this goal?

(A) as it is now
(B) <u>*Frankenstein, Dracula, The Wolfman,* and *The Creature from the Black Lagoon.*</u>
(C) <u>the hundreds of books that he read as a child and adolescent.</u>
(D) <u>the most surprising of these sources being his own sequels.</u>
(E) <u>most notably, his own original stories, created from his vivid imagination.</u>

36. In sentence 6 (reproduced below), the writer is considering which transitional word should be used to begin the sentence:

> *<u>Initially,</u> Carpenter's cinematic accomplishments extended beyond simply being a "slasher movie director."*

Which version of the underlined portion of the sentence provides the most appropriate transition for the content of the sentence?

(A) as it is now
(B) Accordingly
(C) Therefore
(D) However
(E) Consequently

37. Which of the following sentences *does not* serve as a specific example to support the claim that Carpenter is successful in many artistic endeavors and fields?

(A) Initially, Carpenter's cinematic accomplishments extended beyond simply being a "slasher movie director."

(B) First, he composed and performed most of his film's soundtracks, including the haunting and instantly recognizable score for *Halloween*.

(C) Next, Carpenter's filmography contains highly regarded features in a variety of genres, including action (*Assault on Precinct 13* and *Escape from New York*), science fiction (*They Live* and *Starman*), and biography (the made-for-TV movie *Elvis*).

(D) In addition, Carpenter appeared in front of the camera many times, working as an "extra" in many of his movies, and even taking a starring role in the horror/comedy anthology *Body Bags*.

(E) Now that Carpenter is retired from making movies, he continues to compose music (the *Lost Themes* albums), and he performs his pieces with a touring band.

38. The writer's choice of transitional words to begin sentences 7 through 10 ("first," "next," "in addition," and "now") contribute to his desired effect of organizing this portion of the passage by:

(A) Providing causes and effects
(B) Comparing similarities and differences
(C) Listing various examples
(D) Sequencing a narrative
(E) Defining "success"

39. In sentence 9 (reproduced below), which version of the underlined portion of the sentence best maintains the tone of the passage?

> *In addition, Carpenter appeared in front of the camera many times, working as an "extra" in many of his movies, and even taking a starring role* in the horror/comedy anthology Body Bags.

(A) as it is now
(B) hogging the spotlight
(C) flattering himself with a huge role
(D) ridiculously parading himself on stage
(E) honoring his esteemed position by gracing us with his presence

40. The writer wants to avoid expressing the argument of the passage in absolute terms. Which of the following changes should the writer make to sentence 10 (reproduced below) to achieve this goal?

> *Now that Carpenter is retired from making the world's best horror movies, he continues to compose music (the* Lost Themes *albums), and he performs his pieces with a touring band.*

(A) Remove "the world's"
(B) Remove "the world's best"
(C) Remove "the world's best horror"
(D) Add "some of" before "the world's best horror movies"
(E) Add "of all time" after "the world's best horror movies"

Passage 1e: John Henry Newman, *Apologia Pro Vita Sua*[1]

What shall be the special imputation, against which I shall throw myself in these pages, out of the thousand and one which my accuser directs upon me? I mean to confine myself to one, for there is only one about which I much care—the charge of untruthfulness. He may cast upon me as many other imputations as he pleases, and they may stick on me, as long as they 5
can, in the course of nature. They will fall to the ground in their season.

And indeed I think the same of the charge of untruthfulness, and I select it from the rest, not because it is more formidable, but because it is more serious. Like the rest, it may disfigure me for a time, but it will not stain: Archbishop Whately[2] used to say, "Throw dirt enough, and some will 10
stick;" well, will stick, but not stain. I think he used to mean "stain," and I do not agree with him. Some dirt sticks longer than other dirt; but no dirt is immortal. According to the old saying, Prævalebit Veritas[3]. There are virtues indeed, which the world is not fitted to judge about or to uphold, such as faith, hope, and charity: but it can judge about truthfulness; it can 15
judge about the natural virtues, and truthfulness is one of them. Natural virtues may also become supernatural; truthfulness is such; but that does not withdraw it from the jurisdiction of mankind at large. It may be more difficult in this or that particular case for men to take cognizance of it, as it may be difficult for the Court of Queen's Bench at Westminster[4] to try a 20

---

1. Latin for "Apology for his life"

2. an English rhetorician, logician, economist, academic and theologian

3. Latin for "truth will prevail"

4. In England, the Court of Queen's was the name of two courts. They were both senior courts of common law, with civil and criminal jurisdiction, and a jurisdiction to restrain unlawful actions by public authorities. The Court of Queen's Bench in England was abolished in 1875.

case fairly which took place in Hindoostan[5]; but that is a question of capacity, not of right. Mankind has the right to judge of truthfulness in the case of a Catholic, as in the case of a Protestant, of an Italian, or of a Chinese. I have never doubted, that in my hour, in God's hour, my avenger will appear, and the world will acquit me of untruthfulness, even though it be not while I live.

Still more confident am I of such eventual acquittal, seeing that my judges are my own countrymen. I think, indeed, Englishmen the most suspicious and touchy of mankind; I think them unreasonable and unjust in their seasons of excitement; but I had rather be an Englishman (as in fact I am) than belong to any other race under heaven. They are as generous, as they are hasty and burly; and their repentance for their injustice is greater than their sin.

[. . .] I have been treated by contemporary critics in this controversy with great fairness and gentleness, and I am grateful to them for it. However, the decision of the time and mode of my defence has been taken out of my hands; and I am thankful that it has been so. I am bound now as a duty to myself, to the Catholic cause, to the Catholic priesthood, to give account of myself without any delay, when I am so rudely and circumstantially charged with untruthfulness. I accept the challenge; I shall do my best to meet it, and I shall be content when I have done so.

41. The main purpose of the passage is to:
   (A) Extoll the virtue of truthfulness
   (B) Criticize his accuser for making false charges
   (C) Praise the English sentiment that upholds truthfulness as an important virtue
   (D) Prepare to answer charges of untruthfulness that have been made against the speaker
   (E) Argue that the English are more capable of truthfulness than the people of other nationalities

42. In context, "imputation" in line 1 most nearly means:
   (A) Method
   (B) Accusation
   (C) Response
   (D) Form of address
   (E) Insult

---

5. a common geographic term for the northern/northwestern Indian subcontinent

43. In line 6, "season" in "They will fall to the ground in their season" refers to:

(A) Old age
(B) Autumn
(C) Appropriate time
(D) Extended period of time
(E) Recurrent periods of time

44. According to Newman, truthfulness, as defined in lines 16–23, is all of the following *except*:

(A) Open to human judgment
(B) A natural virtue
(C) Capable of becoming supernatural
(D) Out of the jurisdiction of mankind
(E) Sometimes difficult to ascertain

45. The effect of the analogy in lines 20–21, " . . . as it may be difficult for the Court of Queen's Bench at Westminster to try a case fairly which took place in Hindoostan . . . ", is to:

(A) Illustrate the challenge of judging truth out of its context
(B) Illustrate the unfairness of judging truth out of its context
(C) Illustrate the paradoxical nature of judging truth out of its context
(D) Illustrate the impossibility of judging truth out of its context
(E) Illustrate the illegality of judging truth out of its context

46. The speaker regards the English (lines 28–33) with:

(A) Awe
(B) Reverence
(C) Contempt
(D) Ambivalence
(E) Pride

47. Which of the following statements most clearly expresses irony?

  (A) "I have been treated by contemporary critics in this controversy with great fairness and gentleness, and I am grateful to them for it" (lines 34–35)

  (B) "However, the decision of the time and mode of my defence has been taken out of my hands; and I am thankful that it has been so" (lines 35–37)

  (C) "I am bound now as a duty to myself, to the Catholic cause, to the Catholic priesthood, to give account of myself without any delay, when I am so rudely and circumstantially charged with untruthfulness" (lines 37–40)

  (D) "I accept the challenge" (line 40)

  (E) "I shall do my best to meet it, and I shall be content when I have done so" (lines 40–41)

48. The tone of the passage can best be described as:

  (A) Conciliatory

  (B) Irate

  (C) Confident

  (D) Apprehensive

  (E) Mirthful

49. The purpose of the footnotes as a whole is to:

  (A) Provide information that may be pertinent to the reader

  (B) Refute the claims of Whately and other detractors

  (C) Cite the sources of Newman's claims

  (D) Persuade the readers of the veracity of Newman's claims

  (E) Supply needed context of English traditions and beliefs

50. Taken as a whole, the footnotes show the speaker to be all of the following *except*:

  (A) Learned

  (B) Worldly

  (C) Bilingual

  (D) Litigious

  (E) Religious

CHAPTER 2

Biographers and History Writers with Draft Passages

Passage 2a: James Boswell, *Life of Samuel Johnson*

To this may be added the sentiments of the very man whose life I am about to exhibit . . .

But biography has often been allotted to writers, who seem very little acquainted with the nature of their task, or very negligent about the performance. They rarely afford any other account than might be collected from 5 public papers, but imagine themselves writing a life, when they exhibit a chronological series of actions or preferments; and have so little regard to the manners or behaviour of their heroes, that more knowledge may be gained of a man's real character, by a short conversation with one of his servants, than from a formal and studied narrative, begun with his pedigree, 10 and ended with his funeral. . . .

I am fully aware of the objections which may be made to the minuteness on some occasions of my detail of Johnson's conversation, and how happily it is adapted for the petty exercise of ridicule, by men of superficial understanding and ludicrous fancy; but I remain firm and confident in my 15 opinion, that minute particulars are frequently characteristick, and always amusing, when they relate to a distinguished man. I am therefore exceedingly unwilling that any thing, however slight, which my illustrious friend thought it worth his while to express, with any degree of point, should perish. For this almost superstitious reverence, I have found very old and 20 venerable authority, quoted by our great modern prelate, Secker, in whose tenth sermon there is the following passage:

Rabbi David Kimchi, a noted Jewish Commentator, who lived about five hundred years ago, explains that passage in the first Psalm, His leaf also shall not wither, from Rabbis yet older than himself, thus: 25 That even the idle talk, so he expresses it, of a good man ought to be regarded; the most superfluous things he saith are always of some value. And other ancient authours have the same phrase, nearly in the same sense.

Of one thing I am certain, that considering how highly the small por- 30
tion which we have of the table-talk and other anecdotes of our celebrated writers is valued, and how earnestly it is regretted that we have not more, I am justified in preserving rather too many of Johnson's sayings, than too few; especially as from the diversity of dispositions it cannot be known with certainty beforehand, whether what may seem trifling to some and perhaps 35 to the collector himself, may not be most agreeable to many; and the greater number that an authour can please in any degree, the more pleasure does there arise to a benevolent mind.

To those who are weak enough to think this a degrading task, and the time and labour which have been devoted to it misemployed, I shall content 40 myself with opposing the authority of the greatest man of any age, JULIUS CÆSAR, of whom Bacon observes, that "in his book of Apothegms,[1] which he collected, we see that he esteemed it more honour to make himself but a pair of tables, to take the wise and pithy words of others, than to have every word of his own to be made an apothegm or an oracle." 45

51. The major claim of the passage is best stated in the following line:

(A) "But biography has often been allotted to writers, who seem very little acquainted with the nature of their task, or very negligent about the performance." (lines 3–5)

(B) "They rarely afford any other account than might be collected from public papers, but imagine themselves writing a life, when they exhibit a chronological series of actions or preferments . . ." (lines 5–7)

(C) " . . . more knowledge may be gained of a man's real character, by a short conversation with one of his servants, than from a formal and studied narrative, begun with his pedigree, and ended with his funeral." (lines 8–11)

(D) " . . . but I remain firm and confident in my opinion, that minute particulars are frequently characteristick, and always amusing, when they relate to a distinguished man." (lines 15–17)

(E) " . . . considering how highly the small portion which we have of the table-talk and other anecdotes of our celebrated writers is valued, and how earnestly it is regretted that we have not more, I am justified in preserving rather too many of Johnson's sayings, than too few . . . " (lines 30–34)

---

1. Julius Caesar had a book of collected sayings, also known by the Greek title ἀποφθέγματα, or "apothegms"

52. The second paragraph (lines 12–22) begins its argument with the use of:

(A) counterargument
(B) claim
(C) evidence
(D) warrant
(E) logical fallacy

53. In line 14, the pronoun "it" refers to:

(A) objections
(B) minuteness
(C) occasions
(D) details
(E) conversation

54. All of the following are displayed as beneficial to the art of biography by the writer *except*:

(A) minute particulars
(B) idle talk
(C) table talk
(D) a chronological series of actions
(E) anecdotes

55. In context, the word "superfluous" in line 27 most nearly means:

(A) superficial
(B) apparent
(C) arcane
(D) unnecessary
(E) obsolete

56. The tone of the passage can best be described as:

(A) pedantic
(B) detached
(C) confident
(D) flippant
(E) grave

57. The speaker of the passage would most value which of the following in constructing a biography:

(A) detailed genealogy
(B) birth story and circumstances
(C) historical records from the time and place of the subject's life
(D) cultural context
(E) intimate details

58. The pattern of exposition exemplified in the passage can best be described as:

(A) narration
(B) description
(C) process analysis
(D) cause and effect
(E) argument

59. The style of the passage can best be described as:

(A) complex and reasoned
(B) descriptive and evocative
(C) allusive and evocative
(D) symbolic and disjointed
(E) abstract and informal

60. The bulk of this argument is made up of:

(A) an explanation of what biography should and should not include
(B) criticism of other biographies written by Boswell's contemporaries
(C) an appeal to various authorities to justify the writer's choices in writing Samuel Johnson's biography
(D) responses to those who believe that the writer has "misemployed" his time and labor in writing Samuel Johnson's biography
(E) attacks against those who are "negligent" in the task of writing biography

Passage 2b: *Day of the Dead Draft*

(1) The Mexican *Dia de Muertos*—Day of the Dead—is a holiday that occurs right on the tail end of Halloween, extending from November 1 through November 2. (2) One day is dedicated to the remembrance of departed children, and the other is for deceased adults, usually ancestors.

(3) *Dia de Muertos,* a two-day holiday meant to honor deceased loved ones and ancestors, traces its origins as far back as a few millennia, to the Mesoamerican indigenous holiday, when Aztecs and other Nahua people celebrated a feast honoring the dead. (4) As with so many pagan traditions, it became appropriated by the Roman Catholic colonization by Spain, i.e., it was made to coincide with All Saints Day, celebrated by Catholics around the world. (5) Now it is a national public holiday in Mexico.

(6) Day of the Dead is celebrated with colorful remembrance and displays of fearless love for departed relatives, whereas Halloween is a dark, macabre event evoking horror and mischief. (7) The ubiquitous displays of skulls and skeletons—however joyfully presented—have created a false convergence of the two holidays in the minds of many observers, and not just those north of the border. (8) Even Mexican celebrants don zombie attire and makeup that more closely reflect the latter rather than the former.

(9) The Anthropological Museum in Mexico City contains ample evidence of a death-centered religion, including death by human sacrifice. (10) The museum is filled with artistic representations of skulls and skeletal remains of sacrificial victims from pre-Columbian civilizations that flourished long before there was a Mexico.

(11) The element of modern-day *Dia de Muertos* is the construction of household altars with flower arrangements and food items tailored to the special likes and tastes of the departed relatives being honored. (12) Photos of parents, grandparents, and others are posted atop the edible offerings. (13) Special, sweet, delicious bread—a beloved treat—is always included. (14) The dead are remembered and are thought to return in spirit to enjoy the consumption of their favorite foods by their living descendants.

61. The writer is considering adding the following sentence after sentence 2:

> *On November 1, families remember children who have passed away, while on November 2, they spend time remembering the adults closest to them who have died.*

Should the writer make this addition?

(A) Yes, because it helps clarify the different purposes of each day of the holiday

(B) Yes, because it explains why two days are required for the holiday

(C) Yes, because it provides examples that serve to illustrate the point made in the previous sentence

(D) No, because it simply repeats what was said in the previous sentence in slightly different wording

(E) No, because it makes the paragraph too long for an introduction to a passage

62. The writer wants to combine sentences 1 and 2 (reproduced below) into a single sentence.

> *The Mexican* Dia de Muertos—*Day of the Dead*—*is a holiday that occurs right on the tail end of Halloween, extending from November 1 through November 2. One day is dedicated to the remembrance of departed children, and the other is for deceased adults, usually ancestors.*

Which of the following revisions to the underlined portion of sentences 1 and 2 most effectively accomplishes this goal?

(A) is a holiday that occurs right on the tail end of Halloween, extending from November 1 through November 2; one day is dedicated to the remembrance of departed children, and the other is for deceased adults, usually ancestors.

(B) is a holiday that occurs right on the tail end of Halloween, extending from November 1 through November 2, and one day is dedicated to the remembrance of departed children, and the other is for deceased adults, usually ancestors.

(C) is a holiday that occurs right on the tail end of Halloween, extending from November 1 through November 2, with one day dedicated to the remembrance of departed children, and the other to deceased adults, usually ancestors.

(D) is a holiday that occurs right on the tail end of Halloween, extending from November 1 through November 2; however, one day is dedicated to the remembrance of departed children, and the other is for deceased adults, usually ancestors.

(E) is a holiday that occurs right on the tail end of Halloween, extending from November 1 through November 2; although one day is dedicated to the remembrance of departed children, and the other is for deceased adults, usually ancestors.

63. In sentence 3 (reproduced below), the writer is considering deleting the underlined portion, adjusting the punctuation as necessary:

> Dia de Muertos, *a two-day holiday meant to honor deceased loved ones and ancestors*, traces its origins as far back as a few millennia, to the Mesoamerican indigenous holiday, when Aztecs and other Nahua people celebrated a feast honoring the dead.

Should the writer keep or delete the underlined text?

(A) Keep it, because it provides a necessary definition and translation for the Spanish phrase *Dia de Muertos*

(B) Keep it, because it adds to the writer's purpose of informing his audience about the subject

(C) Keep it, because it helps specify the length and function of the holiday

(D) Delete it, because it may be upsetting or offensive to readers who have recently lost family members

(E) Delete it, because a definition of the holiday is not needed after the introductory paragraph

64. The writer is considering changing the underlined portion of sentence 3 (reproduced below) so that it conveys the information in the sentence in the most precise way.

> Dia de Muertos, *a two-day holiday meant to honor deceased loved ones and ancestors*, traces its origins as far back as *a few millennia*, to the Mesoamerican indigenous holiday, when Aztecs and other Nahua people celebrated a feast honoring the dead.

Which version of the underlined portion of the sentence best accomplishes this goal?

(A) as it is now

(B) several centuries ago

(C) many eras ago

(D) 1,000 or 2,000 years ago

(E) prehistoric times

65. The writer is considering rewording the introductory phrase of sentence 4 (reproduced below) to make clear that *Dia de Muertos* is one of many traditions appropriated, or adopted, by European colonizers.

> *As with so many pagan traditions*, *it became appropriated by the Roman Catholic colonization by Spain, i.e., it was made to coincide with All Saints Day, celebrated by Catholics around the world.*

Which version of the underlined portion of the sentence best meets the writer's needs?

(A) as it is now
(B) One of many pagan traditions
(C) Like all pagan traditions
(D) Of the many pagan traditions
(E) Unlike other pagan traditions

66. The writer is considering adding the following sentence before sentence 6:

> Dia de Muertos *is not to be confused with Halloween, although distinctions have blurred in recent years.*

Should the writer make this addition?

(A) Yes, because readers may not be familiar with the particular traditions of Halloween
(B) Yes, because readers may be responsible for blurring the distinctions between these two holidays
(C) Yes, because it introduces the comparison and contrast between Halloween and *Dia de Muertos* explored in this paragraph
(D) No, because it may make it difficult for readers to understand the differences between the two holidays
(E) No, because those who celebrate Halloween do not celebrate Dia de Muertos

67. The writer wants to avoid expressing the claim in sentence 8 (reproduced below) in absolute terms.

> *Even* Mexican celebrants don zombie attire and makeup that more closely reflect the latter rather than the former.

What is the best version of the underlined portion of the sentence to meet the writer's needs?

(A) as it is now
(B) Even some
(C) Even all
(D) However, no
(E) Never would

68. The writer is considering adding the following sentence after sentence 10:

> *The monumental Pyramid of the Sun in Teotihuacan and the Avenue of the Dead connecting it to the nearby Pyramid of the Moon are both thought to have been the sites of human sacrifice.*

Should the writer make this addition?

(A) Yes, because readers will not be able to understand how *Dia de Muertos* is celebrated without this information
(B) Yes, because these sites may be potential tourist attractions for readers
(C) Yes, because these two examples help support the claim made in the topic sentence of this paragraph about a death-centered religion
(D) No, because readers may be confused about which sites are influenced by which traditions and beliefs
(E) No, because only Mexican historians and religious scholars would be interested in this information

69. The writer wants to add an adjective before the word "element" in sentence 11 (reproduced below) to improve the clarity of the claim.

> *The element of modern-day* Dia de Muertos *is the construction of household altars with flower arrangements and food items tailored to the special likes and tastes of the departed relatives being honored.*

Which adjective would best modify that word "element" to reinforce the passage's perspective on the importance of the traditions described to modern-day celebrations of *Dia de Muertos?*

(A) best
(B) loveliest
(C) strangest
(D) surprising
(E) central

70. In sentence 13 (reproduced below), the writer wants to offer the correct terminology to name the item described in the first part of the sentence.

> *Special, sweet, delicious bread—a beloved treat—is always included.*

Which of the following versions of the underlined text best accomplishes this goal?

(A) as it is now
(B) *pan de muerto*
(C) baked with love
(D) made with egg and flour
(E) a long-standing tradition

Passage 2c: Winston Churchill, *The Approaching Conflict*

We are met together at a time when great exertions and a high constancy are required from all who cherish and sustain the Liberal cause. Difficulties surround us and dangers threaten from this side and from that. You know the position which has been created by the action of the House of Lords. Two great political Parties divide all England between them in their 5 conflicts. Now it is discovered that one of these Parties possesses an unfair weapon—that one of these Parties, after it is beaten at an election, after it is deprived of the support and confidence of the country, after it is destitute of a majority in the representative Assembly, when it sits in the shades of Opposition without responsibility, or representative authority, under the 10 frown, so to speak, of the Constitution, nevertheless possesses a weapon, an instrument, a tool, a utensil—call it what you will—with which it can harass, vex, impede, affront, humiliate, and finally destroy the most serious labours of the other. When it is realised that the Party which possesses this prodigious and unfair advantage is in the main the Party of the rich against 15 the poor, of the classes and their dependants against the masses, of the lucky, the wealthy, the happy, and the strong against the left-out and the shut-out millions of the weak and poor, you will see how serious the constitutional situation has become.

A period of supreme effort lies before you. The election with which this 20 Parliament will close, and towards which we are moving, is one which is different in notable features from any other which we have known. Looking back over the politics of the last thirty years, we hardly ever see a Conservative Opposition approaching an election without a programme, on paper at any rate, of social and democratic reform. There was Lord Beaconsfield with 25 his policy of "health and the laws of health." There was the Tory democracy of Lord Randolph Churchill in 1885 and 1886, with large, far-reaching plans of Liberal and democratic reform, of a generous policy to Ireland, of retrenchment and reduction of expenditure upon naval and military armaments—all promises to the people, and for the sake of which he resigned 30 rather than play them false. Then you have the elections of 1892 and 1895. In each the Conservative Party, whether in office or opposition, was, under the powerful influence of Mr. [Joseph] Chamberlain, committed to most extensive social programmes, of what we should call Liberal and Radical reforms, like the Workmen's Compensation Act and Old-Age Pensions, part 35 of which were carried out by them and part by others.

But what social legislation, what plans of reform do the Conservative Party offer now to the working people of England if they will return them to power? I have studied very carefully the speeches of their leaders—if you can call them leaders—and I have failed to discover a single plan of social 40 reform or reconstruction. Upon the grim and sombre problems of the Poor Law they have no policy whatever. Upon unemployment no policy whatever; for the evils of intemperance no policy whatever, except to make sure of the public-house vote; upon the question of the land, monopolised as it is in the hands of so few, denied to so many, no policy whatever; for the 45 distresses of Ireland, for the relations between the Irish and British peoples, no policy whatever unless it be coercion. In other directions where they have a policy, it is worse than no policy. For Scotland the Lords' veto, for Wales a Church repugnant to the conscience of the overwhelming majority of the Welsh people, crammed down their throats at their own expense. 50

71. The function of the passage as a whole is to encourage the audience to:

    (A) support the Welsh people and their church
    (B) question the various forms of reform presented throughout
    (C) insist on a new policy to reduce naval and military expenditures
    (D) think critically about the Conservative party before the election
    (E) accept the Conservative Party's good faith efforts from the years of 1885 to 1895

72. The first sentence of the passage, "We are met together at a time when great exertions and a high constancy are required from all who cherish and sustain the Liberal cause" (lines 1–2), is meant to:

    (A) placate the audience
    (B) galvanize the audience
    (C) rebuke the audience
    (D) frighten the audience
    (E) admonish the audience

73. Churchill offers multiple synonyms for "weapon" and "harass" in lines 11–14 to show:

    (A) the varied and far-reaching effects of the abuse of power discussed
    (B) the disagreement of the different parties involved
    (C) the lack of consensus on how to describe the abuses of power discussed
    (D) the speaker's inner conflict and confusion in trying to describe the abuses of power
    (E) the inability of the speaker to accurately describe the abuses of power

74. At the end of the first paragraph, the writer sets up all of the following oppositions *except*:

    (A) rich vs. poor
    (B) weak vs. strong
    (C) lucky vs. unfair
    (D) wealthy vs. left-out
    (E) happy vs. shut-out

75. Between lines 25 and 36, Churchill offers examples of:

    (A) the current programs that the Conservative party proposes

    (B) the failed social policies of the past

    (C) previous social and democratic reforms of the Conservative party

    (D) the most divisive issues for the political parties

    (E) the programs offered by the opposition

76. The rhetorical question, "But what social legislation, what plans of reform do the Conservative Party offer now to the working people of England if they will return them to power?" (lines 37–39), serves to:

    (A) ask the audience to consider the lack of social reform presented by the Conservative Party

    (B) show Churchill's intimate knowledge of the speeches made by the Conservatives for the current election

    (C) propose social legislation for the working people of England

    (D) ask the audience for ideas for reforms that would be beneficial to the people of England

    (E) ask the audience for financial support in the upcoming election

77. In context, the word "repugnant" in line 49 most nearly means:

    (A) incompatible

    (B) hostile

    (C) offensive

    (D) inconsistent

    (E) provocative

78. The tone of the last paragraph (lines 37–50) can best be described as:

    (A) rapt and engrossed

    (B) didactic and informative

    (C) reverent and timid

    (D) condescending and pedantic

    (E) scornful and critical

79. The effect of the last paragraph (lines 37–50) most heavily relies on:

    (A) figurative language

    (B) outside sources

    (C) expert testimony

    (D) anecdote

    (E) repetition

80. Overall, the speaker can best be described as:
  (A) aloof and detached
  (B) passionate and informed
  (C) calculated and measured
  (D) prudent and judicious
  (E) reserved and cautious

Passage 2d: *Modern Art Draft*

(1) The invention—and widespread use—of the camera in the 19th century led to a change in the way visual art is defined and understood. (2) For the 400 years prior to this, the focus of painting and sculpture was to accurately represent physical reality in the form of portraiture and landscape. (3) Cameras captured a realistic representation more quickly, more easily, and less expensively than painting and sculpture could.

(4) This phenomenon—coupled with the rise of modern philosophies, such as phenomenology, existentialism, and empiricism—encouraged visual artists to use their talents to represent reality in new and innovative ways. (5) A wide array of art movements, such as surrealism, impressionism, and cubism, began to manifest by the end of the century. (6) The radically different visual languages and art techniques of these movements led many to dismiss the work instantly.

(7) Others would say that the impressionism of artists like Vincent Van Gogh and Claude Monet captured "more" realism than that of simple representative art—usually comprised of individual and family portraits and natural landscapes. (8) The modernist formation of psychotherapy in the work of Sigmund Freud and Carl Jung influenced the work of surrealists like Salvador Dali and René Magritte, who turned to the visuals and content of dreams to express greater truths about the human condition. (9) Surrealism was also influenced by the art movement Dada, which rejected the rationalism of direct representation as a part of its core tenet that nonsense and absurdity were more accurate representations of modern life than the rationalism of World War I and capitalism following the Industrial Revolution.

(10) These movements mark the beginning of visual art as a more intellectual and less artisanal pursuit—a tradition that continued throughout the 20th century in the forms of abstract expressionism, pop art, conceptualism, and performance art. (11) For example, the art critic Arthur Danto famously cited Andy Warhol's *Brillo Boxes* as "the end of art"—essentially the creation of an artwork that was more theory and philosophy than necessarily aesthetic beauty and traditional representation.

81. Which of the following sentences can best be described as the writer's thesis?

(A) The invention—and widespread use—of the camera in the 19th century led to a change in the way visual art is defined and understood.

(B) For the 400 years prior to this, the primary focus of painting and sculpture was to accurately represent physical reality in the form of portraiture and landscape.

(C) Cameras captured a realistic representation more quickly, more easily, and less expensively than painting and sculpture could.

(D) This phenomenon—coupled with the rise of modern philosophies, such as phenomenology, existentialism, and empiricism—encouraged visual artists to use their talents to represent reality in new and innovative ways.

(E) A wide array of art movements, such as surrealism, impressionism, and cubism, began to manifest by the end of the century.

82. The writer wants to add an adjective before the word "focus" in sentence 2 (reproduced below) to improve the clarity of the claim.

> For the 400 years prior to this, the focus of painting and sculpture was to accurately represent physical reality in the form of portraiture and landscape.

Which adjective would best modify the word "focus" to reinforce the passage's perspective on the goals of art before the development of the camera?

(A) only

(B) weirdest

(C) valued

(D) desired

(E) primary

83. The writer is considering removing sentence 3 (reproduced below):

> *Cameras captured a realistic representation more quickly, more easily, and less expensively than painting and sculpture could.*

Should the writer remove this sentence?

(A) Yes, because it repeats what was said in sentence 1

(B) Yes, because it contains information that would only be of interest to art critics and historians

(C) Yes, because it contains technical language about art that would not be understood by a general audience

(D) No, because it provides reasons why the camera replaced painting and sculpture as the main medium to capture reality

(E) No, because it provides examples of famous early photographs and photographers

84. The writer would like to include additional information in sentence 4 (reproduced below) to provide a general audience with more contextual background about the other major developments of the time period.

> *This phenomenon—<u>coupled with the rise of modern philosophies, such as phenomenology, existentialism, and empiricism</u>—encouraged visual artists to use their talents to represent reality in new and innovative ways.*

Which version of the underlined portion of the sentence best meets the writer's needs?

(A) as it is now

(B) a remarkable event for its time

(C) unforeseen by art critics

(D) a shift to valuing more expressive art

(E) not enjoyed by all artists, collectors, and connoisseurs

85. The writer is considering adding the following sentence after sentence 6:

> *For example, Henri Matisse was described by critics as painting like a "wild beast" and his branch of impressionism was dubbed* Fauvist *("beastly" in French)—a name that sticks to the movement even to this day.*

Should the writer add the sentence?

(A) Yes, because general audiences may be questioning the artistic merit of modern art

(B) Yes, because it provides a vivid example of the claim made in sentence 6

(C) Yes, because it is a welcome surprise for readers to learn that Matisse was not always appreciated for his style

(D) No, because the use of a French term is not appropriate for a general audience

(E) No, because readers may be offended by the harsh outlook on the esteemed Henri Matisse

86. The writer would like to add an amplification at the end of sentence 7 (reproduced below) that clarifies how impressionism could perhaps capture more reality than some forms of representative art.

> *Others would say that the impressionism of artists like Vincent Van Gogh and Claude Monet captured "more" realism than that of simple representative art—*<u>*usually comprised of individual and family portraits and natural landscapes.*</u>

Which version of the underlined portion of sentence 7 best meets the writer's needs?

(A) as it is now

(B) such as the earlier and more traditional forms of painting and sculpture.

(C) expressing an interior reality, as well as capturing the changing light and subject over time.

(D) an unpopular opinion indeed!

(E) which is, of course, an impossible aim to achieve.

87. The writer is considering removing sentence 8 (reproduced below):

> *The modernist formation of psychotherapy in the work of Sigmund Freud and Carl Jung influenced the work of surrealists like Salvador Dali and René Magritte, who turned to the visuals and content of dreams to express greater truths about the human condition.*

Should the writer remove this sentence?

(A) Yes, because psychotherapy is a highly personal process that may be upsetting for readers with traumatic pasts
(B) Yes, because dreams can be both disturbing and unreliable as a subject or inspiration for art
(C) Yes, because the inclusion of this sentence makes the paragraph too much longer than the other paragraphs in the passage
(D) No, because it provides relevant information on the sources, styles, and practitioners of modern art
(E) No, because Salvador Dali and René Magritte are the most popular artists of that time period and will be familiar names to readers

88. The writer wants to add an adjective before the word "rationalism" in sentence 9 (reproduced below) to improve the clarity of the claim.

> *Surrealism was also influenced by the art movement Dada, which rejected the rationalism of direct representation as a part of its core tenet that nonsense and absurdity were more accurate representations of modern life than the rationalism of World War I and capitalism following the Industrial Revolution.*

Which adjective would best modify the word "rationalism" to reinforce the passage's perspective on the capacity of new forms of art to capture modern reality by casting doubt on the accepted definitions and examples of reality?

(A) preferred
(B) unchanging
(C) supposed
(D) previous
(E) respected

89. All of the following words or phrases are used by the writer in association with modern art *except*:

(A) intellectual
(B) artisanal
(C) theory
(D) philosophy
(E) "the end of art"

90. Which of the following choices for the underlined portion of sentence 11 creates the most logical transition between sentences 10 and 11 (reproduced below)?

> *These movements mark the beginning of visual art as a more intel-lectual and less artisanal pursuit—a tradition that continued throughout the 20th century in the forms of abstract expressionism, pop art, conceptualism, and performance art. For example, the art critic, Arthur Danto, famously cited Andy Warhol's Brillo Boxes as "the end of art"—essentially the creation of an artwork that was more theory and philosophy than necessarily aesthetic beauty and traditional representation.*

(A) as it is now
(B) Finally
(C) Therefore
(D) However
(E) Consequently

Passage 2e: George Trevelyan, *Life and Letters of Lord Macaulay*

He who undertakes to publish the memoirs of a distinguished man may find a ready apology in the custom of the age. If we measure the effective demand for biography by the supply, the person commemorated need pos-sess but a very moderate reputation, and have played no exceptional part, in order to carry the reader through many hundred pages of anecdote, dis- 5
sertation, and correspondence. To judge from the advertisements of our circulating libraries, the public curiosity is keen with regard to some who did nothing worthy of special note, and others who acted so continuously in the face of the world that, when their course was run, there was little left for the world to learn about them. It may, therefore, be taken for granted 10
that a desire exists to hear something authentic about the life of a man who has produced works which are universally known, but which bear little or no indication of the private history and the personal qualities of the author.

This was in a marked degree the case with Lord Macaulay. His two famous contemporaries in English literature have, consciously or unconsciously, told their own story in their books. Those who could see between the lines in "David Copperfield"[1] were aware that they had before them a delightful autobiography; and all who knew how to read Thackeray could trace him in his novels through every stage in his course, on from the day when as a little boy, consigned to the care of English relatives and schoolmasters, he left his mother on the steps of the landing-place at Calcutta. The dates and names were wanting, but the man was there; while the most ardent admirers of Macaulay will admit that a minute study of his literary productions left them, as far as any but an intellectual knowledge of the writer himself was concerned, very much as it found them. A consummate master of his craft, he turned out works which bore the unmistakable marks of the artificer's hand, but which did not reflect his features. It would be almost as hard to compose a picture of the author from the History, the Essays, and the Lays, as to evolve an idea of Shakespeare from *Henry the Fifth* and *Measure for Measure*.

But, besides being a man of letters, Lord Macaulay was a statesman, a jurist, and a brilliant ornament of society, at a time when to shine in society was a distinction which a man of eminence and ability might justly value. In these several capacities, it will be said, he was known well, and known widely. But in the first place, as these pages will show, there was one side of his life (to him, at any rate, the most important,) of which even the persons with whom he mixed most freely and confidentially in London drawing-rooms, in the Indian Council chamber, and in the lobbies and on the benches of the House of Commons, were only in part aware. And in the next place, those who have seen his features and heard his voice are few already and become yearly fewer; while, by a rare fate in literary annals, the number of those who read his books is still rapidly increasing. For everyone who sat with him in private company or at the transaction of public business,—for every ten who have listened to his oratory in Parliament or from the hustings,—there must be tens of thousands whose interest in history and literature he has awakened and informed by his pen, and who would gladly know what manner of man it was that has done them so great a service.

To gratify that most legitimate wish is the duty of those who have the means at their command. His lifelike image is indelibly impressed upon their minds, (for how could it be otherwise with any who had enjoyed so close relations with such a man?) although the skill which can reproduce that image before the general eye may well be wanting. But his own letters will supply the deficiencies of the biographer. Never did any one leave

---

1. The title of a novel by Charles Dickens.

behind him more copious materials for enabling others to put together a narrative which might be the history, not indeed of his times, but of the man himself. For in the first place he so soon showed promise of being one 55 who would give those among whom his early years were passed reason to be proud, and still more certain assurance that he would never afford them cause for shame, that what he wrote was preserved with a care very seldom bestowed on childish compositions; and the value set upon his letters by those with whom he corresponded naturally enough increased as years went 60 on. And in the next place he was by nature so incapable of affectation or concealment that he could not write otherwise than as he felt, and, to one person at least, could never refrain from writing all that he felt; so that we may read in his letters, as in a clear mirror, his opinions and inclinations, his hopes and affections, at every succeeding period of his existence. Such 65 letters could never have been submitted to an editor not connected with both correspondents by the strongest ties; and even one who stands in that position must often be sorely puzzled as to what he has the heart to publish and the right to withhold.

91. The purpose of the passage is to:
    (A) justify the writer's writing a biography of Lord Macaulay
    (B) describe the taste for biographies in the writer's era
    (C) analyze the appropriate reasons for writing a biography
    (D) define the genre of biography
    (E) narrate the accomplishments of Lord Macaulay

92. The major claim of the passage is stated in which of the following lines?
    (A) "He who undertakes to publish the memoirs of a distinguished man may find a ready apology in the custom of the age." (lines 1–2)
    (B) "It may, therefore, be taken for granted that a desire exists to hear something authentic about the life of a man who has produced works which are universally known, but which bear little or no indication of the private history and the personal qualities of the author." (lines 10–13)
    (C) "But, besides being a man of letters, Lord Macaulay was a statesman, a jurist, and a brilliant ornament of society, . . . " (lines 30–31)
    (D) "To gratify that most legitimate wish is the duty of those who have the means at their command." (lines 47–48)
    (E) "Such letters could never have been submitted to an editor not connected with both correspondents by the strongest ties . . . " (lines 65–67)

93. In context, the word "apology" in line 2 most nearly means:
   (A) an admission of error
   (B) an excuse
   (C) an expression of regret
   (D) a justification
   (E) a poor substitute

94. The first line of the second paragraph (line 14) signals a shift in the passage from:
   (A) public to private
   (B) unknown to known
   (C) concrete to abstract
   (D) general to specific
   (E) demand to supply

95. The line "It would be almost as hard to compose a picture of the author from the History, the Essays, and the Lays, as to evolve an idea of Shakespeare from *Henry the Fifth* and *Measure for Measure*" (lines 27–29) uses an analogy for the following purpose:
   (A) to compare the quality of Macaulay's works to those of Shakespeare
   (B) to compare the accuracy of Shakespeare's histories to Macaulay's
   (C) to make a comparison to another author whose life was not apparent in his works
   (D) to compare the intellectual knowledge of Shakespeare to Macaulay's
   (E) to make a comparison to another author who was prolific

96. The primary audience for this passage is:
   (A) "the persons with whom he mixed most freely and confidentially" (line 36)
   (B) "those who have seen his features and heard his voice" (line 39)
   (C) "everyone who sat with him" (lines 41–42)
   (D) "every ten who have listened to his oratory" (line 43)
   (E) "tens of thousands whose interest in history and literature he has awakened and informed by his pen" (lines 44–45)

97. The writer of the passage characterizes himself in the last paragraph (lines 47–69) in all of the following ways *except*:

(A) one who has "means at [his] command"

(B) one who "enjoyed so close relations with such a man" (as Lord Macaulay)

(C) one with skill enough to "reproduce that image" (of Lord Macaulay)

(D) one who is connected "by the strongest ties" (to Lord Macaulay and his correspondent)

(E) one who is "puzzled as to what he has the heart to publish and the right to withhold"

98. The word "affectation" in line 61 is used to mean:

(A) fondness

(B) sincerity

(C) tenderness

(D) artificiality

(E) suppression

99. The speaker regards Lord Macaulay with:

(A) aloof indifference

(B) sordid curiosity

(C) veiled contempt

(D) considerate admiration

(E) skeptical distrust

100. According to the speaker, Macaulay is an ideal subject for a biography because he is both:

(A) open and interesting

(B) prolific and private

(C) eccentric and friendly

(D) beloved and well-known

(E) reserved and terse

CHAPTER 3

Critics with Draft Passages

Passage 3a: Matthew Arnold, *The Function of Criticism at the Current Time*

It has long seemed to me that the burst of creative activity in our literature, through the first quarter of this century, had about it in fact something premature; and that from this cause its productions are doomed, most of them, in spite of the sanguine hopes which accompanied and do still accompany them, to prove hardly more lasting than the productions of far less splendid 5
epochs. And this prematureness comes from its having proceeded without having its proper data, without sufficient materials to work with. In other words, the English poetry of the first quarter of this century, with plenty of energy, plenty of creative force, did not know enough. This makes Byron[1] so empty of matter, Shelley[2] so incoherent, Wordsworth[3] even, profound as 10
he is, yet so wanting in completeness and variety. Wordsworth cared little for books, and disparaged Goethe[4]. I admire Wordsworth, as he is, so much that I cannot wish him different; and it is vain, no doubt, to imagine such a man different from what he is, to suppose that he "could" have been different. But surely the one thing wanting to make Wordsworth an even greater 15
poet than he is,—his thought richer, and his influence of wider application,—was that he should have read more books, among them, no doubt, those of that Goethe whom he disparaged without reading him.

---

1. George Gordon Byron (1788–1824), commonly known as Lord Byron, was an English poet and a leading figure in the Romantic movement.

2. Percy Bysshe Shelley (1792–1822) was one of the major English Romantic poets, and is regarded by some as among the finest poets in the English language.

3. William Wordsworth (1770–1850) was a major English Romantic poet who, with Samuel Taylor Coleridge, helped to launch the Romantic Age in English literature with their joint publication "Lyrical Ballads" (1798).

4. Johann Wolfgang Goethe (1749–1832) was a German writer and statesman. His body of work includes poetry written in a variety of meters and styles, prose and verse dramas, memoirs, an autobiography, and literary criticism.

But to speak of books and reading may easily lead to a misunderstanding here. It was not really books and reading that lacked to our poetry at 20
this epoch: Shelley had plenty of reading, Coleridge[5] had immense reading.
Pindar[6] and Sophocles[7]—as we all say so glibly, and often with so little dis-
cernment of the real import of what we are saying—had not many books;
Shakespeare[8] was no deep reader. True; but in the Greece of Pindar and
Sophocles, in the England of Shakespeare, the poet lived in a current of 25
ideas in the highest degree animating and nourishing to the creative power;
society was, in the fullest measure, permeated by fresh thought, intelligent
and alive. And this state of things is the true basis for the creative power's
exercise, in this it finds its data, its materials, truly ready for its hand; all the
books and reading in the world are only valuable as they are helps to this. 30
Even when this does not actually exist, books and reading may enable a man
to construct a kind of semblance of it in his own mind, a world of knowledge and intelligence in which he may live and work. This is by no means
an equivalent to the artist for the nationally diffused life and thought of the
epochs of Sophocles or Shakespeare; but, besides that it may be a means of 35
preparation for such epochs, it does really constitute, if many share in it, a
quickening and sustaining atmosphere of great value. Such an atmosphere
the many-sided learning and the long and widely combined critical effort
of Germany formed for Goethe, when he lived and worked. There was no
national glow of life and thought there as in the Athens of Pericles or the 40
England of Elizabeth. That was the poet's weakness. But there was a sort of
equivalent for it in the complete culture and unfettered thinking of a large
body of Germans. That was his strength. In the England of the first quarter
of this century there was neither a national glow of life and thought, such
as we had in the age of Elizabeth, nor yet a culture and a force of learning 45
and criticism such as were to be found in Germany. Therefore the creative
power of poetry wanted, for success in the highest sense, materials and a
basis; a thorough interpretation of the world was necessarily denied to it.

---

5. Samuel Taylor Coleridge (1772–1834) was an English poet, literary critic and philosopher
who, with his friend William Wordsworth, was a founder of the Romantic Movement in England
and a member of the Lake Poets.

6. Pindar (c. 522-c. 443 BC) was an Ancient Greek lyric poet from Thebes. Of the major nine
lyric poets of ancient Greece, his work is the best preserved.

7. Sophocles (c. 497/6–406/5 BC) is one of three ancient Greek tragedians whose plays have
survived. His plays were written in verse.

8. William Shakespeare (1564–1616) was an English poet, playwright, and actor. He is widely
regarded as the greatest writer in the English language and the world's best dramatist.

101. The primary purpose of the passage as a whole is to:

(A) argue for the inability of reading to compensate for a lack in fresh thought

(B) argue for the importance of criticism for literature in a time that may lack a "national glow of life"

(C) argue that Wordsworth is one of the misinformed poets of the epoch

(D) argue that Greece is superior to England in "national glow of life"

(E) argue that the literature of Germany is superior to the literature of England

102. In context, the word "sanguine" in line 4 most nearly means:

(A) optimistic

(B) inevitable

(C) exhilarating

(D) doubtful

(E) infallible

103. The writer uses the word "data" to encompass all of the following *except*:

(A) materials

(B) a current of ideas

(C) creative force

(D) fresh thought

(E) a national glow of life

104. In line 15, "wanting" is used to mean:

(A) desiring

(B) coveting

(C) envying

(D) obstructing

(E) lacking

105. The purpose of the sentence "But to speak of books and reading may easily lead to a misunderstanding here," (lines 19–20) at the beginning of paragraph 2, is to:

(A) refute Arnold's major claim
(B) reiterate Arnold's major claim
(C) provide a counter-example
(D) acknowledge and refute a potential counterargument
(E) provide an example for Arnold's major claim

106. The phrase "a current of ideas" is a metaphor that compares ideas to a current to show their _____ nature:

(A) fleeting
(B) powerful
(C) perilous
(D) omnipresent
(E) depleting

107. According to the author, Germany was advanced in its body of:

(A) poetry
(B) philosophy
(C) criticism
(D) reading
(E) creativity

108. The tone of the passage can best be described as:

(A) melancholy and lugubrious
(B) confident and polemical
(C) sardonic and irreverent
(D) detached and aloof
(E) somber and grave

109. Each footnote provides all of the following information *except*:

(A) full name
(B) life span
(C) nationality
(D) occupation
(E) titles of written work

110. The information from the footnotes confirms that all of the people mentioned are:

(A) English

(B) of the 17th century

(C) critics

(D) poets

(E) in agreement with Arnold

Passage 3b: *Diverse Characters in Children's Literature Draft*

(1) Many libraries and classrooms today are striving to fill their bookshelves with diverse literature for children. (2) Teachers, librarians, and parents with the best of intentions often struggle to find the best approach to discuss race with their students and children. (3) Books provide a wonderful opportunity to start the conversation and answer the questions some of us didn't even realize we had.

(4) For years, diverse characters did not exist widely in children's literature. (5) It was impossible to find characters of color depicted in a picture book, unless they represented some aspect of poverty, crime, or struggle. (6) If characters of color did appear, often the focus would be on history pertaining to slavery or the civil rights movement, a struggle for social justice that occurred during the 1950s and 1960s for Black Americans to gain equal rights under the law in the United States, rather than just a child enjoying and experiencing the many lessons to be learned when growing up.

(7) As the civil rights movement of the 1960s marched on, children's literature slowly started to catch up. (8) Some of the earlier authors who started introducing characters of color include Ezra Jack Keats (*The Snowy Day*, 1962) and Don Freeman (*Corduroy*,1968). (9) In these books, you could find a character playing in the snow or picking out a new toy from a department store. (10) However simple these stories seem, these groundbreaking books spoke to parents and children like never before.

(11) The various themes in these books are woven with concepts and illustrations as beautiful as tapestries. (12) *The Snowy Day* was not just a story about a boy in the snow. (13) This story invited children to open their eyes to the wonder and possibilities beyond the blanket of white that surrounded them on cold winter days. (14) And Corduroy was an adorable bear that any child would love! (15) Yet, before *Corduroy*, there were fewer young black children who had seen themselves depicted in a story showing a black mother with a full purse able to make this luxurious purchase. (16) Therefore, the shift had begun.

(17) Today, diversity is represented in hundreds of beautiful children's books. (18) Now, countless books celebrating different skin colors and shades, hairstyles, body types, and mind-sets from any and every culture imaginable are so abundant that the struggle has become budgeting to buy them all rather than finding the needle in the haystack.

111. The writer wants to combine sentences 2 and 3 (reproduced below) in a way that makes clear the relationship between the claims made in these two sentences:

> *Teachers, librarians, and parents with the best of intentions often struggle to find the best approach to discuss race with their students and children. Books provide a wonderful opportunity to start the conversation and answer the questions some of us didn't even realize we had.*

Which version of the combined sentences below best meets the needs of the writer?

(A) Teachers, librarians, and parents with the best of intentions often struggle to find the best approach to discuss race with their students and children, but books provide a wonderful opportunity to start the conversation and answer the questions some of us didn't even realize we had.

(B) Teachers, librarians, and parents with the best of intentions often struggle to find the best approach to discuss race with their students and children; however, books provide a wonderful opportunity to start the conversation and answer the questions some of us didn't even realize we had.

(C) Teachers, librarians, and parents with the best of intentions often struggle to find the best approach to discuss race with their students and children, and books provide a wonderful opportunity to start the conversation and answer the questions some of us didn't even realize we had.

(D) Teachers, librarians, and parents with the best of intentions often struggle to find the best approach to discuss race with their students and children; books provide a wonderful opportunity to start the conversation and answer the questions some of us didn't even realize we had.

(E) Teachers, librarians, and parents with the best of intentions often struggle to find the best approach to discuss race with their students and children; therefore, books provide a wonderful opportunity to start the conversation and answer the questions some of us didn't even realize we had.

112. The writer wants to avoid expressing the claim in sentence 5 (reproduced below) in absolute terms.

> *It was impossible to even find characters of color depicted in a picture book, unless they represented some aspect of poverty, crime, or struggle.*

What is the best revision of the sentence to meet the writer's needs?

(A) as it is now
(B) Add "nearly" before the word "impossible"
(C) Add "completely" before "impossible"
(D) Replace "impossible" with "possible"
(E) Add "not" before "impossible"

113. The writer is considering deleting the clause "a struggle for social justice that occurred during the 1950s and 1960s for Black Americans to gain equal rights under the law in the United States," in sentence 6 (reproduced below).

> *If characters of color did appear, often the focus would be on history pertaining to slavery or the civil rights movement, a struggle for social justice that occurred during the 1950s and 1960s for Black Americans to gain equal rights under the law in the United States, rather than just a child enjoying and experiencing the many lessons to be learned when growing up.*

Which of the following factors is most important for the writer to consider when deciding whether to keep or delete the clause?

(A) Whether the audience agrees with the aims of the civil rights movement
(B) Which other American historical movements the audience is likely to be aware of
(C) What else was happening during the world during the civil rights movement
(D) Whether the audience is likely to have a basic knowledge of what the civil rights movement is
(E) Whether the literary critics of the time wrote extensively on the diversity of characters in childrens' books

114. The writer is considering removing sentence 8 (reproduced below):

> *Some of the earlier authors who started introducing characters of color include Ezra Jack Keats (*The Snowy Day, *1962) and Don Freeman (*Corduroy, *1968).*

Should the writer remove this sentence?

(A) Yes, because the specific authors and titles are irrelevant to the claim that diverse characters began to appear in children's books

(B) Yes, because only librarians and educators would be interested in knowing the titles and years of publication of these specific books

(C) Yes, because it shifts the tone by providing the readers with emotional and personal reactions to these particular stories

(D) No, because these examples support the claim provided in the preceding sentence with specific details

(E) No, because everyone has read these books and enjoys hearing about their authors and dates of publication

115. To which earlier sentence does sentence 15 (reproduced below) most clearly respond?

> *Yet, before* Corduroy, *there were fewer young black children who had seen themselves depicted in a story showing a black mother with a full purse able to make this luxurious purchase.*

(A) Many libraries and classrooms today are striving to fill their bookshelves with diverse literature for children.

(B) Teachers, librarians, and parents with the best of intentions often struggle to find the best approach to discuss race with their students and children.

(C) Books provide a wonderful opportunity to start the conversation and answer the questions some of us didn't even realize we had.

(D) For years, diverse characters did not exist widely in children's literature.

(E) It was impossible to find characters of color depicted in a picture book, unless they represented some aspect of poverty, crime, or struggle.

116. The writer wants to revise the transition used in sentence 16 (reproduced below):

> *Therefore,* the shift had begun.

Which version of the underlined portion best transitions from sentence 15 to sentence 16?

(A) as it is now
(B) Finally,
(C) Accordingly,
(D) Consequently,
(E) Surprisingly,

117. The writer is considering removing the adjective "beautiful" from sentence 17 (reproduced below):

> *Today, diversity is represented in hundreds of beautiful children's books.*

Should the writer remove the word "beautiful"?

(A) Yes, because it is not appropriate to include opinion in this type of piece on diversity in literature
(B) Yes, because some readers may disagree that the books are beautiful
(C) Yes, because it causes too large a shift in tone between the preceding paragraph and this paragraph
(D) No, because positive language has been used throughout the passage and this description fits the writer's perspective on the subject
(E) No, because those who disagree that the books are beautiful should not be reading this passage

118. The writer is considering adding the following sentence after
sentence 17:

> *One example is* Jabari Jumps, *which introduces the simple yet very
> real accomplishment of jumping off a diving board, inviting chil-
> dren to swim in the hope of achieving their goals and overcoming
> their fears.*

Should the writer add this sentence?

(A) Yes, because while *The Snowy Day* has a wintry setting, this
example provides a necessary summer setting

(B) Yes, because jumping off a diving board is a real and common
fear for many children

(C) Yes, because this sentence provides a recent example that
matches the shift to the present discussed in sentence 17

(D) No, because a third example of a book with diverse characters is
more than is necessary to make the writer's point

(E) No, because of the newness of this book, readers may not be
familiar with it

119. The writer is considering removing the word "countless" before "books"
in sentence 18 (reproduced below):

> *Now, countless books celebrating different skin colors and shades,
> hairstyles, body types, and mind-sets from any and every culture
> imaginable are so abundant that the struggle has become budgeting
> to buy them all rather than finding the needle in the haystack.*

Should the writer remove the word "countless" from sentence 18?

(A) Yes, because it is imprecise and should be replaced with an
exact number

(B) Yes, because it shifts the tone of the piece too dramatically at
this late point in the passage

(C) Yes, because it is an unnecessary adjective to describe books
because of the use of "so abundant" later in the sentence

(D) No, because it provides the sentence with an enjoyable rhythm
for readers reading the passage aloud

(E) No, because writers should always place descriptive words
before nouns like "books"

120. The writer wants to use a word in sentence 18 (reproduced below) that communicates the positive light in which diversity is being presented in today's childrens' books.

> *Now, countless books <u>celebrating</u> different skin colors and shades, hairstyles, body types, and mind-sets from any and every culture imaginable are so abundant that the struggle has become budgeting to buy them all rather than finding the needle in the haystack.*

Which version of the underlined portion of the sentence best achieves this purpose?

(A) as it is now
(B) displaying
(C) presenting
(D) showing
(E) sharing

Passage 3c: William Hazlitt, *On Poetry in General*

Poetry is the language of the imagination and the passions. It relates to whatever gives immediate pleasure or pain to the human mind. It comes home to the bosoms and businesses of men; for nothing but what so comes home to them in the most general and intelligible shape, can be a subject for poetry. Poetry is the universal language which the heart holds with nature 5 and itself. He who has a contempt for poetry, cannot have much respect for himself, or for any thing else. It is not a mere frivolous accomplishment, (as some persons have been led to imagine) the trifling amusement of a few idle readers or leisure hours—it has been the study and delight of mankind in all ages. Many people suppose that poetry is something to be found only 10 in books, contained in lines of ten syllables, with like endings: but wherever there is a sense of beauty, or power, or harmony, as in the motion of a wave of the sea, in the growth of a flower that "spreads its sweet leaves to the air, and dedicates its beauty to the sun,"—there is poetry, in its birth. If history is a grave study, poetry may be said to be a graver: its materials lie deeper, 15 and are spread wider. History treats, for the most part, of the cumbrous and unwieldly masses of things, the empty cases in which the affairs of the world are packed, under the heads of intrigue or war, in different states, and from century to century: but there is no thought or feeling that can have entered into the mind of man, which he would be eager to communicate to 20 others, or which they would listen to with delight, that is not a fit subject for poetry. It is not a branch of authorship: it is "the stuff of which our life is made." The rest is "mere oblivion," a dead letter: for all that is worth remembering in life, is the poetry of it. Fear is poetry, hope is poetry, love is poetry, hatred is poetry; contempt, jealousy, remorse, admiration, wonder, 25 pity, despair, or madness, are all poetry. Poetry is that fine particle within us, that expands, rarefies, refines, raises our whole being: without it "man's life is poor as beast's." Man is a poetical animal: and those of us who do not study the principles of poetry, act upon them all our lives, like Molière's "Bourgeois Gentilhomme", who had always spoken prose without know- 30 ing it. The child is a poet in fact, when he first plays at hide-and-seek, or repeats the story of Jack the Giant-killer; the shepherd-boy is a poet, when he first crowns his mistress with a garland of flowers; the countryman, when he stops to look at the rainbow; the city-apprentice, when he gazes after the Lord-Mayor's show; the miser, when he hugs his gold; the courtier, 35 who builds his hopes upon a smile; the savage, who paints his idol with blood; the slave, who worships a tyrant, or the tyrant, who fancies himself a god;—the vain, the ambitious, the proud, the choleric man, the hero and the coward, the beggar and the king, the rich and the poor, the young and the old, all live in a world of their own making; and the poet does no more 40 than describe what all the others think and act. If his art is folly and madness, it is folly and madness at second hand. "There is warrant for it." Poets alone have not "such seething brains, such shaping fantasies, that apprehend more than cooler reason" can.

121. The purpose of the passage can best be characterized as to:
    (A) defend poetry against its harshest critics
    (B) explore what poetry is
    (C) argue that poetry is more important than history
    (D) display the many uses for and types of poetry
    (E) describe the many types of poets

122. In defining what poetry is, the speaker also defines what poetry is not. He includes all of the following *except*:
    (A) poetry is not a frivolous accomplishment
    (B) poetry is not just amusement for some idle readers
    (C) poetry is not a branch of authorship
    (D) poetry is not only found in books
    (E) poetry is not a fit subject

123. In context, the word "grave" in line 15 most nearly means:

(A) deep
(B) wide
(C) dignified
(D) somber
(E) momentous

124. The sentence "Fear is poetry, hope is poetry, love is poetry, hatred is poetry; contempt, jealousy, remorse, admiration, wonder, pity, despair, or madness, are all poetry" in lines 24–26 uses repetition and listing to return most directly to the idea presented in the following line:

(A) "Poetry is the language of the imagination and the passions" (line 1)
(B) "He who has a contempt for poetry, cannot have much respect for himself, or for anything else" (lines 6–7)
(C) " . . . it has been the study and delight of mankind in all ages" (lines 9–10)
(D) "Many people suppose poetry is something to be found only in books" (lines 10–11)
(E) " . . . its materials lie deeper, and are spread wider" (lines 15–16)

125. All of the following are set up in opposition to one another *except*:

(A) slave and tyrant
(B) hero and coward
(C) beggar and king
(D) rich and poor
(E) young and old

126. The main idea of the last sentence, "Poets alone have not 'such seething brains, such shaping fantasies, that apprehend more than cooler reason' can," (lines 42–44) can be understood as expressing the thought that:

(A) poets are not the only source of poetry
(B) poets can understand more than the rational man can
(C) poets have imagination and passion above regular men
(D) poets have keen and perceptive brains
(E) poets do not have insight, imagination, and understanding

127. The passage's major claim is developed by all of the following *except*:

(A) allusion
(B) example
(C) figurative language
(D) quotations
(E) anecdote

128. The structure and style of the passage as a whole have the effect of impressing upon the reader which of the following traits of poetry?

(A) its elitism
(B) its formality
(C) its intellect
(D) its variance
(E) its superiority

129. The writer would most likely describe poetry as most importantly:

(A) a product of skill and practice
(B) able to transform people's lives
(C) all that is beautiful and powerful in life
(D) evidence of man's respect for himself
(E) a distinction between us and animals

130. The tone of the passage can best be described as:

(A) benevolent
(B) effusive
(C) whimsical
(D) elated
(E) facetious

Passage 3d: *Kurt Gödel Draft*

(1) Kurt Gödel was born in 1906 in Austria-Hungary. (2) According to today's political borders, his birthplace is inside the Czech Republic. (3) He moved to the United States in 1940. (4) Gödel joined up with the Institute for Advanced Study (IAS) shortly before immigrating to the United States, so he took up residence in Princeton, New Jersey, where the IAS is head-quartered, when he relocated here. (5) He lived in Princeton until his death in 1978.

(6) Gödel's main accomplishments were in the area of mathematical logic. (7) The mid-20th century was a time when mathematicians placed

heavy emphasis on discrete math topics like set theory and logic. (8) These subjects are related to the issues examined in the field of philosophy. (9) Nevertheless, major contributors to these areas, like Gödel and Bertrand Russell, are often considered to be philosophers just as much as mathematicians.

(10) The first of these is often called Gödel's undecidability theorem. (11) In plain language, this states that whenever a system is defined by a set of axioms, there will be questions that cannot be answered, proven, or disproven strictly by using the system's set of axioms. (12) The second is generally known as Gödel's incompleteness theorem, which postulates that whenever a system is defined by a set of axioms, and that system requires all questions to be answerable, then some mathematical statements will contradict each other. (13) Given that these theorems altered mathematicians' concept of certainty resulting from logical deduction, Gödel's work also greatly influenced proof theory.

131. The writer wants to combine sentences 1 and 2 (reproduced below) in a way that makes clear the relationship between the claims made in these two sentences.

> *Kurt Gödel was born in 1906 in Austria-Hungary. According to today's political borders, his birthplace is inside the Czech Republic.*

Which version of the combined sentences below best meets the needs of the writer?

(A) Kurt Gödel was born in 1906 in Austria-Hungary; according to today's political borders, his birthplace is inside the Czech Republic.

(B) Kurt Gödel was born in 1906 in Austria-Hungary, and according to today's political borders, his birthplace is inside the Czech Republic.

(C) Kurt Gödel was born in 1906 in Austria-Hungary, but according to today's political borders, his birthplace is inside the Czech Republic.

(D) Kurt Gödel was born in 1906 in Austria-Hungary, so according to today's political borders, his birthplace is inside the Czech Republic.

(E) Kurt Gödel was born in 1906 in Austria-Hungary, which according to today's political borders, his birthplace is inside the Czech Republic.

132. The writer is considering adding an introductory clause or phrase, adjusting punctuation and capitalization as necessary, to sentence 3 (reproduced below) that provides some contextual information about Godel's life.

> *He moved to the United States in 1940.*

Which underlined introductory clause or phrase best meets the writer's needs?

(A) <u>After establishing himself as a prominent mathematician and philosopher in Europe,</u> he moved to the United States in 1940.

(B) <u>Toward the beginning of World War II,</u> he moved to the United States in 1940.

(C) <u>At the start of a new decade,</u> he moved to the United States in 1940.

(D) <u>In the aftermath of the Great Depression,</u> he moved to the United States in 1940.

(E) <u>After careful thought and consideration,</u> he moved to the United States in 1940.

133. In sentence 4 (reproduced below), which version of the underlined text best maintains the tone of the passage?

> *Gödel <u>joined up with</u> the Institute for Advanced Study (IAS) shortly before immigrating to the United States, so he took up residence in Princeton, New Jersey, where the IAS is headquartered, when he relocated here.*

(A) as it is now

(B) hung out with members of

(C) became a member of

(D) spent time with guys in

(E) linked up with

134. Which of the following can best be described as the writer's thesis?

(A) He lived in Princeton until his death in 1978.

(B) Gödel's main accomplishments were in the area of mathematical logic.

(C) The mid-20th century was a time when mathematicians placed heavy emphasis on discrete math topics like set theory and logic.

(D) These subjects are closely related to the issues examined in the field of philosophy.

(E) Nevertheless, major contributors to these areas, like Gödel and Bertrand Russell, are often considered to be philosophers just as much as mathematicians.

135. The writer wants to add a word before "related" in sentence 8 (reproduced below) that will further define the connection between these two fields of study.

> *These subjects are related to the issues examined in the field of philosophy.*

Which word if inserted before "related" will best meet the writer's needs?

(A) somewhat

(B) barely

(C) nearly

(D) closely

(E) almost

136. The writer is considering revising the transition used in sentence 9 (reproduced below).

> *Nevertheless, major contributors to these areas, like Gödel and Bertrand Russell, are often considered to be philosophers just as much as mathematicians.*

Which underlined portion of the sentence provides the best transition to show the relationship between sentences 8 and 9?

(A) as it is now

(B) However, major contributors to these areas, like Gödel and Bertrand Russell, are often considered to be philosophers just as much as mathematicians.

(C) Additionally, major contributors to these areas, like Gödel and Bertrand Russell, are often considered to be philosophers just as much as mathematicians.

(D) Furthermore, major contributors to these areas, like Gödel and Bertrand Russell, are often considered to be philosophers just as much as mathematicians.

(E) Consequently, major contributors to these areas, like Gödel and Bertrand Russell, are often considered to be philosophers just as much as mathematicians.

137. The writer is considering adding a sentence before sentence 10 that will serve as a topic sentence for the third paragraph.

Which of the following sentences can best serve the writer's needs?

(A) Gödel's largest contribution to logic and philosophy was a pair of theorems that challenged our basic assumptions about math, knowledge, reasoning, and certainty.

(B) Gödel is more widely known than Russell and more widely regarded for his contributions to the worlds of philosophy and mathematics.

(C) Gödel's first major theorem is called the undecidability theorem.

(D) Gödel's life was almost evenly split between Europe and the United States.

(E) It is hard to overstate how important Gödel has been to the fields of mathematics and philosophy.

138. The writer is considering removing sentence 11 (reproduced below):

> *In plain language, this states that whenever a system is defined by a set of axioms, there will be questions that cannot be answered, proven, or disproven strictly by using the system's set of axioms.*

Should the writer remove this sentence?

(A) Yes, because its technical language will not be understood by a general audience

(B) Yes, because its mathematical information will only be of interest to those advanced in mathematical studies

(C) Yes, because it makes the paragraph too much longer than the previous two paragraphs

(D) No, because its explanation is necessary to clarify the theorem introduced in the previous sentence

(E) No, because the audience consists of only advanced math students and their instructors, who would be interested in this information

139. The writer is considering removing the underlined portion of sentence 12 (reproduced below):

> *The second is generally known as Gödel's incompleteness theorem, <u>which postulates that whenever a system is defined by a set of axioms, and that system requires all questions to be answerable, then some mathematical statements will contradict each other.</u>*

Should the writer remove the underlined portion of sentence 12?

(A) Yes, because the sentence is too long compared to the other sentences in paragraph 3

(B) Yes, because only mathematicians would be interested in learning about Gödel's incompleteness theorem

(C) Yes, because it is only necessary to explain one of the two theorems named in the paragraph

(D) No, because the paragraph would be too short without this added portion of the sentence

(E) No, because the explanation of the theorem is necessary for both clarity and coherence with the rest of the paragraph

140. The writer wants to avoid expressing the claim in sentence 13 (reproduced below) in absolute terms.

> *Given that these theorems altered mathematicians' concept of cer-tainty resulting from logical deduction, <u>Gödel's work also greatly influenced proof theory</u>.*

Which version of the underlined portion of the sentence avoids expressing the claim in absolute terms?

(A) as it is now
(B) Gödel's work is considered the most important influence on proof theory.
(C) Gödel's work completely redefined proof theory.
(D) Gödel's work was the original and sole source of proof theory.
(E) Gödel's work was solely responsible for the creation of proof theory.

Passage 3e: John Ruskin, *Of the Pathetic Fallacy*

Now, therefore, putting these tiresome and absurd words[1] quite out of our way, we may go on at our ease to examine the point in question,—namely, the difference between the ordinary, proper, and true appearances of things to us; and the extraordinary, or false appearances, when we are under the influence of emotion, or contemplative fancy; false appearances, I say, as being entirely unconnected with any real power or character in the object, and only imputed to it by us.

For instance—

The spendthrift crocus, bursting through the mould
Naked and shivering, with his cup of gold[2].

This is very beautiful, and yet very untrue. The crocus is not a spendthrift, but a hardy plant; its yellow is not gold, but saffron. How is it that we enjoy so much the having it put into our heads that it is anything else than a plain crocus?

It is an important question. For, throughout our past reasonings about art, we have always found that nothing could be good or useful, or ulti-mately pleasurable, which was untrue. But here is something pleasurable in written poetry which is nevertheless untrue. And what is more, if we think

5

10

15

1. Three short sections discussing the use of the terms "Objective" and "Subjective" have been omitted from the beginning of this chapter.
2. Holmes (Oliver Wendell), quoted by Miss Mitford in her *Recollections of a Literary Life*. [Ruskin.] From "Astræa, a Poem" delivered before the Phi Beta Kappa Society of Yale College. The passage in which these lines are found was later published as "Spring."

over our favourite poetry, we shall find it full of this kind of fallacy, and that we like it all the more for being so.   20

It will appear also, on consideration of the matter, that this fallacy is of two principal kinds. Either, as in this case of the crocus, it is the fallacy of wilful fancy, which involves no real expectation that it will be believed; or else it is a fallacy caused by an excited state of the feelings, making us, for the time, more or less irrational. Of the cheating of the fancy we shall   25 have to speak presently; but, in this chapter, I want to examine the nature of the other error, that which the mind admits when affected strongly by emotion. Thus, for instance, in Alton Locke,—They rowed her in across the rolling foam—

The cruel, crawling foam[3].   30

The foam is not cruel, neither does it crawl. The state of mind which attributes to it these characters of a living creature is one in which the reason is unhinged by grief. All violent feelings have the same effect. They produce in us a falseness in all our impressions of external things, which I would   35 generally characterize as the "pathetic fallacy."

Now we are in the habit of considering this fallacy as eminently a character of poetical description, and the temper of mind in which we allow it, as one eminently poetical, because passionate. But I believe, if we look well into the matter, that we shall find the greatest poets do not often admit   40 this kind of falseness,—that it is only the second order of poets who much delight in it[4].

---

3. Kingsley's *Alton Locke*, chap. 26.

4. I admit two orders of poets, but no third; and by these two orders I mean the creative (Shakspere, Homer, Dante), and Reflective or Perceptive (Wordsworth, Keats, Tennyson). But both of these must be first-rate in their range, though their range is different; and with poetry second-rate in quality no one ought to be allowed to trouble mankind. There is quite enough of the best,— much more than we can ever read or enjoy in the length of a life; and it is a literal wrong or sin in any person to encumber us with inferior work. I have no patience with apologies made by young pseudo-poets, "that they believe there is some good in what they have written: that they hope to do better in time," etc. Some good! If there is not all good, there is no good. If they ever hope to do better, why do they trouble us now? Let them rather courageously burn all they have done, and wait for the better days. There are few men, ordinarily educated, who in moments of strong feeling could not strike out a poetical thought, and afterwards polish it so as to be presentable. But men of sense know better than so to waste their time; and those who sincerely love poetry, know the touch of the master's hand on the chords too well to fumble among them after him. Nay, more than this, all inferior poetry is an injury to the good, inasmuch as it takes away the freshness of rhymes, blunders upon and gives a wretched commonalty to good thoughts; and, in general, adds to the weight of human weariness in a most woful and culpable manner. There are few thoughts likely to come across ordinary men, which have not already been expressed by greater men in the best possible way; and it is a wiser, more generous, more noble thing to remember and point out the perfect words, than to invent poorer ones, wherewith to encumber temporarily the world. [Ruskin.]

141. The writer would most likely agree with which of the following remarks?

(A) Reason is stronger than emotion
(B) Grief is the strongest of all emotions
(C) The greatest poets rely heavily on the pathetic fallacy
(D) Feelings make us irrational
(E) Authors intentionally mislead readers to experience the same emotions as them

142. Taken as a whole, the passage is best described as:

(A) an angry response to a personal attack
(B) a researched presentation of facts
(C) an informal reaction to a common problem
(D) an extended narrative about several known writers
(E) an argument employing illustrative quotations

143. Much of the meaning of the passage relies on the author's use of:

(A) refuting the claims of other authors
(B) calling on expert testimony from renowned people in the field
(C) extensively quoting the work of first order poets
(D) defining the term "pathetic fallacy"
(E) celebrating the profound impact of figurative language on readers

144. The author classifies all of the following *except*:

(A) true and false appearances
(B) fallacy caused by wilful fancy and fallacy caused by an excited state of the feelings
(C) creative and receptive or perceptive poets
(D) good and inferior poetry
(E) grief and violent feelings

145. In context, the word "pathetic" in line 36 most nearly means:

(A) caused by feelings
(B) absurd and laughable
(C) marked by sorrow
(D) having the ability to move to pity
(E) pitifully inferior

146. The tone of the passage (not including the footnotes) can best be described as:

(A) incredulous
(B) scornful
(C) evasive
(D) didactic
(E) curt

147. The major claim of the passage is:

(A) the pathetic fallacy is a character of poetical description
(B) the pathetic fallacy can be classified into two types
(C) the pathetic fallacy is mostly used by the reflective and perceptive poets
(D) the pathetic fallacy is exclusively used by inferior poets
(E) the pathetic fallacy is believed by readers overwhelmed by strong feelings

148. The first quoted lines are written by:

(A) Holmes
(B) Oliver
(C) Wendell
(D) Mitford
(E) Ruskin

149. The second quoted lines are written by:

(A) Ruskin
(B) Kingsley
(C) Alton
(D) Locke
(E) Mitford

150. The tone of footnote 4 can be described as:

(A) apprehensive
(B) belligerent
(C) condescending
(D) desperate
(E) fatalistic

CHAPTER 4

Essayists and Fiction Writers
with Draft Passages

Passage 4a: Joseph Addison, *True and False Humour*

Among all kinds of writing, there is none in which authors are more apt to miscarry than in works of humour, as there is none in which they are more ambitious to excel. It is not an imagination that teems with monsters, a head that is filled with extravagant conceptions, which is capable of furnishing the world with diversions of this nature; and yet, if we look into the 5 productions of several writers, who set up for men of humour, what wild, irregular fancies, what unnatural distortions of thought do we meet with? If they speak nonsense, they believe they are talking humour; and when they have drawn together a scheme of absurd, inconsistent ideas, they are not able to read it over to themselves without laughing. These poor gentle- 10 men endeavour to gain themselves the reputation of wits and humorists, by such monstrous conceits as almost qualify them for Bedlam[1]; not considering that humour should always lie under the check of reason, and that it requires the direction of the nicest judgment, by so much the more as it indulges itself in the most boundless freedoms. There is a kind of nature that 15 is to be observed in this sort of compositions, as well as in all other; and a certain regularity of thought which must discover the writer to be a man of sense, at the same time that he appears altogether given up to caprice. For my part, when I read the delirious mirth of an unskilful author, I cannot be so barbarous as to divert myself with it, but am rather apt to pity the man, 20 than to laugh at anything he writes.

The deceased Mr. Shadwell, who had himself a great deal of the talent which I am treating of, represents an empty rake, in one of his plays, as very much surprised to hear one say that breaking of windows was not humour; and I question not but several English readers will be as much startled to 25 hear me affirm, that many of those raving, incoherent pieces, which are

---

1. (archaic) an institution for the care of mentally ill people

often spread among us, under odd chimerical titles, are rather the offsprings of a distempered brain than works of humour.

It is, indeed, much easier to describe what is not humour than what is; and very difficult to define it otherwise than as Cowley[2] has done wit, by negatives. Were I to give my own notions of it, I would deliver them after Plato's manner, in a kind of allegory, and, by supposing Humour to be a person, deduce to him all his qualifications, according to the following genealogy. Truth was the founder of the family, and the father of Good Sense. Good Sense was the father of Wit, who married a lady of a collateral line called Mirth, by whom he had issue Humour. Humour therefore being the youngest of this illustrious family, and descended from parents of such different dispositions, is very various and unequal in his temper; sometimes you see him putting on grave looks and a solemn habit, sometimes airy in his behaviour and fantastic in his dress; insomuch that at different times he appears as serious as a judge, and as jocular as a merry-andrew. But, as he has a great deal of the mother in his constitution, whatever mood he is in, he never fails to make his company laugh.

But since there is an impostor abroad, who takes upon him the name of this young gentleman, and would willingly pass for him in the world; to the end that well-meaning persons may not be imposed upon by cheats, I would desire my readers, when they meet with this pretender, to look into his parentage, and to examine him strictly, whether or no he be remotely allied to Truth, and lineally descended from Good Sense; if not, they may conclude him a counterfeit. They may likewise distinguish him by a loud and excessive laughter, in which he seldom gets his company to join with him. For as True Humour generally looks serious while everybody laughs about him, False Humour is always laughing whilst everybody about him looks serious. I shall only add, if he has not in him a mixture of both parents—that is, if he would pass for the offspring of Wit without Mirth, or Mirth without Wit, you may conclude him to be altogether spurious and a cheat.

151. The primary purpose of the passage as a whole is to:

    (A) narrate a humorous story

    (B) describe a humorous scenario

    (C) classify the common types of humor

    (D) define what humor is

    (E) analyze the causes of humor

---

2. Abraham Cowley (1618–1667), one of the leading English poets of the 17th century, wrote a poem, "Ode of Wit," which defines wit by what it is not.

152. According to the claim in the first sentence of the passage:
- (A) authors are ambitious to excel in all kinds of writing
- (B) authors are likely to fail when writing humor
- (C) authors are not likely to fail when writing humor
- (D) there is no kind of writing in which authors are more likely to fail than any other
- (E) there is no kind of writing in which authors are more ambitious than any other

153. According to the first paragraph (lines 1–21), humor is:
- (A) filled with extravagant conceptions
- (B) the product of wild, irregular fancies
- (C) from unnatural distortions of thought
- (D) absurd and inconsistent
- (E) required to be reasonable

154. In context, the word "barbarous" in line 20 most nearly means:
- (A) aggressive
- (B) cruel
- (C) violent
- (D) uncivilized
- (E) ignorant

155. In paragraph three (lines 29–43), the writer seeks to prove his claim with the use of:
- (A) literary example
- (B) inductive reasoning
- (C) deductive reasoning
- (D) allegory
- (E) anecdote

156. The second "him" of the last paragraph, in line 45, refers to:
- (A) an impostor
- (B) humor
- (C) wit
- (D) good sense
- (E) truth

157. In context, the word "spurious" in line 56 most nearly means:

(A) counterfeit
(B) facetious
(C) deceptive
(D) authentic
(E) artless

158. The tone of the passage can best be described as:

(A) self-assured
(B) sympathetic
(C) acerbic
(D) somber
(E) frantic

159. According to the passage as a whole, humor must be all of the following *except*:

(A) rational and truthful
(B) amusing to the writer
(C) amusing to the reader
(D) clear and cohesive
(E) both serious and jovial

160. Taken as a whole, the purpose of the footnotes is to:

(A) cite sources of information
(B) furnish biographical information
(C) provide information about the proper nouns that the author alludes to within the passage
(D) supply archaic definitions that would not be known to contemporary readers
(E) refute Cowley's definition of wit

Passage 4b: *Thailand Travel Blog Draft*

(1) As soon as the villa host at the <u>Banyan Tree Samui</u> asked us to choose our pillow foam, linen scent, sleep essential oil, and incense stick, I knew this would be a special place. (2) Having dreamed of visiting Thailand for many years, I had built up the experience in my head. (3) Koh Samui, a 1.5-hour flight from <u>Bangkok</u> and 18 hours from my home in New York, over exceeded my expectations in every way.

(4) Sitting in an infinity pool outside the villa on the cliff overlooking the Gulf of Thailand, the two-day journey to get there seemed like a distant memory. (5) We got over our jet lag by going straight to a Muay Thai boxing class (one of the many complimentary classes included in our stay) to bring up our energy levels. (6) This was followed by the hour-long rainforest spa experience, which includes an indoor rainforest shower, steam, sauna, multi-jet pool massage, waterfall swim, heated lounge chair, and rock garden walk.

(7) If you are looking for a honeymoon retreat where you can just enjoy the privacy of your villa, a sunset cruise, a guided snorkel along the coast, and some morning yoga and Pilates, then you can find this and so much more here. (8) For families, the Octopus Kids Club, kayaks at the beach, oversized two-bedroom family villas, and hammocks in the garden will keep children of all ages occupied for days. (9) Groups of friends can try the Banyan tree mixology and cooking classes, outdoor ping pong and pool tables, and various restaurant options—a casual meal on the beach at The Sands or a fine dining offering at Saffron. (10) Highlights at Saffron include the duck breast with tamarind sauce, multiple curry options, crabmeat spring rolls, and taro dumplings with purple potato ice cream for dessert. (11) It also offers gluten-free bread and many bountiful salads for those watching what they eat.

(12) When you are ready to venture off the property, Koh Samui has a lot to offer guests by day and by night. (13) A full-day snorkeling and kayak trip at Angthong National Marine Park is a great way to explore nature and see the exotic fish and coral. (14) You can also fish on Koh Tan Island for barracuda, snapper, shark, mackerel, and more, which is great for people of any age and experience level. (15) Those who wish to stay on land can see the Namuang waterfall or visit the Buddha's magic garden, a beautiful sight to behold!

161. Which of the following can best be described as the writer's thesis?

(A) As soon as the villa host at the <u>Banyan Tree Samui</u> asked us to choose our pillow foam, linen scent, sleep essential oil, and incense stick, I knew this would be a special place.

(B) Having dreamed of visiting Thailand for many years, I had built up the experience in my head.

(C) Koh Samui, a 1.5-hour flight from <u>Bangkok</u> and 18 hours from my home in New York, over exceeded my expectations in every way.

(D) Sitting in an infinity pool outside the villa on the cliff overlooking the Gulf of Thailand, the two-day journey to get there seemed like a distant memory.

(E) We got over our jet lag by going straight to a Muay Thai boxing class (one of the many complimentary classes included in our stay) to bring up our energy levels.

162. The author is considering combining sentences 2 and 3 (reproduced below):

> *Having dreamed of visiting Thailand for many years, <u>I had built up the experience in my head.</u> Koh Samui, a 1.5-hour flight from Bangkok and 18 hours from my home in New York, over exceeded my expectations in every way.*

What is the best version of the underlined portion of these sentences?

(A) I had built up the experience in my head; however, Koh Samui
(B) I had built up the experience in my head; therefore, Koh Samui
(C) I had built up the experience in my head, but Koh Samui
(D) I had built up the experience in my head, and Koh Samui
(E) I had built up the experience in my head, so Koh Samui

163. The writer is considering removing the word "over" before "exceeded" in sentence 3 (reproduced below):

> *Koh Samui, a 1.5-hour flight from Bangkok and 18 hours from my home in New York, over exceeded my expectations in every way.*

Should the writer remove "over" from sentence 3?

(A) Yes, because "exceeded" already communicates that Koh Samui surpassed the writer's expectations
(B) Yes, because the reader may be confused by the use of "over," which is usually used to indicate position
(C) Yes, because it causes an abrupt shift in tone that is not aligned with the writer's purpose
(D) No, because it keeps the sentence's parallel structure intact
(E) No, because the reader may not understand the meaning of the sentence without it

164. In sentence 5 (reproduced below), which version of the underlined text best maintains the tone of the passage?

> We _got over_ our jet lag by going straight to a Muay Thai boxing class (one of the many complimentary classes included in our stay) to bring up our energy levels.

(A) as it is now
(B) recovered from
(C) dramatically and precipitously reduced
(D) beat
(E) destroyed

165. The writer is considering adding the following sentence after sentence 6:

> To complete the experience, I chose a one-hour Thai classic massage with oil, which began with a foot scrub with flowers and ended with warm towels, hot tea, and a relaxed mind.

Should the writer add the sentence?

(A) Yes, because the readers may not know what a massage is
(B) Yes, because people who travel to Thailand are going for the famous Thai classic massages
(C) Yes, because it completes the narrative of the first day of the trip and concludes paragraph 2
(D) No, because not all travelers are interested in the massage offerings in Thailand
(E) No, because some travelers are more interested in hiking and adventures and do not want to read about spa treatments and relaxation

166. The writer is considering adding the following sentence before sentence 7:

> *Banyan Tree offers options for all types of travelers.*

Should the writer add the sentence?

(A) Yes, because it serves as a unifying main idea to begin the paragraph and connects the supporting details presented in sentences 7 through 11

(B) Yes, because the previous two paragraphs have led readers to believe that Banyan Tree is only for families

(C) No, because it provides irrelevant and unnecessary information for potential travelers

(D) No, because it makes the paragraph too much longer than the previous paragraphs

(E) No, because the writer cannot have personal experience traveling with all these types of travelers

167. The writer is considering removing sentence 10 (reproduced below):

> *Highlights at Saffron include the duck breast with tamarind sauce, multiple curry options, crabmeat spring rolls, and taro dumplings with purple potato ice cream for dessert.*

Should the writer remove sentence 10?

(A) Yes, because not all travelers can eat all of those menu offerings due to various allergies and preferences

(B) Yes, because readers may be unfamiliar with the foods listed, such as "tamarind sauce," "curry," and "taro dumplings"

(C) Yes, because the menu offerings at Saffron are irrelevant to the passage as a whole

(D) No, because providing some of the food options is important to readers understanding the experience offered at Banyan Tree and is typical for a travel blog

(E) No, because readers have no other means of learning about what kind of food is available to them at Banyan Tree

168. The writer wants to avoid expressing the claim in sentence 12 (reproduced below) in absolute terms:

> *When you are ready to venture off the property, Koh Samui has a lot to offer guests by day and by night.*

Which version of the underlined portion of the sentence meets the writer's needs?

(A) as it is now
(B) everything a traveler could ever dream of
(C) the best activities available anywhere in the world
(D) all any traveler could hope for
(E) the most incredible offerings of any location

169. The writer is considering removing the underlined portion of sentence 14 (reproduced below).

> *You can also fish on Koh Tan Island for barracuda, snapper, shark, mackerel, and more, which is great for people of any age and experience level.*

Should the writer remove the underlined portion of the sentence?

(A) Yes, because the sentence already provides the types of fish and is long enough as is
(B) Yes, because the age and experience level of the potential fishers is irrelevant to the passage
(C) Yes, because readers interested in fishing are of only one age range and experience level
(D) No, because age and experience level for different activities, such as fishing, are of interest to potential travelers to the area
(E) No, because fishing is enjoyed by all people of varying ages and experience levels

170. In sentence 15 (reproduced below), the writer wants to provide additional information to help readers to know what to expect if they choose to visit Buddha's magic garden.

> *Those who wish to stay on land can see the Namuang waterfall or visit the Buddha's magic garden, a beautiful sight to behold!*

Which of the following versions of the underlined text best accomplishes this goal?

(A) as it is now
(B) also known as Heaven's Garden.
(C) which was founded in 1976.
(D) which was created by an old Samui fruit farmer, Nim Thongsuk.
(E) hidden high up in the hills and offering majestic views and an unusual collection of statues in the midst of the jungle.

Passage 4c: G. K. Chesterton, *A Defence of Baby-Worship*

The two facts which attract almost every normal person to children are, first, that they are very serious, and, secondly, that they are in consequence very happy. They are jolly with the completeness which is possible only in the absence of humour. The most unfathomable schools and sages have never attained to the gravity which dwells in the eyes of a baby of three 5 months old. It is the gravity of astonishment at the universe, and astonishment at the universe is not mysticism, but a transcendent common-sense. The fascination of children lies in this: that with each of them all things are remade, and the universe is put again upon its trial. As we walk the streets and see below us those delightful bulbous heads, three times too big for the 10 body, which mark these human mushrooms, we ought always primarily to remember that within every one of these heads there is a new universe, as new as it was on the seventh day of creation[1]. In each of those orbs there is a new system of stars, new grass, new cities, a new sea.

There is always in the healthy mind an obscure prompting that religion 15 teaches us rather to dig than to climb; that if we could once understand the common clay of earth we should understand everything. Similarly, we have the sentiment that if we could destroy custom at a blow and see the stars as a child sees them, we should need no other apocalypse. This is the great truth which has always lain at the back of baby-worship, and which will support 20 it to the end. Maturity, with its endless energies and aspirations, may easily be convinced that it will find new things to appreciate; but it will never be

---

1. From the Book of Genesis of the Bible. After God creates Heaven and Earth, makes animals, and breathes his own breath into clay to make man, he rests on the seventh day.

convinced, at bottom, that it has properly appreciated what it has got. We may scale the heavens and find new stars innumerable, but there is still the new star we have not found—that on which we were born.   25

But the influence of children goes further than its first trifling effort of remaking heaven and earth. It forces us actually to remodel our conduct in accordance with this revolutionary theory of the marvellousness of all things. We do (even when we are perfectly simple or ignorant)—we do actually treat talking in children as marvellous, walking in children as   30 marvellous, common intelligence in children as marvellous. The cynical philosopher fancies he has a victory in this matter—that he can laugh when he shows that the words or antics of the child, so much admired by its worshippers, are common enough. The fact is that this is precisely where baby-worship is so profoundly right. Any words and any antics in a lump of   35 clay are wonderful, the child's words and antics are wonderful, and it is only fair to say that the philosopher's words and antics are equally wonderful.

171. The primary purpose of the passage is to:
   (A) defend the worship of babies
   (B) apologize for the worship of babies
   (C) persuade people to worship babies
   (D) explain why people worship babies
   (E) dissuade people from worshipping babies

172. Which of the following merely contributes to the reasons we worship babies, and is not worthy of worship as an isolated characteristic?
   (A) they are very serious
   (B) they are very happy
   (C) in them, everything is new
   (D) they help us treat simple actions as marvelous
   (E) they are capable of appreciating everything

173. The sentence "They are jolly with the completeness which is possible only in the absence of humour" (lines 3–4) uses the rhetorical technique of:
   (A) allusion
   (B) analogy
   (C) paradox
   (D) anaphora
   (E) antithesis

174. The metaphor of "these human mushrooms" in line 11 to describe babies serves to make clear their:

(A) physical dimensions
(B) innate intelligence
(C) fragile nature
(D) quick growth
(E) sturdy composition

175. The last line of the first paragraph, "In each of those orbs there is a new system of stars, new grass, new cities, a new sea," (lines 13–14) uses repetition to underscore:

(A) the novelty of all that is around us
(B) the awe of how many new things are created all the time
(C) the enjoyment of all that nature has to offer
(D) the wonder of the baby's astonishment with the world
(E) our pride in our many and varied man-made creations

176. In context, the word "custom" in line 18 most nearly means:

(A) a practice followed by a particular group of people
(B) a ritual performed at certain times
(C) a habitual practice
(D) a routine done with monotony
(E) an inherited tradition

177. The word "trifling" (in line 26), meaning unimportant or trivial, is used here to express:

(A) surprise
(B) annoyance
(C) sarcasm
(D) disappointment
(E) disbelief

178. The effect of children upon adults is a:

(A) deeper appreciation of how little time we have in our lives
(B) deeper appreciation of the love that brings children into the world
(C) deeper appreciation of the marvels of inventions and human ingenuity
(D) deeper appreciation of the goodness of humanity
(E) deeper appreciation of what we normally treat as ordinary

179. The references to clay in lines 17 and 36 refer back to:

    (A) gravity
    (B) creation
    (C) mysticism
    (D) sages
    (E) the universe

180. The tone of the passage can best be described as:

    (A) irreverent and sarcastic
    (B) moralistic and restrained
    (C) sentimental and poignant
    (D) contentious and irate
    (E) thoughtful and jocular

Passage 4d: *Birthday Problem Draft*

(1) Let's say you're in a class with 29 classmates, a total of 30 students. (2) What's the probability that at least two students in the class share a birthday?

(3) You probably suspect the probability is extremely low. (4) After all, isn't it exceedingly rare to find someone who shares your birthday?

(5) A superior alternative exists when analyzing this particular situation. (6) First, let's call you Student #1, and let's also say your birthday is May 30. (7) If you randomly select a classmate (Student #2), the probability that he or she does *not* share your birthday is $\frac{364}{365}$. (8) For the sake of argument, let's say Student #2's birthday is May 11. (9) Now, if you select another student at random, the probability that Student #3's birthday is *neither* May 30 *nor* May 11 is $\frac{363}{365}$. (10) The joint probability of multiple consecutive independent events is the product of the probabilities of each event. (11) Thirdly, if we repeat this process for all 30 students, the probability that *no* two students in the class share a birthday is:

$$P\ (no\ two\ share) = \frac{364}{365} \times \frac{363}{365} \times \cdots \times \frac{336}{365} = 0.294 = 29.4\%$$

(12) And we are interested in the probability that at least two students *do* share the same birthday:

$$P\ (at\ least\ two\ share) = 1 - p\ (no\ two\ share) = 1 - 0.294 = 70.6\%$$

(13) Yes, you read that correctly: there is a 70.6% chance that, in a group of 30 people, at least two of them share a birthday. (14) One important lesson from this fun exercise is that, when it comes to probability and statistics, it's always smart to ignore your mind and trust the calculations instead. 20

181. The writer is considering combining sentences 1 and 2 (reproduced below) to communicate the ideas expressed as simply as possible.

> *Let's say you're in a class with 29 classmates, a total of 30 students. What's the probability that at least two students in the class share a birthday?*

Which of the following options is the best combination of sentences 1 and 2 to meet the writer's needs?

(A) Let's say you're in a class with 29 classmates, a total of 30 students, but what's the probability that at least two students in the class share a birthday?

(B) Let's say you're in a class with 29 classmates, a total of 30 students, and what's the probability that at least two students in the class share a birthday?

(C) What's the probability that at least two students in a class of 30 students share a birthday?

(D) What's the probability that at least two students in a class of 30 students share a birthday if you are in the class, so you are one of the 30 students?

(E) What's the probability that at least two students in a class of 30 students, in which you are a student too, share a birthday?

182. Which of the following sentences can best be described as the writer's thesis?

(A) Let's say you're in a class with 29 classmates, a total of 30 students.

(B) What's the probability that at least two students in the class share a birthday?

(C) You probably suspect the probability is extremely low.

(D) But we are interested in the probability that at least two students *do* share the same birthday.

(E) Yes, you read that correctly: there is a 70.6% chance that, in a group of 30 people, at least two of them share a birthday.

183. The writer is considering revising sentence 5 (reproduced below) to make sure it is consistent with the tone of the passage.

> *A superior alternative exists when analyzing this particular situation.*

Which version of sentence 5 is most consistent with the tone of the rest of the passage?

(A) as it is now
(B) Here's a better approach.
(C) One should be made aware that more efficacious perspectives are in existence.
(D) Please consider a shift to a more enlightened viewpoint when pondering the current problem and its complexities.
(E) Check this out!

184. The writer is considering revising the transition used to begin sentence 6 (reproduced below).

> *First, let's call you Student #1, and let's also say your birthday is May 30.*

Which option below is the best transition for the underlined portion of the sentence?

(A) as it is now
(B) Therefore,
(C) Furthermore,
(D) However,
(E) Moreover,

185. The writer is considering removing sentence 8 (reproduced below).

> *For the sake of argument, let's say Student #2's birthday is May 11.*

Should the writer remove this sentence?

(A) Yes, because the birthdate of May 11 is presented in the following sentence
(B) Yes, because the birthdate of Student #2 is irrelevant to solving the shared birthday probability of the class of all 30 students
(C) Yes, because Student #1's birthday is also in May
(D) No, because the example of Student #2's birthday helps clarify the steps of solving the problem and is referred to in sentence 9
(E) No, because the reader should be made aware of each student's birthday in the class in order to understand the probability

186. The writer is considering revising the transition used to begin sentence 11 (reproduced below).

> *Thirdly, if we repeat this process for all 30 students, the probability that no two students in the class share a birthday is:*

$$P \, (\textit{no two share}) = \frac{364}{365} \times \frac{363}{365} \times \cdots \times \frac{336}{365} = 0.294 = 29.4\%$$

Which option below is the best transition for the underlined portion of the sentence?

(A) as it is now
(B) Therefore,
(C) Furthermore,
(D) However,
(E) Moreover,

187. The writer is considering revising the transition used to begin sentence 12 (reproduced below).

> *And we are interested in the probability that at least two students do share the same birthday.*

Which option below is the best transition for the underlined portion of the sentence?

(A) as it is now
(B) Therefore,
(C) Furthermore,
(D) However,
(E) Moreover,

188. The writer wants to alter the passage for an audience that is unfamiliar with the concept of probability. Which of the following changes best accomplishes this goal?

(A) Add "or likelihood" after the word "probability" in sentence 2
(B) Add "a branch of mathematics" after the word "probability" in sentence 3
(C) Add "which was developed by Middle Eastern mathematicians" after the word "probability" in sentence 7
(D) Add "founded between the 8th and 13th centuries" after the word "probability" in sentence 10
(E) Add "which is applied in everyday life" after the word "probability" in sentence 10

189. The writer wants to replace the underlined word in sentence 14 (reproduced below) with a more precise word, taking into account the context of the paragraph.

> *One important lesson from this fun exercise is that, when it comes to probability and statistics, it's always smart to ignore your* __mind__ *and trust the calculations instead.*

Which version of the underlined word best accomplishes this goal?

(A) ideas
(B) brain
(C) intuitions
(D) thoughts
(E) feelings

190. The writer is considering removing sentence 14 (reproduced below).

> *One important lesson from this fun exercise is that, when it comes to probability and statistics, it's always smart to ignore your mind and trust the calculations instead.*

Should the writer remove this sentence?

(A) Yes, because the solution to the problem has already been presented to the reader

(B) Yes, because readers may not be interested in other topics or questions in probability and statistics

(C) Yes, because not all readers know how to do these calculations on their own

(D) No, because it is impossible to understand the probability of 30 people sharing a birthday without this final thought

(E) No, because this sentence communicates that "the birthday problem" is one example, and the reader should apply this type of problem solving to other probability and statistics questions as well

Passage 4e: Michel de Montaigne, *Of the Punishment of Cowardice*

I once heard of a prince, and a great captain, having a narration given him as he sat at table of the proceeding against Monsieur de Vervins, who was sentenced to death for having surrendered Boulogne to the English,—[To Henry VIII, in 1544]—openly maintaining that a soldier could not justly be put to death for want of courage. And, in truth, 'tis reason that a man   5 should make a great difference betwixt faults that merely proceed from infirmity, and those that are visibly the effects of treachery and malice: for, in the last, we act against the rules of reason that nature has imprinted in us; whereas, in the former, it seems as if we might produce the same nature, who left us in such a state of imperfection and weakness of courage, for our   10 justification. Insomuch that many have thought we are not fairly questionable for anything but what we commit against our conscience; and it is partly upon this rule that those ground their opinion who disapprove of capital or sanguinary punishments inflicted upon heretics and misbelievers; and theirs also who advocate or a judge is not accountable for having from   15 mere ignorance failed in his administration.

But as to cowardice, it is certain that the most usual way of chastising it is by ignominy and it is supposed that this practice brought into use by the legislator Charondas; and that, before his time, the laws of Greece punished

those with death who fled from a battle; whereas he ordained only that they 20
be for three days exposed in the public dressed in woman's attire, hoping
yet for some service from them, having awakened their courage by this
open shame:

> "Suffundere malis homims sanguinem, quam effundere."
> ["Rather bring the blood into a man's cheek than let it out of his body." 25
> Tertullian in his *Apologetics*.]

It appears also that the Roman laws did anciently punish those with death
who had run away; for Ammianus Marcellinus says that the Emperor Julian
commanded ten of his soldiers, who had turned their backs in an encounter against the Parthians, to be first degraded, and afterward put to death, 30
according, says he, to the ancient laws,—[Ammianus Marcellinus, xxiv. 4;
xxv. i.]—and yet elsewhere for the like offence he only condemned others
to remain amongst the prisoners under the baggage ensign. The severe punishment the people of Rome inflicted upon those who fled from the battle
of Cannae, and those who ran away with Aeneius Fulvius at his defeat, did 35
not extend to death. And yet, methinks, 'tis to be feared, lest disgrace should
make such delinquents desperate, and not only faint friends, but enemies.

Of late memory,—[In 1523]—the Seigneur de Frauget, lieutenant to the
Mareschal de Chatillon's company, having by the Mareschal de Chabannes
been put in government of Fuentarabia in the place of Monsieur de Lude, 40
and having surrendered it to the Spaniard, he was for that condemned to be
degraded from all nobility, and both himself and his posterity declared igno-
ble, taxable, and for ever incapable of bearing arms, which severe sentence
was afterwards accordingly executed at Lyons.—[In 1536]—And, since that,
all the gentlemen who were in Guise when the Count of Nassau entered 45
into it, underwent the same punishment, as several others have done since
for the like offence. Notwithstanding, in case of such a manifest ignorance
or cowardice as exceeds all ordinary example, 'tis but reason to take it for a
sufficient proof of treachery and malice, and for such to be punished.

191. The overall purpose of the passage as a whole is to:
- (A) debunk the myth that people are punished for cowardice
- (B) analyze the effects on society of the practice of punishing
  cowardice
- (C) provide a series of examples to refute the process of punishing
  cowardice
- (D) support the practice of punishing cowardice
- (E) argue to abolish the practice of punishing cowardice

192. The writer classifies faults from infirmity (or weakness) and malice (or ill will) to express his acceptance that:

  (A) faults from infirmity are more common so we should be more accepting of them

  (B) faults from infirmity are innate while faults from malice are learned

  (C) faults from malice can be corrected while faults from infirmity are immutable

  (D) faults from infirmity trouble men in their younger years while faults of malice occur in their later years

  (E) faults from infirmity are more pardonable because they do not go against human nature

193. The rhetorical function of the sentence "And, in truth, 'tis reason . . . for our justification" in lines 5–11 is to:

  (A) acknowledge the validity of one of the claims of the counterargument

  (B) put into words the unspoken assumption shared by the writer and his audience

  (C) provide evidence to support the major claim of the passage

  (D) qualify the original claim of the passage so that the audience will be persuaded

  (E) establish the credibility of the writer as an expert on the subject

194. In context, the word "questionable" in lines 11–12 most nearly means:

  (A) of doubtful integrity

  (B) uncertain

  (C) debatable

  (D) difficult to decide

  (E) capable of being inquired of

195. According to the first paragraph (lines 1–16), cowardice is:

  (A) just cause for capital punishment

  (B) a product of frailty

  (C) a product of ill will

  (D) against nature

  (E) against our conscience

196. The quote in the passage, "Rather bring the blood into a man's cheek than let it out of his body," (line 25) is an aphorism meaning:

(A) it is better to shame a man than kill him
(B) it is better to momentarily harm a man than kill him
(C) it is better to injure a man's face than his body
(D) it is preferable to be shamed rather than killed
(E) it is preferable to be harmed momentarily rather than killed

197. The last sentence of the passage, "Notwithstanding . . . punished" in lines 47–49 _____ the earlier claim of the prince mentioned in the first sentence: "that a soldier could not justly be put to death for want of courage" (lines 4–5).

(A) agrees with
(B) disagrees with
(C) qualifies
(D) refutes with counterargument
(E) supports with examples

198. The use of brackets in the passage does all of the following *except*:

(A) provide more information than given in the body of the passage
(B) provide citations for the material in the passage
(C) provide translations of material presented in Latin
(D) provide dates for when the examples occurred
(E) provide personal commentary on the historical information given

199. In building his argument, the speaker mostly relies on:

(A) contemporary illustrations
(B) expert testimony
(C) a collection of clarifying analogies
(D) a range of historical examples
(E) figurative language

200. The tone for the majority of the passage can best be described as:

(A) incredulous
(B) ambivalent
(C) objective
(D) exasperated
(E) relieved

Journalists and Science and Nature Writers with Draft Passages

Passage 5a: Margaret Fuller, *At Home and Abroad; or, Things and Thoughts in America and Europe*

In the afternoon we went on shore at the Manitou Islands, where the boat stops to wood. No one lives here except wood-cutters for the steamboats. I had thought of such a position, from its mixture of profound solitude with service to the great world, as possessing an ideal beauty. I think so still, even after seeing the wood-cutters and their slovenly huts. 5

In times of slower growth, man did not enter a situation without a certain preparation or adaptedness to it. He drew from it, if not to the poetical extent, at least in some proportion, its moral and its meaning. The wood-cutter did not cut down so many trees a day, that the Hamadryads[1] had not time to make their plaints heard; the shepherd tended his sheep, and did no 10 jobs or chores the while; the idyl had a chance to grow up, and modulate his oaten pipe. But now the poet must be at the whole expense of the poetry in describing one of these positions; the worker is a true Midas[2] to the gold he makes. The poet must describe, as the painter sketches Irish peasant-girls and Danish fishwives, adding the beauty, and leaving out the dirt. 15

I come to the West prepared for the distaste I must experience at its mushroom growth. I know that, where "go ahead" is tire only motto, the village cannot grow into the gentle proportions that successive lives and the gradations of experience involuntarily give. In older countries the house of the son grew from that of the father, as naturally as new joints on a bough, 20 and the cathedral crowned the whole as naturally as the leafy summit the tree. This cannot be here. The march of peaceful is scarce less wanton than

---

1. Hamadryads are Greek mythological beings that live in trees. They are a particular type of dryad, and dryads are a type of nymph.

2. King Midas is popularly remembered in Greek mythology for his ability to turn everything he touched into gold. This came to be called the golden touch, or the Midas touch.

that of warlike invasion. The old landmarks are broken down, and the land, for a season, bears none, except of the rudeness of conquest and the needs of the day, whose bivouac-fires blacken the sweetest forest glades. I have come prepared to see all this, to dislike it, but not with stupid narrowness to distrust or defame. On the contrary, while I will not be so obliging as to confound ugliness with beauty, discord with harmony, and laud and be contented with all I meet, when it conflicts with my best desires and tastes, I trust by reverent faith to woo the mighty meaning of the scene, perhaps to foresee the law by which a new order, a new poetry, is to be evoked from this chaos, and with a curiosity as ardent, but not so selfish, as that of Macbeth[3], to call up the apparitions of future kings from the strange ingredients of the witch's caldron. Thus I will not grieve that all the noble trees are gone already from this island to feed this caldron, but believe it will have Medea's[4] virtue, and reproduce them in the form of new intellectual growths, since centuries cannot again adorn the land with such as have been removed.

201. The "slovenly huts" (line 5) are used as an example of:
  - (A) the profound solitude of the wood-cutters
  - (B) the service to the great world done by the wood-cutters
  - (C) the beauty added by the poet
  - (D) the dirt left out by the poet
  - (E) the ideal beauty of the lives of the wood-cutters

202. The writer presents the wood-cutter and the shepherd as examples of all of the following *except*:
  - (A) men with the time to reflect on their positions
  - (B) men that are prepared for and adapted to their situations
  - (C) men who drew the moral and meaning from their positions
  - (D) men living in a time of slower growth
  - (E) men who must be at the full expense in describing their position

---

3. Macbeth is Shakespeare's shortest tragedy, and tells the story of a brave Scottish general named Macbeth who receives a prophecy from a trio of witches that one day he will become King of Scotland.

4. in Greek mythology, Medea is a sorceress who was the daughter of King Aeëtes of Colchis, niece of Circe, granddaughter of the sun god Helios, and later wife to the hero Jason. In Euripides's play Medea, Jason leaves Medea when Creon, king of Corinth, offers him his daughter, Glauce. The play tells of Medea avenging her husband's betrayal by killing their children.

203. Because of the rapid growth of the present times, poets must:

  (A) describe the lives of workers because workers don't have the time to reflect on their positions
  (B) be prepared for the distaste that they will experience
  (C) see the lives of wood-cutters as possessing an ideal beauty
  (D) trust by faith to be able to make meaning from their surroundings
  (E) reproduce the past with a new form of poetry

204. The primary purpose of paragraph two (lines 6–15) is:

  (A) to narrate a typical day of woodcutters and shepherds
  (B) to describe times of slower growth
  (C) to analyze the effects of more rapid growth on the lives and jobs of poets
  (D) to define the poet
  (E) to classify the types of poets

205. In the first sentence of paragraph three (lines 16–17), "mushroom" is used to figuratively modify "growth" as being:

  (A) natural
  (B) dark
  (C) hidden
  (D) fast
  (E) spreading

206. In context, the word "confound" in line 28 most nearly means:

  (A) combine
  (B) confuse
  (C) distinguish
  (D) abash
  (E) ruin

207. Which of the following lines expresses irony:
- (A) "In times of slower growth, man did not enter a situation without a certain preparation or adaptedness to it" (6–7)
- (B) "The poet must describe, as the painter sketches Irish peasant-girls and Danish fishwives, adding the beauty, and leaving out the dirt" (14–15)
- (C) "I come to the West prepared for the distaste I must experience at its mushroom growth." (16–17)
- (D) "The march of peaceful is scarce less wanton than that of warlike invasion." (22–23)
- (E) "I have come prepared to see all this, to dislike it, but not with stupid narrowness to distrust or defame." (25–27)

208. The footnotes are used to:
- (A) refute earlier claims
- (B) cite scholarship on the subject
- (C) increase the author's credibility
- (D) show how the author's opinion has shifted since writing this piece
- (E) clarify allusions

209. The style of the passage can best be described as:
- (A) disjointed and complex
- (B) terse and dramatic
- (C) descriptive and allusive
- (D) abstract and informal
- (E) colloquial and evocative

210. The tone of the passage can best be described as:
- (A) bittersweet
- (B) skeptical
- (C) derisive
- (D) curt
- (E) moralistic

Passage 5b: *Teaching Philosophy Draft*

(1) As a teacher, I must accept that not all students naturally and automatically share my love of math and science. (2) In fact, the opposite is often the case. (3) My primary responsibility is to make sure my students learn.

(4) I wish I could say I have an infallible, one-size-fits-all formula that works perfectly for all classes, but the truth is that I have a set of ideas, techniques, and tools that I utilize on a class-by-class and day-by-day basis. (5) For example, to stimulate students' interest in the topic being discussed, I incorporate examples of real-world applications into lessons whenever possible—for example, teaching that suspension bridge cables are parabolas governed by quadratic equations. (6) Next, I never teach via straight lecture; rather, I frequently offer students hands-on practice by incorporating problem sets through which I can guide and "scaffold" them during class. (7) To activate students' natural curiosity and inquisitiveness, I regularly pepper my instruction with higher-order thinking questions such as "So what do you predict will happen if this term becomes infinitely large?" or "Can you think of a different way to factor this polynomial?"

(8) Furthermore, I involve a variety of instructional technologies like the Active Board, the TI-84 calculator's Smart View software, embedded animations in presentations, and the web-based Skyward system. (9) In addition, I have students work at the board and explain their answers to the class at least once or twice in every class meeting. (10) This rarely fails to get the class smiling, chattering (about the material!), animated, and engaged. (11) Finally, I employ traditional summative assessments like tests and quizzes, and formative assessments such as nightly homework, which is graded on effort, not on accuracy.

211. Which of the following sentences can best be described as a thesis for the passage?

(A) As a teacher, I must accept that not all students naturally and automatically share my love of math and science.

(B) In fact, the opposite is often the case.

(C) My primary responsibility is to make sure my students learn.

(D) I wish I could say I have an infallible, one-size-fits-all formula that works perfectly for all classes, but the truth is that I have a set of ideas, techniques, and tools that I utilize on a class-by-class and day-by-day basis.

(E) For example, to stimulate students' interest in the topic being discussed, I incorporate examples of real-world applications into lessons whenever possible—for example, teaching that suspension bridge cables are parabolas governed by quadratic equations.

212. The writer would like to combine sentences 1 and 2 (reproduced below).

> *As a teacher, I must accept that not all students naturally and automatically share my love of math and science. In fact, the opposite is often the case.*

Which of the following is the best combination of these sentences?

(A) As a teacher, I must accept that not all students naturally and automatically share my love of math and science, for in fact, the opposite is often the case.

(B) As a teacher, I must accept that not all students naturally and automatically share my love of math and science, nor in fact, the opposite is often the case.

(C) As a teacher, I must accept that not all students naturally and automatically share my love of math and science, but in fact, the opposite is often the case.

(D) As a teacher, I must accept that not all students naturally and automatically share my love of math and science, or in fact, the opposite is often the case.

(E) As a teacher, I must accept that not all students naturally and automatically share my love of math and science, so in fact, the opposite is often the case.

213. The writer would like to add a transition at the beginning of sentence 3 (reproduced below) that communicates its relationship to the sentences that came before it.

> *My primary responsibility is to make sure my students learn.*

Which of the following transitions, if placed at the beginning of the sentence, adjusting capitalization and punctuation as needed, best meets the writer's needs?

(A) Therefore,

(B) Moreover,

(C) Furthermore,

(D) Additionally,

(E) Regardless,

214. The writer is considering removing sentence 5 (reproduced below):

> *For example, to stimulate students' interest in the topic being discussed, I incorporate examples of real-world applications into lessons whenever possible—for example, teaching that suspension bridge cables are parabolas governed by quadratic equations.*

Should the writer remove sentence 5?

(A) Yes, because only some students will learn about suspension bridge cables
(B) Yes, because some students have not encountered quadratic equations yet
(C) Yes, because student interest varies widely from topic to topic
(D) No, because all students need to master the concept of parabolas
(E) No, because the sentence provides a clarifying illustration of the claim made in sentence 4

215. The writer is considering adding the underlined phrase to sentence 6 (reproduced below):

> *Next, I never teach via straight lecture, <u>an educational talk to an audience</u>; rather, I frequently offer students hands-on practice by incorporating problem sets through which I can guide and "scaffold" them during class.*

Should the writer add the underlined portion to sentence 6?

(A) Yes, because the writer should not assume that the audience has heard that term before
(B) Yes, because "lecture" is considered jargon that is specific to mathematics education
(C) Yes, because the audience is clearly students who have not had any educational experience
(D) No, because the audience is probably familiar with the term, and the second half of the sentence provides context clues through counterexamples
(E) No, because the writer does not have the educational expertise to define a term like "lecture" for the audience

216. The writer would like to add a transition at the beginning of sentence 7 (reproduced below) that communicates its relationship to the sentences that came before it.

> *To activate students' natural curiosity and inquisitiveness, I regularly pepper my instruction with higher-order thinking questions such as "So what do you predict will happen if this term becomes infinitely large?" or "Can you think of a different way to factor this polynomial?"*

Of the following transitions, with the proper adjustments for capitalization and punctuation, would *not* meet the writer's needs if added to the beginning of the sentence?

(A) Also,
(B) Additionally,
(C) Furthermore,
(D) Moreover,
(E) However,

217. The writer is considering adding the underlined information to sentence 8 (reproduced below):

> *Furthermore, <u>to appeal to today's technology-loving students</u>, I involve a variety of instructional technologies like the Active Board, the TI-84 calculator's Smart View software, embedded animations in presentations, and the web-based Skyward system.*

Should the writer add the underlined portion to the sentence?

(A) Yes, because all students love technology and are adept at using it
(B) Yes, because it provides the writer's rationale for using these technologies and helps support the major claim that the writer does what is necessary to make sure the students learn
(C) Yes, readers may be unfamiliar with these forms of technology and need this added information as clarification
(D) No, because not all students love technology, and this added information may make those students feel left out
(E) No, because the use of technology is not appropriate or relevant for the writer's discussion of teaching techniques

218. The writer would like to combine sentences 9 and 10 (reproduced below):

> *In addition, I have students work at the board and explain their answers to the class at least once or twice in every class meeting. This rarely fails to get the class smiling, chattering (about the material!), animated, and engaged.*

Which version below does not serve as an effective combination of these sentences?

(A) In addition, I have students work at the board and explain their answers to the class at least once or twice in every class meeting, and this rarely fails to get the class smiling, chattering (about the material!), animated, and engaged.

(B) In addition, I have students work at the board and explain their answers to the class at least once or twice in every class meeting; this rarely fails to get the class smiling, chattering (about the material!), animated, and engaged.

(C) In addition, I have students work at the board and explain their answers to the class at least once or twice in every class meeting, which rarely fails to get the class smiling, chattering (about the material!), animated, and engaged.

(D) In addition, I have students work at the board and explain their answers to the class at least once or twice in every class meeting, but this rarely fails to get the class smiling, chattering (about the material!), animated, and engaged.

(E) In addition, I have students work at the board and explain their answers to the class at least once or twice in every class meeting, a tactic that rarely fails to get the class smiling, chattering (about the material!), animated, and engaged.

219. The writer is considering revising the transition at the beginning of sentence 11 (reproduced below):

Finally, I employ traditional summative assessments like tests and quizzes, and formative assessments such as nightly homework, which is graded on effort, not on accuracy.

Which of the following words is the best transition for this last sentence of the passage?

(A) as it is now
(B) Consequently,
(C) Therefore,
(D) Furthermore,
(E) Nevertheless,

220. The writer is considering adding the following sentence after sentence 11:

Debates exist about whether homework should be graded on effort or accuracy; while some believe students need actionable feedback based on their accuracy in demonstrating understanding of the material, or lack thereof, others believe that students should receive credit for their time and effort in trying to understand the material to the best of their ability.

Should the writer add this sentence?

(A) Yes, because readers may be unfamiliar with the debate around grading for effort or accuracy
(B) Yes, because the homework grading policy is a key detail in support of the writer's major claim about the responsibility of the teacher to do everything possible to aid students' learning
(C) Yes, because the passage ends abruptly and needs this final sentence as a conclusion for the reader's satisfaction
(D) No, because this information is irrelevant to the major claim, and this proposed sentence begins a new topic, which is not appropriate for a final sentence
(E) No, because readers are not interested in homework policies and would have a difficult time understanding the information presented about effort and accuracy

Passage 5c: Charles Darwin, *On the Origin of Species*

In considering the Origin of Species, it is quite conceivable that a naturalist, reflecting on the mutual affinities of organic beings, on their embryological relations, their geographical distribution, geological succession, and other such facts, might come to the conclusion that each species had not been independently created, but had descended, like varieties, from other species. 5 Nevertheless, such a conclusion, even if well founded, would be unsatisfactory, until it could be shown how the innumerable species inhabiting this world have been modified, so as to acquire that perfection of structure and coadaptation which most justly excites our admiration. Naturalists continually refer to external conditions, such as climate, food, etc., as the only 10 possible cause of variation. In one very limited sense, as we shall hereafter see, this may be true; but it is preposterous to attribute to mere external conditions, the structure, for instance, of the woodpecker, with its feet, tail, beak, and tongue, so admirably adapted to catch insects under the bark of trees. In the case of the misseltoe which draws its nourishment from certain 15 trees, which has seeds that must be transported by certain birds, and which has flowers with separate sexes absolutely requiring the agency of certain insects to bring pollen from one flower to the other, it is equally preposterous to account for the structure of this parasite, with its relations to several distinct organic beings, by the effects of external conditions, or of habit, or 20 of the volition of the plant itself.

The author of the *Vestiges of Creation* would, I presume, say that, after a certain unknown number of generations, some bird had given birth to a woodpecker, and some plant to the misseltoe, and that these had been produced perfect as we now see them; but this assumption seems to me 25 to be no explanation, for it leaves the case of the coadaptations of organic beings to each other and to their physical conditions of life, untouched and unexplained.

It is, therefore, of the highest importance to gain a clear insight into the means of modification and coadaptation. At the commencement of my 30 observations it seemed to me probable that a careful study of domesticated animals and of cultivated plants would offer the best chance of making out this obscure problem. Nor have I been disappointed; in this and in all other perplexing cases I have invariably found that our knowledge, imperfect though it be, of variation under domestication, afforded the best and 35 safest clue. I may venture to express my conviction of the high value of such studies, although they have been very commonly neglected by naturalists.

221. The function of the passage as a whole is to:
- (A) admonish the naturalists for the logical fallacies in their arguments
- (B) propose that we disregard all of what naturalists have offered on the origin of species
- (C) acknowledge the limited usefulness of the studies that we have of modification and coadaptation
- (D) point out the shortcomings in the arguments of naturalists and encourage more review
- (E) express the value and completeness of our existing studies

222. In context, the word "affinities" in line 2 most nearly means:
- (A) feelings of kinship
- (B) natural attractions
- (C) relationships
- (D) counterparts
- (E) resemblances in structure

223. According to the passage, the problem with the "conclusion that each species had not been independently created, but had descended, like varieties, from other species" (lines 4–5) is that:
- (A) it is begging the question (assuming something is true before it is proven)
- (B) it is a hasty generalization (concluding something without sufficient evidence)
- (C) it is ad hominem (attacking the person rather than the argument)
- (D) it is post hoc (something that happens before an event is assumed to be a cause)
- (E) it is non sequitur (the conclusion does not logically follow the evidence)

224. The sentences "Naturalists continually refer to external conditions, such as climate, food, etc., as the only possible cause of variation. In one very limited sense, as we shall hereafter see, this may be true; but it is preposterous to attribute to mere external conditions, the structure, for instance, of the woodpecker, with its feet, tail, beak, and tongue, so admirably adapted to catch insects under the bark of trees," (lines 9–15) are provided by the writer as:

(A) counterargument
(B) an underlying assumption (warrant)
(C) a rebuttal
(D) data
(E) claim

225. While discussing the woodpecker and the misseltoe in paragraph one, the writer's tone can best be described as:

(A) jovial
(B) sanguine
(C) awed
(D) conciliatory
(E) nostalgic

226. The subject and predicate of the last sentence (lines 15–21) of the first paragraph are:

(A) case draws
(B) seeds transported
(C) flowers requiring
(D) it is
(E) relations effects

227. The third paragraph (lines 29–36) can best be described as:

(A) a reasoned introduction to an argument
(B) an impassioned appeal to the audience
(C) a dramatic narrative
(D) a historical commentary
(E) a personal reflection on a problem

228. In context, the word "obscure" in line 33 most nearly means:

    (A) dark

    (B) faint

    (C) mysterious

    (D) remote

    (E) ambiguous

229. "Coadaptation" in a species refers to:

    (A) the effects of geographical distribution

    (B) the effects of embryological relations

    (C) the effects of geological succession

    (D) the effects of relationships with other organic beings and life

    (E) the effects of having descended from other species

230. The tone of the last paragraph (lines 29–37) can best be described as:

    (A) forthright

    (B) poignant

    (C) evasive

    (D) acerbic

    (E) ominous

Passage 5d: *Barefoot in Boca Travel Blog Draft*

(1) A Florida hotspot, <u>Boca Raton Resort & Club, a Waldorf Astoria Resort,</u> will over exceed your expectations for a convenient and luxurious family get-away. (2) With 30 tennis courts, 13 bars and restaurants, seven pools, two championship golf courses, a FlowRider wave simulator and Surf School, the lavish Waldorf Astoria Spa, and two health clubs, your days can be filled with hours of relaxation and memorable family experiences.

(3) After undergoing a 120-million-dollar renovation several years ago, Boca Beach Club reopened with a barefoot luxury vibe and 45 poolside cabanas, two beachfront cafés, remodeled guest rooms, and the stunning SeaGrille, celebrating its new chef Jordan Lerman. (4) Boca Beach Club is set up with pools for adults only, children only, and both. (5) The rooms are conveniently located steps away from the pool and beach, making daytime naps and breaks from the sun easy with kids in tow.

(6) The shuttle and ferry will take you back and forth from the Boca Beach Club to the main resort (Boca Raton Resort & Club) to visit the spa and gym as well as the Morimoto sushi bar, the fabulous Italian restaurant Lucca, and Serendipity 3. (7) In 2018, The Yacht Club, located at the main

resort, underwent an 8.2-million-dollar redesign to become South Florida's most luxurious boutique waterfront hotel, with 112 guestrooms. (8) The resort features 11 boutiques, a full-service 32-slip marina, a bocce court and croquet lawn, daily aerobic classes, tennis courts, and the world's most exclusive Waldorf Astoria Spa with over 40 treatment rooms, a beautiful garden, outdoor waterfall hot tubs, and the Ritual Bath experience.

(9) The FlowRider wave simulator and Surf School provides hours of entertainment, and the water sports desk will rent you paddleboards, Jet Skis, small motorboats, or large catamarans, if you want to explore the area. (10) Mizner's Quest Club includes a daily supervised camp, with an arcade center, sports deck, and scavenger-like program with interactive learning experiences. (11) Days filled with soccer, yoga, fishing, life-size lawn chess, kite flying, and more make the property kid-friendly, even though the pools have a live DJ on the weekends for adult-only parties. (12) The rock-climbing wall and Rec-Deck with remote-controlled racing boats, a basketball hoop, and table tennis are just a few of the activities teenagers can take advantage of while Mom and Dad enjoy a spa treatment, round of golf, or game of tennis.

231. The writer is considering removing the underlined portion of sentence 1 (reproduced below):

> *A Florida hotspot, Boca Raton Resort & Club, a Waldorf Astoria Resort,* will over exceed your expectations for a convenient and luxurious family getaway.

Should the writer remove the underlined portion of the sentence?

(A) Yes, because all readers will already know that Boca Raton Resort & Club is a Florida hotspot

(B) Yes, because readers may be unfamiliar with the term "hotspot"

(C) Yes, because the phrase makes the sentence too long for an opening line

(D) No, because it adds relevant information about the Boca Raton Resort & Club, including its location and classification as a hotspot

(E) No, because readers will assume that Boca Raton Resort & Club is a location in New York City without the phrase "A Florida hotspot"

232. The writer is considering removing the word "over" before "exceed" in sentence 1 (reproduced below):

A Florida hotspot, <u>Boca Raton Resort & Club, a Waldorf Astoria Resort</u>, will over exceed your expectations for a convenient and luxurious family getaway.

Should the writer remove "over" from sentence 1?

(A) Yes, because "over" is redundant and unnecessary when placed before "exceeded"

(B) Yes, because the reader may believe that the use of "over" changes the meaning of the word "exceeded"

(C) Yes, because it causes a shift in the tone of the passage

(D) No, because it helps to develop the writer's voice and the passage's style

(E) No, because the reader may not know the definition of "exceeded" and may be relying on "over" as a context clue

233. Which of the following can best be described as the writer's thesis?

(A) A Florida hotspot, <u>Boca Raton Resort & Club, a Waldorf Astoria Resort</u>, will over exceed your expectations for a convenient and luxurious family getaway.

(B) With 30 tennis courts, 13 bars and restaurants, seven pools, two championship golf courses, a FlowRider wave simulator and Surf School, the lavish Waldorf Astoria Spa, and two health clubs, your days can be filled with hours of relaxation and memorable family experiences.

(C) After undergoing a 120-million-dollar renovation several years ago, Boca Beach Club reopened with a barefoot luxury vibe and 45 poolside cabanas, two beachfront cafés, remodeled guest rooms, and the stunning SeaGrille celebrating its new chef Jordan Lerman.

(D) Boca Beach Club is set up with pools for adults only, children only, and both.

(E) The rooms are conveniently located steps away from the pool and beach, making daytime naps and breaks from the sun easy with kids in tow.

234. The writer is considering removing sentence 4 (reproduced below):

> *Boca Beach Club is set up with pools for adults only, children only, and both.*

Should the writer remove sentence 4?

(A) Yes, because this travel blog is for families with children, so readers do not need to know about pools for adults only

(B) Yes, because the information about the pools is irrelevant to those who may consider planning a trip to Boca Raton Resort & Club

(C) Yes, because travelers to that area of Florida are interested in going to the beach, not swimming in the resort's pools

(D) No, because travelers with children will not want to go to a resort that has a pool only for adults

(E) No, because readers of a travel blog are most likely interested in how the resort is designed for different types of potential travelers

235. In sentence 5 (reproduced below), the writer wants to ensure that the connotation of the underlined word is appropriate to the context of the sentence.

> *The rooms are <u>conveniently</u> located steps away from the pool and beach, making daytime naps and breaks from the sun easy with kids in tow.*

Which of the following versions of the underlined word would best accomplish this goal?

(A) as it is now
(B) closely
(C) nearly
(D) adjacently
(E) practically

236. The writer is considering adding the underlined phrase to sentence 6 (reproduced below):

> *The shuttle and ferry will take you back and forth from the Boca Beach Club to the main resort (Boca Raton Resort & Club) to visit the spa and gym as well as the Morimoto sushi bar, the fabulous Italian restaurant Lucca, and Serendipity 3, <u>a whimsical spot for casual eats and sweet treats.</u>*

Should the writer add the underlined phrase to sentence 6?

(A) Yes, because readers will be familiar with Serendipity 3 from New York City and will be glad to see it described

(B) Yes, because, unlike Morimoto and Lucca, it is unclear from the sentence what type of food Serendipity 3 offers

(C) Yes, because readers are not interested in fine dining and want to know more about the casual food offerings

(D) No, because readers can infer that Serendipity 3 offers casual food and desserts from its name

(E) No, because travelers will use room service if they want this type of food on vacation

237. The writer wants to avoid expressing the claim in sentence 8 (reproduced below) in absolute terms:

> *The resort features 11 boutiques, a full-service 32-slip marina, a bocce court and croquet lawn, daily aerobic classes, tennis courts, and <u>the world's most exclusive</u> Waldorf Astoria Spa with over 40 treatment rooms, a beautiful garden, outdoor waterfall hot tubs, and the Ritual Bath experience.*

Which version of the underlined portion of the sentence meets the writer's needs?

(A) as it is now

(B) the world's best

(C) the award-winning

(D) the most highly regarded

(E) the nation's nicest

238. The writer is considering adding the following sentence before sentence 9:

> *Among this luxury, the offerings for children and families are plentiful.*

Should the writer add this sentence?

(A) Yes, because it serves as a topic sentence for the final paragraph, which details the activity options for children and families

(B) Yes, because children have not been mentioned up until this point in the passage

(C) Yes, because families with young children and teenagers are the only potential guests of the Boca Raton Resort & Club

(D) No, because children should not be guests at such a luxurious location, where they may be bored or disruptive

(E) No, because children have been mentioned enough already in this passage

239. The writer is considering replacing the underlined phrase in sentence 11 (reproduced below):

> *Days filled with soccer, yoga, fishing, life-size lawn chess, kite flying, and more make the property kid-friendly, even though the pools have a live DJ on the weekends for adult-only parties.*

Which version of the underlined portion of sentence 11 best communicates the relation between the parts of the sentence?

(A) as it is now

(B) although

(C) however

(D) nevertheless

(E) even when

240. The writer is considering adding the following sentence after sentence 12:

> *Highly recommended for a family vacation, the property exudes a sense of ease and elegance with five-star service that leaves you looking forward to your next visit back.*

Should the writer add the sentence?

(A) Yes, because the sentence communicates the writer's appreciation for the resort and clarifies his or her positive outlook on the property

(B) Yes, because the sentence serves as a strong conclusion for both the paragraph and the passage as a whole

(C) Yes, because the paragraph's major claim was not sufficiently supported with details, and this sentence provides those details

(D) No, because the writer's recommendation is inappropriate for an objective description of the location

(E) No, because this sentence breaks from the established tone and dominant impression of the passage

Passage 5e: Charles Lyell, *The Student's Elements of Geology*

Of what materials is the earth composed, and in what manner are these materials arranged? These are the first inquiries with which Geology is occupied, a science which derives its name from the Greek ge, the earth, and logos, a discourse. Previously to experience we might have imagined that investigations of this kind would relate exclusively to the mineral kingdom, 5
and to the various rocks, soils, and metals, which occur upon the surface of the earth, or at various depths beneath it. But, in pursuing such researches, we soon find ourselves led on to consider the successive changes which have taken place in the former state of the earth's surface and interior, and the causes which have given rise to these changes; and, what is still more singu- 10
lar and unexpected, we soon become engaged in researches into the history of the animate creation, or of the various tribes of animals and plants which have, at different periods of the past, inhabited the globe.

All are aware that the solid parts of the earth consist of distinct substances, such as clay, chalk, sand, limestone, coal, slate, granite, and the 15
like; but previously to observation it is commonly imagined that all these had remained from the first in the state in which we now see them—that they were created in their present form, and in their present position. The geologist soon comes to a different conclusion, discovering proofs that the external parts of the earth were not all produced in the beginning of things 20

in the state in which we now behold them, nor in an instant of time. On the contrary, he can show that they have acquired their actual configuration and condition gradually, under a great variety of circumstances, and at successive periods, during each of which distinct races of living beings have flourished on the land and in the waters, the remains of these creatures still 25 lying buried in the crust of the earth.

By the "earth's crust," is meant that small portion of the exterior of our planet which is accessible to human observation. It comprises not merely all of which the structure is laid open in mountain precipices, or in cliffs overhanging a river or the sea, or whatever the miner may reveal in artificial 30 excavations; but the whole of that outer covering of the planet on which we are enabled to reason by observations made at or near the surface. These reasonings may extend to a depth of several miles, perhaps ten miles; and even then it may be said, that such a thickness is no more than 1/400 part of the distance from the surface to the centre. The remark is just: but although 35 the dimensions of such a crust are, in truth, insignificant when compared to the entire globe, yet they are vast, and of magnificent extent in relation to man, and to the organic beings which people our globe. Referring to this standard of magnitude, the geologist may admire the ample limits of his domain, and admit, at the same time, that not only the exterior of the 40 planet, but the entire earth, is but an atom in the midst of the countless worlds surveyed by the astronomer.

241. The main function of the first paragraph (lines 1–13) is:
   (A) to argue against those who would simplify the study of geology
   (B) to describe the investigations into the mineral kingdom
   (C) to define geology as a field of study
   (D) to classify the types of materials of which the earth is composed
   (E) to analyze the process of changes of the earth's surface and interior

242. The major claim of the first paragraph (lines 1–13) is that:

    (A) although geology was first thought to be a study of minerals, further study shows that animals, plants, and evolution are part of the subject as well

    (B) although geology was first thought to be a study of minerals, further study shows that rocks, soils, and metals are part of the subject as well

    (C) although geology was first thought to be a study of the earth's surface, further study shows that the depths beneath the surface are part of the subject as well

    (D) although geology was first thought to be a study of the changes that have taken place in the earth, further study shows that the history of animals and plants is part of the subject as well

    (E) although geology was first thought to be a study of the history of creation, further study shows that animals and plants are part of the subject as well

243. The first sentence of paragraph two, "All are aware that the solid parts of the earth consist of distinct substances, such as clay, chalk, sand, limestone, coal, slate, granite, and the like; but previously to observation it is commonly imagined that all these had remained from the first in the state in which we now see them—that they were created in their present form, and in their present position," (lines 14–18) serves to:

    (A) provide an exhaustive list of the solid parts of the earth

    (B) admonish those who hold the belief that the materials of the earth are unchanged

    (C) provide the latest research on geology

    (D) clear up a common misconception

    (E) argue against the categories of the solid parts of the earth

244. The last sentence of paragraph two, "On the contrary, he can show that they have acquired their actual configuration and condition gradually, under a great variety of circumstances, and at successive periods, during each of which distinct races of living beings have flourished on the land and in the waters, the remains of these creatures still lying buried in the crust of the earth," (lines 21–26) is an example of a cumulative sentence that has the effect of:

(A) providing incomplete thoughts
(B) asking questions of the reader
(C) commanding the reader to listen
(D) supplying a direct and simple statement
(E) beginning with a main idea and adding detailed descriptions of that claim

245. In context, the word "artificial" in line 30 most nearly means:

(A) produced by humans rather than nature
(B) made in imitation of something
(C) feigned
(D) not genuine
(E) affected

246. In context, the word "just" in line 35 most nearly means:

(A) impartial
(B) morally upright
(C) equitable; fair
(D) accurate
(E) deserved

247. In the last paragraph of the passage (lines 27–42), the author defines the "earth's crust" through his use of all of the following *except*:

(A) denotation, or objective definition
(B) boundaries of what it is and is not
(C) a personal interpretation of the phrase
(D) measurements of the earth's crust
(E) reflections on its scope

248. According to the last sentence (lines 38–42), the geologist views the earth with:

(A) frustration and bewilderment
(B) awe and humility
(C) fervor and hostility
(D) mirth and irreverence
(E) elation and skepticism

249. Overall, the passage can be described as:

(A) lyrical
(B) logical
(C) abstract
(D) provocative
(E) controversial

250. The primary purpose of the passage is to:

(A) inform
(B) persuade
(C) entertain
(D) refute
(E) defend

CHAPTER 6

Political Writers with Draft Passages

Passage 6a: Thomas Jefferson, *Sixth State of the Union Address*

It would have given me, fellow citizens, great satisfaction to announce in the moment of your meeting that the difficulties in our foreign relations existing at the time of your last separation had been amicably and justly terminated. I lost no time in taking those measures which were most likely to bring them to such a termination—by special missions charged with such powers and instructions as in the event of failure could leave no imputation on either our moderation or forbearance. The delays which have since taken place in our negotiations with the British Government appear to have proceeded from causes which do not forbid the expectation that during the course of the session I may be enabled to lay before you their final issue. What will be that of the negotiations for settling our differences with Spain nothing which had taken place at the date of the last dispatches enables us to pronounce. On the western side of the Mississippi she advanced in considerable force, and took post at the settlement of Bayou Pierre, on the Red River. This village was originally settled by France, was held by her as long as she held Louisiana, and was delivered to Spain only as a part of Louisiana. Being small, insulated, and distant, it was not observed at the moment of redelivery to France and the United States that she continued a guard of half a dozen men which had been stationed there. A proposition, however, having been lately made by our commander in chief to assume the Sabine River as a temporary line of separation between the troops of the two nations until the issue of our negotiations shall be known, this has been referred by the Spanish commandant to his superior, and in the mean time he has withdrawn his force to the western side of the Sabine River. The correspondence on this subject now communicated will exhibit more particularly the present state of things in that quarter.

The nature of that country requires indispensably that an unusual proportion of the force employed there should be cavalry or mounted infantry. In order, therefore, that the commanding officer might be enabled to act with effect, I had authorized him to call on the governors of Orleans and

Mississippi for a corps of 500 volunteer cavalry. The temporary arrangement he has proposed may perhaps render this unnecessary; but I inform you with great pleasure of the promptitude with which the inhabitants of those Territories have tendered their services in defense of their country. It has done honor to themselves, entitled them to the confidence of their fellow citizens 35 in every part of the Union, and must strengthen the general determination to protect them efficaciously under all circumstances which may occur.

Having received information that in another part of the United States a great number of private individuals were combining together, arming and organizing themselves contrary to law, to carry on a military expedition 40 against the territories of Spain, I thought it necessary, by proclamation as well as by special orders, to take measures for preventing and suppressing this enterprise, for seizing the vessels, arms, and other means provided for it, and for arresting and bringing to justice its authors and abettors. It was due to that good faith which ought ever to be the rule of action in pub- 45 lic as well as in private transactions, it was due to good order and regular government, that while the public force was acting strictly on defensive and merely to protect our citizens from aggression the criminal attempts of private individuals to decide for their country the question of peace or war by commencing active and unauthorized hostilities should be promptly and 50 efficaciously suppressed.

251. The primary purpose of paragraph one (lines 1–26) is to:

(A) inform listeners of of the present situation in foreign relations, especially with Spain

(B) persuade listeners of the need for them to act on the present situation with Spain

(C) entertain listeners with a rousing story of how the speaker negotiated the present situation of foreign relations

(D) refute the claim that the speaker did not try hard enough to settle the conflict with Spain

(E) defend the speaker's decision to delay negotiations with Spain

252. The tone of the first sentence (lines 1–4) can best be described as one of:

(A) indignation

(B) resignation

(C) disappointment

(D) resolution

(E) mirth

253. The relationship between the first sentence (lines 1–4) and second sentence (lines 4–7) of the first paragraph is:

(A) the second sentence gives examples of the claim presented in the first

(B) the second sentence elaborates on the steps taken to reach the intended outcome described in the first

(C) the second sentence refutes the claim made in the first

(D) the second sentence provides the effects of the event presented in the first

(E) the second sentence contradicts the logic laid out in the first

254. In context, the word "promptitude" in line 33 most nearly means:

(A) fearlessness

(B) quickness to respond

(C) bravery

(D) fortitude

(E) selflessness

255. The sentence "It has done honor to themselves, entitled them to the confidence of their fellow citizens in every part of the Union, and must strengthen the general determination to protect them efficaciously under all circumstances which may occur" (lines 34–37) serves to:

(A) persuade listeners to follow the example of these volunteers in their own hometowns

(B) persuade listeners to collect payment for these volunteers who bravely gave of themselves without compensation

(C) persuade listeners that these volunteers are outstanding citizens who are worthy of our help and protection

(D) persuade listeners to keep the confidence of these volunteers by not gossiping or spreading the story too liberally

(E) persuade listeners to figure out their own ways to pay tributes to these brave and helpful volunteers

256. The first sentence of paragraph three (lines 38–44) is used primarily to transition from:

(A) Orleans and Mississippi to other parts of the country
(B) five hundred volunteer cavalry to a great number of private individuals
(C) temporary to more permanent arrangements
(D) special orders to good faith
(E) legal to illegal resistance

257. In context, the word "efficaciously" in lines 37 and 51 most nearly means:

(A) feasibly
(B) with futility
(C) effectively
(D) expeditiously
(E) fruitlessly

258. The primary purpose of paragraph three (lines 38–51) is to:

(A) inform listeners of the situation with Spain
(B) persuade listeners of the need to be self-reliant in times of adversity
(C) entertain listeners with an anecdote of those who rose up of their own accord
(D) refute the claim that citizens are incapable of resisting force when necessary
(E) defend the speaker's choice to disarm the people who were trying to fight the Spanish without sanction

259. The tone of paragraph three (lines 38–51) can best be described as:

(A) fervent
(B) tranquil
(C) compassionate
(D) introspective
(E) sentimental

260. The speaker of the passage can best be described as:

(A) authoritative and decisive
(B) reflective and introspective
(C) sardonic and derisive
(D) paternalistic and empathetic
(E) condescending and scornful

Passage 6b: *The Birth of Quantum Physics Draft*

(1) Since the time of Thomas Young, a hundred years earlier, light was known to behave like a longitudinal wave. (2) However, in 1905, Albert Einstein's discovery of the photoelectric effect demonstrated that light also acts like a cluster of particles, the singular of which physicists dubbed "photon" or "quantum." (3) Experts attempted to resolve this seeming contradiction by theorizing that light travels as a wave, but it arrives as particles.

(4) In 1924, the physicist Louis de Broglie shocked the world by proposing the basic concept of quantum theory: all matter, including light, has both wave and particle properties. (5) His theories about matter's wave-particle duality were confirmed experimentally in 1927 by the famous double-slit experiment of scientists Clinton Davisson and Lester Germer. (6) Davisson and Germer revealed that electrons, previously thought of exclusively as particles, exhibit wave properties too, such as diffraction and interference. (7) Additional investigations showed increasingly zany results, such as single "particles" interfering with themselves the way waves do, and beams of subatomic matter appearing to "choose" when to act like particles and when to act like waves.

(8) The solidity and repeatability of these experiments convinced scientists that quantum theory had dethroned classical physics. (9) Therefore, given the bizarre nature of these experimental results, physicists have struggled to interpret them ever since. (10) A century later, we can still agree with quantum pioneer Neils Bohr's statement that "anyone who is not shocked by quantum theory has not understood it."

261. The writer would like to add a sentence before sentence 1 to engage the reader by providing some context for the paragraph that follows. Which sentence best meets the writer's needs?

(A) Thomas Young made important contributions to the fields of vision, light, and energy.

(B) Inquiries into the nature of light brought physics to a crossroads in the early 20th century.

(C) Have you ever wondered about how light travels?

(D) Light behaves in peculiar ways!

(E) Thomas Young was born in 1773 and lived until 1829.

262. The writer is considering adding the following sentence after sentence 1:

> *That is, scientists measured and analyzed properties like wavelength and amplitude for traveling light.*

Should the writer add the proposed sentence after sentence 1?

(A) Yes, because the sentence clears up a misconception raised in the previous sentence by offering a differing perspective on the topic of light

(B) Yes, because the sentence offers an illustrative example of the major claim made in the previous sentence and supports the writer's thesis

(C) Yes, because the sentence provides a helpful explanation and amplification of the previous sentence for an audience that may be unfamiliar with the idea that light was known to behave like a longitudinal wave

(D) No, because only scientists would be interested in reading about the measurement and analysis of wavelength and amplitude

(E) No, because readers of this passage will already be familiar with the fact that scientists measured and analyzed wavelength and amplitude for traveling light

263. The writer is considering revising the transition at the beginning of sentence 2 (reproduced below):

> *However, in 1905, Albert Einstein's discovery of the photoelectric effect demonstrated that light also acts like a cluster of particles, the singular of which physicists dubbed "photon" or "quantum."*

Which version of the underlined portion of the sentence best serves as a transition between sentences 1 and 2?

(A) as it is now

(B) For example,

(C) Secondly,

(D) Consequently,

(E) Finally,

264. The writer is considering adding the underlined portion to sentence 4 (reproduced below):

> *In 1924, the physicist Louis de Broglie, <u>who studied physics in the 20th century,</u> shocked the world by proposing the basic concept of quantum theory: all matter, including light, has both wave and particle properties.*

Should the writer add the underlined portion to sentence 4?

(A) Yes, because readers may not be familiar with Louis de Broglie, and those who are may appreciate a reminder of his life span and work

(B) Yes, because it is the first time that the writer is introducing Louis de Broglie, and each time an individual is introduced in a passage, it is appropriate to describe that person for readers

(C) Yes, because those familiar with Thomas Young and Albert Einstein have probably not had the opportunity to study French physicists as well

(D) No, because the year and Louis de Broglie's role as a physicist are already presented before his name is provided in the sentence, and this information is redundant

(E) No, because the timing of the discovery and the background of the man who made it are irrelevant to the writer's communicating the enormous shock that the concept of quantum theory had on the world

265. The writer wants to avoid expressing the claim in sentence 5 (reproduced below) in absolute terms:

> *His theories about matter's wave-particle duality were confirmed experimentally in 1927 by the <u>famous</u> double-slit experiment of scientists Clinton Davisson and Lester Germer.*

(A) as it is now

(B) most influential

(C) most important

(D) best known

(E) world's most prominent

266. The writer is considering removing the underlined portion of sentence 6 (reproduced below):

> *Davisson and Germer revealed that electrons, previously thought of exclusively as particles, exhibit wave properties too, <u>such as diffraction and interference</u>.*

Should the writer remove the underlined portion of the sentence?

(A) Yes, because readers cannot be expected to know about diffraction and interference

(B) Yes, because the mention of diffraction and interference detracts from the discussion of wave properties

(C) Yes, because the underlined phrase makes the sentence too long when compared to the other sentences in the paragraph

(D) No, because it provides useful examples of wave properties, with which readers may not be overly familiar

(E) No, because this portion of the sentence is a necessary rebuttal to the claim made earlier in the sentence

267. In sentence 7 (reproduced below), the writer wants to ensure that the connotation and tone of the underlined word is appropriate to the context of the sentence and passage.

> *Additional investigations showed increasingly <u>zany</u> results, such as single "particles" interfering with themselves the way waves do, and beams of subatomic matter appearing to "choose" when to act like particles, and when to act like waves.*

Which of the following versions of the underlined word would best accomplish this goal?

(A) as it is now

(B) wacky

(C) funny

(D) freaky

(E) strange

268. In sentence 7 (reproduced below), the writer has used quotation marks for the word "choose" (underlined below) for which of the following reasons?

> *Additional investigations showed increasingly zany results, such as single "particles" interfering with themselves the way waves do, and beams of subatomic matter appearing to "choose" when to act like particles and when to act like waves.*

(A) Because the writer disagrees with the use of the word in this context

(B) Because the word was used elsewhere and is being quoted and cited here

(C) Because the writer wants to indicate the break in tone that occurs when using this word

(D) Because beams of subatomic matter are inanimate, and the term is being used figuratively

(E) Because readers will object to the term, and the writer wants to anticipate that objection

269. The writer is considering revising the transition at the beginning of sentence 9 (reproduced below):

> *Therefore, given the bizarre nature of these experimental results, physicists have struggled to interpret them ever since.*

Which version of the underlined portion of the sentence best serves as a transition between sentences 8 and 9?

(A) as it is now

(B) For example,

(C) Secondly,

(D) Consequently,

(E) However,

270. The writer is considering removing sentence 10 (reproduced below):

> *A century later, we can still agree with quantum pioneer Neils Bohr's statement that "anyone who is not shocked by quantum theory has not understood it."*

Should the writer remove sentence 10?

(A) Yes, because most readers will not recognize who Neil Bohr is
(B) Yes, because the writer has not included a quotation up until this point, and it is inappropriate to do so in the final sentence
(C) Yes, because it does not add any new information to the paragraph or passage
(D) No, because the sentence effectively concludes the paragraph and passage by highlighting how shocking and revolutionary quantum physics is
(E) No, because the passage has been focused on the past, and this sentence disruptively and confusingly brings the passage into the present

Passage 6c: Thomas Paine, *Common Sense*

Some writers have so confounded society with government, as to leave little or no distinction between them; whereas they are not only different, but have different origins. Society is produced by our wants, and government by our wickedness; the former promotes our happiness POSITIVELY by uniting our affections, the latter NEGATIVELY by restraining our vices. 5
The one encourages intercourse, the other creates distinctions. The first a patron, the last a punisher.
    Society in every state is a blessing, but government even in its best state is but a necessary evil; in its worst state an intolerable one; for when we suffer, or are exposed to the same miseries BY A GOVERNMENT, which 10 we might expect in a country WITHOUT GOVERNMENT, our calamity is heightened by reflecting that we furnish the means by which we suffer. Government, like dress, is the badge of lost innocence; the palaces of kings are built on the ruins of the bowers of paradise. For were the impulses of conscience clear, uniform, and irresistibly obeyed, man would need no other 15 lawgiver; but that not being the case, he finds it necessary to surrender up a part of his property to furnish means for the protection of the rest; and this he is induced to do by the same prudence which in every other case advises him out of two evils to choose the least. WHEREFORE, security being the true design and end of government, it unanswerably follows, that whatever 20 FORM thereof appears most likely to ensure it to us, with the least expense and greatest benefit, is preferable to all others.

In order to gain a clear and just idea of the design and end of government, let us suppose a small number of persons settled in some sequestered part of the earth, unconnected with the rest; they will then represent the first 25 peopling of any country, or of the world. In this state of natural liberty, society will be their first thought. A thousand motives will excite them thereto, the strength of one man is so unequal to his wants, and his mind so unfitted for perpetual solitude, that he is soon obliged to seek assistance and relief of another, who in his turn requires the same. Four or five united would be 30 able to raise a tolerable dwelling in the midst of a wilderness, but one man might labour out of the common period of life without accomplishing any thing; when he had felled his timber he could not remove it, nor erect it after it was removed; hunger in the mean time would urge him from his work, and every different want call him a different way. Disease, nay even 35 misfortune would be death, for though neither might be mortal, yet either would disable him from living, and reduce him to a state in which he might rather be said to perish than to die.

Thus necessity, like a gravitating power, would soon form our newly arrived emigrants into society, the reciprocal blessings of which, would 40 supersede, and render the obligations of law and government unnecessary while they remained perfectly just to each other; but as nothing but heaven is impregnable to vice, it will unavoidably happen, that in proportion as they surmount the first difficulties of emigration, which bound them together in a common cause, they will begin to relax in their duty and attachment to 45 each other; and this remissness will point out the necessity of establishing some form of government to supply the defect of moral virtue.

271. The speaker is reacting to writers who:
- (A) have solely focused on society
- (B) have solely focused on government
- (C) describe society in unrealistic terms
- (D) don't acknowledge the difference between society and government
- (E) argue that government is unnecessary

272. In context, the word "confounded" in line 1 most nearly means:
- (A) combined
- (B) destroyed
- (C) confused
- (D) refuted
- (E) frustrated

273. The differences between society and government are presented as all of the following oppositions in paragraph one (lines 1–7) *except*:

(A) wants and wickedness
(B) affections and vices
(C) intercourse and distinctions
(D) encourages and creates
(E) uniting and restraining

274. In describing society and government in the last line of paragraph one, "The first a patron, the last a punisher," (lines 6–7) the writer uses:

(A) apostrophe
(B) oxymoron
(C) simile
(D) metaphor
(E) personification

275. According to the writer, the suffering described in paragraph two (lines 8–22) is made worse by the fact that it is:

(A) inevitable
(B) self-inflicted
(C) surprising
(D) ceaseless
(E) expected

276. The sentence "Government, like dress, is the badge of lost innocence; the palaces of kings are built on the ruins of the bowers of paradise" (lines 13–14) uses a biblical allusion to show that government is necessary due to man's:

(A) fallibility
(B) ignorance
(C) laziness
(D) violent nature
(E) unerring ways

277. The primary purpose of paragraphs two and three (lines 8–38) is to:

(A) refute the claim that government is a necessary evil
(B) describe typical societies and governments
(C) analyze the effects of government on various societies
(D) define society and government
(E) analyze the process of building a government

278. The first sentence of paragraph three, "In order to gain a clear and just idea of the design and end of government, let us suppose a small number of persons settled in some sequestered part of the earth, unconnected with the rest; they will then represent the first peopling of any country, or of the world," (lines 23–27) transitions in all of the following ways *except*:

(A) defining to providing examples
(B) abstract to concrete terms
(C) discussing to illustrating
(D) confirming to refuting
(E) theoretical claims to ideas in action

279. The primary purpose of paragraph three (lines 23–38) is to:

(A) define natural liberty
(B) classify the different types of societies
(C) analyze the causes of creating governments
(D) describe the earliest society
(E) illustrate what men can do together and how they need each other

280. The major claim of the passage as a whole is that:

(A) government is a necessary evil
(B) government is avoidable in truly civilized societies
(C) government robs men of their security
(D) government is synonymous with society
(E) government is unnecessary because men are inherently good

Passage 6d: *Educational Philosophy Draft*

(1) In my earlier years as a teacher, I used to assess if students could remember and recall details about the texts that we would read together. (2) These quizzes and tests were almost always summative assessments. (3) In my own metacognition, I asked myself if *I* would do well on my own exams. (4) I recognized that I would not succeed if asked to recall details about plot.

(5) I would not be able to show mastery in that way. (6) I decided it was unjust to ask students to do well on an assessment on which I would do poorly. (7) Assessments must give accurate information about what students understand by being meaningful and by accounting for different learning styles.

(8) I have grown to learn that I do not want to privilege the teaching of the content of a text over more transferable skills. (9) Then I think about providing students with the opportunities to practice their listening, speaking, reading, and writing, but the common denominator is always sharpening their thinking skills. (10) When I plan my instruction, I try to clearly define the purpose of my lessons and units and to think about how this work will help my students with the next text and topic, even how it will help them in other classes. (11) I want to help build a generation of thoughtful citizens through my classes by teaching careful thinking and by celebrating the values of diversity, collaboration, and inquiry.

281. Which sentence below can best be described as the writer's thesis?

(A) In my own metacognition, I asked myself if *I* would do well on my own exams.
(B) I recognized that I would not succeed if asked to recall details about plot.
(C) I would not be able to show mastery in that way.
(D) I decided it was unjust to ask students to do well on an assessment on which I would do poorly.
(E) Assessment must give accurate information about what students understand by being meaningful and by accounting for different learning styles.

282. The writer is considering removing the underlined portion of sentence 1 (reproduced below):

> In my earlier years as a teacher, I used to assess if students could <u>remember and</u> recall details about the texts that we would read together.

Should the writer remove the underlined portion of sentence 1?

(A) Yes, because it is redundant when placed next to "recall"
(B) Yes, because it is irrelevant whether students could remember the details for these assessments
(C) Yes, because recalling details is more important than remembering them
(D) No, because remembering and recalling are separate actions
(E) No, because different questions are used to assess whether students remember or recall plot details

283. The writer is considering removing sentence 2 (reproduced below):

These quizzes and tests were almost always summative assessments.

Should the writer remove sentence 2?

(A) Yes, because quizzes and tests are too similar to be discussed separately
(B) Yes, because the categorization of assessments is not discussed beyond this sentence
(C) Yes, because formative assessments are not given equal treatment in the passage and paragraph
(D) No, because it is crucial to explain the types of assessments provided by teachers to students
(E) No, because readers will be wondering if the assessments provided were formative or summative

284. The writer is considering providing the following definition for "metacognition" in sentence 3:

the understanding of one's own thought processes

Should the writer build this definition into sentence 3?

(A) Yes, because it is a difficult word that will be unfamiliar to all readers
(B) Yes, because it is key to understanding the writer's thesis
(C) Yes, because it is the first time that the writer is introducing this term
(D) No, because the second part of the sentence makes clear that the term refers to some sort of understanding of self
(E) No, because all readers will understand and know how to use this term

285. The writer would like to combine sentences 4 and 5 (reproduced below):

> *I recognized that I would not succeed if asked to recall details about plot. I would not be able to show mastery in that way.*

Which of the following options is the best combination of sentences 4 and 5?

(A) I recognized that I would not succeed if asked to recall details about plot, and I would not be able to show mastery in that way.

(B) I recognized that I would not succeed if asked to recall details about plot, so I would not be able to show mastery in that way.

(C) I recognized that I would not succeed if asked to recall details about plot, but I would not be able to show mastery in that way.

(D) I recognized that I would not succeed if asked to recall details about plot, or I would not be able to show mastery in that way.

(E) I recognized that I would not succeed if asked to recall details about plot, yet I would not be able to show mastery in that way.

286. The writer is considering adding a sentence after sentence 7 that provides examples of the types of assessments described in that sentence. Which of the following sentences helps meet the writer's needs?

(A) Assessments should be given regularly to get the most recent information about students' progress.

(B) Learning styles include visual, verbal, physical, and others.

(C) Students should be given the option to revise previous assessments to show growth.

(D) Essays, projects, and assessments that provide choices can all provide students with the chance to demonstrate their understanding.

(E) Assessment results must be provided quickly to have an impact on students' learning.

287. The writer is considering adding the following sentence before sentence 8:

> *Besides a shift in thinking about assessment, I have developed a new perspective on my goals for instruction.*

Should the writer add this sentence before sentence 8?

(A) Yes, because readers will be more interested in reading about instruction than assessment

(B) Yes, because readers may want to stop reading at this point if their interest is in assessment and not instructional goals

(C) Yes, because it serves as a helpful topic sentence that signals a transition and unifies the rest of the paragraph

(D) No, because sentence 8 makes the topic clear when it identifies content to be taught

(E) No, because readers will be bothered by the intrusion of including another sentence at this point

288. The writer is considering revising the transition at the beginning of sentence 9 (reproduced below):

> <u>Then</u> *I think about providing students with the opportunities to practice their listening, speaking, reading, and writing, but the common denominator is always sharpening their thinking skills.*

Which of the following is the best transition to begin sentence 9?

(A) as it is now

(B) However,

(C) Nevertheless,

(D) First

(E) Now,

289. The writer is considering revising the underlined word in sentence 10 (reproduced below):

> *When I plan my instruction, I try to clearly <u>define</u> the purpose of my lessons and units and to think about how this work will help my students with the next text and topic, even how it will help my students in other classes.*

Which word is the best fit for the underlined word in sentence 10?

(A) as it is now
(B) describe
(C) explain
(D) clarify
(E) defend

290. The writer is considering removing the underlined portion of sentence 11 (reproduced below):

> *I want to help build a generation of thoughtful citizens <u>through my classes</u> by teaching careful thinking and by celebrating the values of diversity, collaboration, and inquiry.*

Should the writer remove the underlined portion of sentence 11?

(A) Yes, because it is redundant when placed next to "by teaching"
(B) Yes, because it is possible that the writer may have this impact through others' classes
(C) Yes, because this type of development and learning does not only happen in the classroom
(D) No, because it helps clarify the process by which this development will happen
(E) No, because this phrase helps to develop the writer's voice in this concluding remark

Passage 6e: Mary Wollstonecraft, *A Vindication of the Rights of Woman*

After considering the historic page, and viewing the living world with anxious solicitude, the most melancholy emotions of sorrowful indignation have depressed my spirits, and I have sighed when obliged to confess, that either nature has made a great difference between man and man, or that the civilization, which has hitherto taken place in the world, has been very partial. I have turned over various books written on the subject of education, and patiently observed the conduct of parents and the management of schools; but what has been the result? a profound conviction, that the

5

neglected education of my fellow creatures is the grand source of the misery I deplore; and that women in particular, are rendered weak and wretched by a variety of concurring causes, originating from one hasty conclusion. The conduct and manners of women, in fact, evidently prove, that their minds are not in a healthy state; for, like the flowers that are planted in too rich a soil, strength and usefulness are sacrificed to beauty; and the flaunting leaves, after having pleased a fastidious eye, fade, disregarded on the stalk, long before the season when they ought to have arrived at maturity. One cause of this barren blooming I attribute to a false system of education, gathered from the books written on this subject by men, who, considering females rather as women than human creatures, have been more anxious to make them alluring mistresses than rational wives; and the understanding of the sex has been so bubbled by this specious homage, that the civilized women of the present century, with a few exceptions, are only anxious to inspire love, when they ought to cherish a nobler ambition, and by their abilities and virtues exact respect.

In a treatise, therefore, on female rights and manners, the works which have been particularly written for their improvement must not be over-looked; especially when it is asserted, in direct terms, that the minds of women are enfeebled by false refinement; that the books of instruction, written by men of genius, have had the same tendency as more frivolous productions; and that, in the true style of Mahometanism[1], they are only considered as females, and not as a part of the human species, when improv-able reason is allowed to be the dignified distinction, which raises men above the brute creation, and puts a natural sceptre in a feeble hand.

Yet, because I am a woman, I would not lead my readers to suppose, that I mean violently to agitate the contested question respecting the equality and inferiority of the sex; but as the subject lies in my way, and I cannot pass it over without subjecting the main tendency of my reasoning to mis-construction, I shall stop a moment to deliver, in a few words, my opinion. In the government of the physical world, it is observable that the female, in general, is inferior to the male. The male pursues, the female yields—this is the law of nature; and it does not appear to be suspended or abrogated in favour of woman. This physical superiority cannot be denied—and it is a noble prerogative! But not content with this natural pre-eminence, men endeavour to sink us still lower, merely to render us alluring objects for a moment; and women, intoxicated by the adoration which men, under the influence of their senses, pay them, do not seek to obtain a durable interest in their hearts, or to become the friends of the fellow creatures who find amusement in their society.

---

1. archaic term for Muslim

291. After reading history and making observations around her, the writer of the passage has concluded all of the following to be true *except*:

(A) there are differences between people that are attributable to nature

(B) there are differences in treatment that have resulted from civilization

(C) the disparities between people are saddening

(D) the disparities between people are infuriating

(E) the past has little to teach us about the present conditions of people

292. In context, the word "solicitude" in line 2 most nearly means:

(A) attention

(B) isolation

(C) unity

(D) discourse

(E) petition

293. According to the first paragraph (lines 1–24), the primary cause of the disparate conditions of people is:

(A) government

(B) parents and family

(C) civilization

(D) education

(E) women

294. The sentence "The conduct and manners of women, in fact, evidently prove, that their minds are not in a healthy state; for, like the flowers that are planted in too rich a soil, strength and usefulness are sacrificed to beauty; and the flaunting leaves, after having pleased a fastidious eye, fade, disregarded on the stalk, long before the season when they ought to have arrived at maturity" (lines 11–16) uses an analogy to elucidate:

(A) the effects of too much pressure on women

(B) the effects of the limited goals of education on women

(C) the effects of women's having choice in education

(D) the effects of too much rigor in education

(E) the effects of starting women's education too early

295. The writer finds fault with the education of women for all of the following reasons *except*:

    (A) it teaches women to please rather than to be useful

    (B) it teaches women to value love over respect

    (C) it is self-inflicted by women

    (D) it does not consider women people

    (E) it weakens women's minds

296. What may be considered ironic by current-day readers is the fact that the writer claims:

    (A) women are inferior to men

    (B) women ought to be taught to have more noble goals

    (C) women are enfeebled by the education provided for them

    (D) men are not satisfied with their physical dominance

    (E) men are responsible for keeping women down

297. In context, the word "society" in line 48 most nearly means:

    (A) a group of humans

    (B) a group of people with a common culture

    (C) a group of people with a common interest

    (D) the privileged social class

    (E) company or companionship

298. The primary purpose of the passage is to:

    (A) inform

    (B) entertain

    (C) persuade

    (D) refute

    (E) defend

299. The speaker can best be described as:

    (A) hostile and vehement

    (B) detached and logical

    (C) aloof and condescending

    (D) reasonable and observant

    (E) patronizing and derisive

300. The tone of the passage can best be described as:

- (A) measured indignation
- (B) cautious admonition
- (C) incredulous bewilderment
- (D) unapologetic criticism
- (E) irreverent sarcasm

16th and 17th Centuries
with Draft Passages

Passage 7a: Niccolo Machiavelli, *The Prince*

Commencing then with the first of the above-named characteristics, I say that it would be well to be reputed liberal. Nevertheless, liberality[1] exercised in a way that does not bring you the reputation for it, injures you; for if one exercises it honestly and as it should be exercised, it may not become known, and you will not avoid the reproach of its opposite. Therefore, any 5 one wishing to maintain among men the name of liberal is obliged to avoid no attribute of magnificence; so that a prince thus inclined will consume in such acts all his property, and will be compelled in the end, if he wish to maintain the name of liberal, to unduly weigh down his people, and tax them, and do everything he can to get money. This will soon make him 10 odious to his subjects, and becoming poor he will be little valued by any one; thus, with his liberality, having offended many and rewarded few, he is affected by the very first trouble and imperiled by whatever may be the first danger; recognizing this himself, and wishing to draw back from it, he runs at once into the reproach of being miserly. 15

Therefore, a prince, not being able to exercise this virtue of liberality in such a way that it is recognized, except to his cost, if he is wise he ought not to fear the reputation of being mean, for in time he will come to be more considered than if liberal, seeing that with his economy his revenues are enough, that he can defend himself against all attacks, and is able to 20 engage in enterprises without burdening his people; thus it comes to pass that he exercises liberality towards all from whom he does not take, who are numberless, and meanness towards those to whom he does not give, who are few.

We have not seen great things done in our time except by those who 25 have been considered mean; the rest have failed. Pope Julius the Second was

---

1. liberality: giving or spending freely; generosity

assisted in reaching the papacy by a reputation for liberality, yet he did not strive afterwards to keep it up, when he made war on the King of France; and he made many wars without imposing any extraordinary tax on his subjects, for he supplied his additional expenses out of his long thriftiness. The 30 present King of Spain would not have undertaken or conquered in so many enterprises if he had been reputed liberal. A prince, therefore, provided that he has not to rob his subjects, that he can defend himself, that he does not become poor and abject, that he is not forced to become rapacious, ought to hold of little account a reputation for being mean, for it is one of those 35 vices which will enable him to govern.

And if any one should say: Caesar obtained empire by liberality, and many others have reached the highest positions by having been liberal, and by being considered so, I answer: Either you are a prince in fact, or in a way to become one. In the first case this liberality is dangerous, in the second 40 it is very necessary to be considered liberal; and Caesar was one of those who wished to become pre-eminent in Rome; but if he had survived after becoming so, and had not moderated his expenses, he would have destroyed his government. And if any one should reply: Many have been princes, and have done great things with armies, who have been considered very liberal, 45 I reply: Either a prince spends that which is his own or his subjects' or else that of others. In the first case he ought to be sparing, in the second he ought not to neglect any opportunity for liberality. And to the prince who goes forth with his army, supporting it by pillage, sack, and extortion, handling that which belongs to others, this liberality is necessary, otherwise he 50 would not be followed by soldiers. And of that which is neither yours nor your subjects' you can be a ready giver, as were Cyrus, Caesar, and Alexander; because it does not take away your reputation if you squander that of others, but adds to it; it is only squandering your own that injures you.

And there is nothing wastes so rapidly as liberality, for even whilst 55 you exercise it you lose the power to do so, and so become either poor or despised, or else, in avoiding poverty, rapacious and hated. And a prince should guard himself, above all things, against being despised and hated; and liberality leads you to both. Therefore it is wiser to have a reputation for meanness which brings reproach without hatred, than to be compelled 60 through seeking a reputation for liberality to incur a name for rapacity which begets reproach with hatred.

301. In order for being liberal to have positive results for the prince, it must be enacted with:

(A) consistency
(B) dishonesty
(C) honesty
(D) free will
(E) obligation

302. The primary purpose of the first paragraph (lines 1–15) is:

(A) to narrate a particularly disastrous story about a prince's liberality
(B) to describe the ways in which a prince can be liberal
(C) to analyze the effects of practicing liberality
(D) to argue that liberality is the best policy for a ruler
(E) to equally compare and contrast the states of being liberal and miserly

303. According to the first paragraph (lines 1–15), being liberal (as a prince) leads to all of the following results *except*:

(A) being loved
(B) becoming poor
(C) being despised
(D) being in danger
(E) being considered miserly

304. In context, the word "odious" in line 11 most nearly means:

(A) pitied
(B) valued
(C) sympathetic
(D) detestable
(E) patronizing

305. The major claim of the second paragraph (lines 16–24) is that not being liberal has all of the following effects *except*:

(A) an initial reputation for meanness
(B) the ability to defend himself against all attacks
(C) a lack of burden placed on his people
(D) an economy in which his revenues are enough
(E) a fleeting reputation for generosity

306. The third paragraph (lines 25–36) is developed by:
  (A) moving figurative language that is meant to persuade readers to accept the speaker's claims
  (B) a series of closely associated supporting ideas to support the main claim
  (C) historical scholarship from experts in the field
  (D) a collection of compelling anecdotes on practicing liberality
  (E) examples of those who didn't freely exercise liberality and were successful as a result

307. Paragraph four (lines 37–54) is primarily developed by the use of:
  (A) addressing and refuting counterargument
  (B) classifying types of liberality
  (C) presenting examples of deductive logic
  (D) narrating a series of anecdotes that are enlightening on the topic of generosity
  (E) refuting the claim that the appearance of liberality is what helps rulers succeed

308. The writer's major claim that being liberal is dangerous and disastrous, as presented in the sentence "And a prince should guard himself, above all things, against being despised and hated; and liberality leads you to both," is effective because of its:
  (A) unlikely use of adjectives
  (B) paradoxical nature
  (C) use of common sense
  (D) stirring figurative language
  (E) use of allusions

309. The speaker of the piece can best be described as:
  (A) empathetic
  (B) practical
  (C) vindictive
  (D) jocular
  (E) reticent

310. The tone of the passage can best be described as:
- (A) poignant
- (B) solemn
- (C) forthright
- (D) despairing
- (E) aloof

Passage 7b: *Tim Burton Draft*

(1) Surrealist and multimedia artist Tim Burton is the subject of a major exhibition at New York City's MoMA that must be seen by everyone interested in pop culture. (2) One of the first things one notices is the enormous body of work that he has churned out over the years. (3) Known mainly for motion pictures, which feature his eccentric design style, Burton is also revealed to have been amazingly prolific and gifted with ink and paint, on paper and on canvas, since very early in his life. (4) His witty and light-hearted drawings are filled with fantasy creatures that have dislocated eyeballs and menacing clowns with pointy teeth.

(5) The lightly colored pen-and-ink drawings include recognizable personalities. (6) Others are anonymous humans with distorted body parts, aggressive toys, or nightmarish yet comical fantasy creatures. (7) They are typically composed of weirdly proportioned, wiggly shapes that might have been drawn by Aubrey Beardsley intoxicated with absinthe, or by Edward Gorey if he executed them with his left hand. (8) Many are hilarious visual puns. (9) One entitled "Tongue-twister" displays a creature maliciously twisting a man's tongue as if wringing out a washrag. (10) Some of these have been translated by sculptors into jaw-dropping constructions and assemblages.

(11) More than 700 pieces are on exhibit and include concept drawings for the characters in his movies, recognizable iconic mannequins, costumes, and statuettes from both his animated and his live-action films. (12) The monstrous, menacing Jack O'Lantern from *Nightmare* stands 10 feet above the milling crowd of spectators. (13) A crude ape head with wooden-branch antlers from *Planet of the Apes* is mounted high on a wall, evoking the feeling of strange otherworldliness.

(14) Tim Burton has spent a lifetime arduously and playfully exploring the borderland between the naive fun and the malignant fears of childhood that continue to haunt us well into adulthood.

311. Which sentence below can best be described as the writer's thesis?

   (A) Surrealist and multimedia artist Tim Burton is the subject of a major exhibition at New York City's MoMA that must be seen by everyone interested in pop culture.

   (B) One of the first things one notices is the enormous body of work that he has churned out over the years.

   (C) Known mainly for motion pictures, which feature his eccentric design style, Burton is also revealed to have been amazingly prolific and gifted with ink and paint, on paper and on canvas, since very early in his life.

   (D) His witty and light-hearted drawings are filled with fantasy creatures that have dislocated eyeballs and menacing clowns with pointy teeth.

   (E) The lightly colored pen-and-ink drawings include recognizable personalities.

312. Judging from the information provided in sentence 1 (reproduced below), the writer expects an audience that has which of the following characteristics?

> *Surrealist and multimedia artist Tim Burton is the subject of a major exhibition at New York City's MoMA that must be seen by everyone interested in pop culture.*

   (A) An intense appreciation of Tim Burton's early work

   (B) A basic working knowledge and potential interest in art

   (C) A blind devotion to all of the surrealist artists

   (D) A deep distaste for the practitioners of pop art

   (E) A complete love of all multimedia artists and their works of art

313. The writer is considering removing sentence 4 (reproduced below):

> *His witty and light-hearted drawings are filled with fantasy creatures that have dislocated eyeballs and menacing clowns with pointy teeth.*

Should the writer remove sentence 4?

(A) Yes, because the images presented are too gruesome for the readers

(B) Yes, because the sentence does not support the claim that he is known mainly for his motion pictures

(C) Yes, because not all of these drawings have been made into sculptures

(D) No, because it provides examples of his talent with ink and paper

(E) No, because he is best known for these successful drawings

314. The writer is considering adding the underlined portion to sentence 5 (reproduced below):

> *The lightly colored pen-and-ink drawings include recognizable personalities, <u>such as Joey Ramone, Vincent Price, and Alice Cooper</u>.*

Should the writer add the underlined portion to sentence 5?

(A) Yes, because readers of this passage will be fans of Joey Ramone, Vincent Price, and Alice Cooper

(B) Yes, because it provides useful examples of people who are recognizable personalities

(C) Yes, these three people have never been rendered in pen-and-ink drawings before

(D) No, because the audience may not recognize all of these people

(E) No, because readers may not be fans of Joey Ramone, Vincent Price, and Alice Cooper

315. The writer would like to combine sentences 8 and 9 (reproduced below):

> *Many are hilarious visual puns. One entitled "Tongue-twister" displays a creature maliciously twisting a man's tongue as if wringing out a washrag.*

Which is the best combination of the two sentences?

(A) Many are hilarious visual puns; however, one entitled "Tongue-twister" displays a creature maliciously twisting a man's tongue as if wringing out a washrag.

(B) Many are hilarious visual puns, but one entitled "Tongue-twister" displays a creature maliciously twisting a man's tongue as if wringing out a washrag.

(C) Many are hilarious visual puns, yet one entitled "Tongue-twister" displays a creature maliciously twisting a man's tongue as if wringing out a washrag.

(D) Many are hilarious visual puns, so one entitled "Tongue-twister" displays a creature maliciously twisting a man's tongue as if wringing out a washrag.

(E) Many are hilarious visual puns, and one entitled "Tongue-twister" displays a creature maliciously twisting a man's tongue as if wringing out a washrag.

316. Which of the following sentences, if added after sentence 11, would effectively offer examples of the range of artworks from Burton's films on display at the exhibit?

(A) His most famous movies include *Edward Scissorhands* and *The Nightmare Before Christmas*.

(B) Among them are Catwoman's costume, a life-size effigy of Edward Scissorhands, and numerous statuettes representing the various creatures in the stop-action movie *The Nightmare Before Christmas*.

(C) His pre-production illustrations for many of his films are on display for visitors.

(D) You can see his collaborations on costume design with many of the premiere designers in the industry.

(E) His storyboarding illustrations are a sight to behold!

317. The writer wants to revise the underlined word in sentence 12 (reproduced below) to match the tone of the rest of the sentence and paragraph:

> *The monstrous, menacing Jack O'Lantern from* Nightmare <u>*stands*</u> *10 feet above the milling crowd of spectators.*

Which option below best captures the tone of the rest of the sentence and paragraph?

(A) as it is now
(B) hovers
(C) is located
(D) is situated
(E) is positioned

318. Which of the following words should be placed at the beginning of sentence 13 (reproduced below) to demonstrate a connection to the previous sentence?

> *A crude ape head with wooden-branch antlers from* Planet of the Apes *is mounted high on a wall, evoking the feeling of strange otherworldliness.*

(A) However,
(B) Regardless,
(C) Thus,
(D) Nonetheless,
(E) Additionally,

319. In sentence 14 (reproduced below), the writer wants to ensure that the connotation of the underlined word is appropriate to the context of the sentence.

> *Tim Burton has spent a lifetime arduously and playfully <u>exploring</u> the borderland between the naive fun and the malignant fears of childhood that continue to haunt us well into adulthood.*

Which of the following versions of the underlined word would best accomplish this goal?

(A) as it is now
(B) studying
(C) mapping
(D) presenting
(E) inspecting

320. The writer wants to add a concluding sentence after sentence 14 that specifically communicates what the exhibit offers viewers. Which of the following sentences best meets the writer's needs?

(A) This exhibit ran from November 2009 until April 2010.
(B) This exhibition tells us much about postmodern culture, about ourselves, and about the creative process.
(C) You will definitely not be bored if you visit this exhibit!
(D) Be sure to watch Tim Burton's *Corpse Bride* and *Beetlejuice*, two of my favorites.
(E) I highly recommend this exhibit to all who enjoy Burton's extensive body of work.

Passage 7c: Thomas Hobbes, *Leviathan*

It is true, that certain living creatures, as Bees, and Ants, live sociably one with another, (which are therefore by Aristotle numbered amongst Political creatures;) and yet have no other direction, than their particular judgments and appetites; nor speech, whereby one of them can signify to another, what he thinks expedient for the common benefit: and therefore some man   5
may perhaps desire to know, why Man-kind cannot do the same. To which I answer,

First, that men are continually in competition for Honour and Dignity, which these creatures are not; and consequently amongst men there ariseth on that ground, Envy and Hatred, and finally Warre; but amongst these   10
not so.

Secondly, that amongst these creatures, the Common good different not from the Private; and being by nature inclined to their private, they procure thereby the common benefit. But man, whose Joy consisteth in comparing himselfe with other men, can relish nothing but what is eminent. 15

Thirdly, that these creatures, having not (as man) the use of reason, do not see, nor think they see any fault, in the administration of their common businesses: whereas amongst men, there are very many, that think themselves wiser, and abler to govern the Publique, better than the rest; and these strive to reforme and innovate, one this way, another that way; and thereby 20 bring it into Distraction and Civill warre.

Fourthly, that these creatures, though they have some use of voice, in making knowne to one another their desires, and other affections; yet they want that art of words, by which some men can represent to others, that which is Good, in the likenesse of Evill; and Evill, in the likenesse of Good; 25 and augment, or diminish the apparent greatnesse of Good and Evill; discontenting men, and troubling their Peace at their pleasure.

Fiftly, irrationall creatures cannot distinguish betweene Injury, and Dammage; and therefore as long as they be at ease, they are not offended with their fellowes: whereas Man is then most troublesome, when he is most 30 at ease: for then it is that he loves to shew his Wisdome, and controule the Actions of them that governe the Common-wealth.

Lastly, the agreement of these creatures is Naturall; that of men, is by Covenant only, which is Artificiall: and therefore it is no wonder if there be somewhat else required (besides Covenant) to make their Agreement 35 constant and lasting; which is a Common Power, to keep them in awe, and to direct their actions to the Common Benefit.

321. The overall purpose of the passage as a whole is to:
- (A) inform readers why men cannot live sociably with one another
- (B) argue that men are incapable of living sociably with one another
- (C) refute the argument that men can live sociably with one another
- (D) describe the ways in which men cannot live sociably with one another
- (E) entertain readers with narrative accounts of men not living sociably with one another

322. The speaker begins the passage by addressing:

(A) a claim from Aristotle
(B) an inaccurate system of classification
(C) a faulty comparison between political creatures and men
(D) long-standing criticism from his enemies
(E) flawed scholarship on the topic of political creatures

323. According to the first paragraph (lines 1–7) of the passage, what does it mean that mankind cannot "do the same"?

(A) mankind cannot live sociably one with another
(B) mankind cannot have direction
(C) mankind cannot be directed by his particular judgments and appetites
(D) mankind cannot signify to another
(E) mankind cannot speak what he feels expedient for the common benefit

324. In context, the word "want" in line 24 most nearly means to:

(A) require
(B) desire
(C) request
(D) lack
(E) seek

325. The pronouns "their" and "their" in line 27 refer to:

(A) men
(B) others
(C) creatures and men, respectively
(D) men and others, respectively
(E) others and men, respectively

326. In paragraph six, the statement "whereas Man is then most troublesome, when he is most at ease" (line 30) can be described as:

(A) figurative
(B) ironic
(C) antithetical
(D) sarcastic
(E) facetious

327. The creatures capable of living sociably with one another are described as all of the following *except*:

(A) political
(B) ambitious
(C) irrational
(D) communicative
(E) at ease

328. The overall structure of the passage is accomplished by:

(A) chronological sequence
(B) enumeration
(C) movement from general to specific
(D) movement from specific to general
(E) movement from brief to long

329. The style of the passage can best be described as:

(A) allusive
(B) systematic
(C) abstract
(D) descriptive
(E) disjointed

330. The tone of the passage as a whole can best be described as:

(A) bantering
(B) indifferent
(C) patronizing
(D) poignant
(E) learned

Passage 7d: *Park City Travel Log Draft*

(1) <u>Park City</u> is nestled among the Wasatch Mountains, only 35 minutes from the <u>Salt Lake City International Airport</u>. (2) The charming Utah town was founded in the late 1800s as a mining town and was home to the 2002 Olympic Winter Games. (3) Shopping, galleries, great dining, a historic Old Town, and the famous <u>Sundance Film Festival</u> have put Park City on the map as a premiere ski town and year-round destination. (4) Perfectly located for the best of what Park City has to offer, the Waldorf Astoria Park City is an ideal place to call home while exploring this picture-perfect destination.

(5) <u>Summer</u> in Park City is full of outdoor fun, street fairs, and farmers markets. (6) Countless activities include hot-air balloon rides, kayaking, river rafting, hiking, and fly-fishing. (7) Mountain biking is a must-do during the Park City summertime as Park City Mountain Resort provides lift service and well-maintained bike trails. (8) Other fun things to try are stand-up paddle (SUP) boarding or a round at Canyons Golf Course, located directly behind Waldorf Astoria Park City. (9) If you're looking for a less fun activity, there are many concerts at the Canyons Village base of the resort throughout the entire summer, or you can check out the farmers market that happens every Wednesday. (10) "Park City is truly a four-season destination," shares Danielle Summers. (11) "What makes Park City so superior in the summer is the perfect weather consisting of 75-degree days, no humidity, and endless sunshine."

(12) With the recent acquisition by Vail Resorts of Park City Mountain Resort, skiing and snowboarding in Park City and the Canyons has never been better. (13) If you have not yet purchased your Epic Pass for this next season, here are two more reasons why you should: legendary deep, dry powder and exciting nightlife at après-ski venues. (14) Located at the base of the new Park City Mountain Resort, now the largest ski and snowboard resort in the country, Waldorf Astoria Park City offers prime access to a myriad of year-round outdoor activities.

(15) "We are very excited about our partnership with Vail Resorts because similar to Waldorf Astoria, Vail Resorts is known for being the best in class in what they do," states Kerry Hing, general manager of the Waldorf Astoria Park City. (16) "Waldorf Astoria Park City is fortunate to be the only Forbes four-star luxury hotel located at the base of the resort, which makes for a very elite partnership that will afford both Vail Resorts and Waldorf Astoria great opportunity."

331. Which sentence below can best be described as the writer's thesis?

(A) <u>Park City</u> is nestled among the Wasatch Mountains, only 35 minutes from the <u>Salt Lake City International Airport</u>.

(B) The charming Utah town was founded in the late 1800s as a mining town and was home to the 2002 Olympic Winter Games.

(C) Shopping, galleries, great dining, a historic Old Town, and the famous <u>Sundance Film Festival</u> have put Park City on the map as a premiere ski town and year-round destination.

(D) Perfectly located for the best of what Park City has to offer, the Waldorf Astoria Park City is an ideal place to call home while exploring this picture-perfect destination.

(E) <u>Summer</u> in Park City is full of outdoor fun, street fairs, and farmers markets.

332. The writer is considering removing sentence 5 (reproduced below):

<u>Summer</u> in Park City is full of outdoor fun, street fairs, and farmers markets.

Should the writer remove sentence 5?

(A) Yes, because potential visitors to Park City are interested in skiing, not summer activities

(B) Yes, because many readers will not be interested in street fairs and farmers markets.

(C) Yes, because it is obvious from the rest of the paragraph that the topic is summer activities

(D) No, because it serves as a topic sentence for paragraph 2, making clear the focus on summertime offerings in Park City

(E) No, because potential visitors to Park City are only interested in the summertime offerings of the locale

333. The writer wants to revise the underlined word in sentence 7 (reproduced below) to match the tone of the rest of the sentence and paragraph:

> *Mountain biking is a <u>must-do</u> during the Park City summertime as Park City Mountain Resort provides lift service and well-maintained bike trails.*

Which option below best captures the tone of the rest of the sentence and paragraph?

(A) as it is now
(B) requirement
(C) obligation
(D) necessity
(E) duty

334. The writer wants to replace the underlined word in sentence 9 (reproduced below) with one that is precise and has a neutral connotation.

> *If you're looking for a less <u>fun</u> activity, there are many concerts at the Canyons Village base of the resort throughout the entire summer, or you can check out the farmers market that happens every Wednesday.*

Which word below best meets the writer's needs?

(A) as it is now
(B) exciting
(C) youthful
(D) strenuous
(E) exhausting

335. The writer is considering adding the underlined portion to sentence 10 (reproduced below):

> *"Park City is truly a four-season destination,"* shares Danielle Summers, <u>*public relations & marketing manager at Waldorf Astoria Park City*</u>.

Should the writer add the underlined portion to sentence 10?

(A) Yes, because readers may need definitions for what public relations and marketing are

(B) Yes, because it is helpful to readers to provide the titles and identifying information for speakers of quotations, who may be unfamiliar

(C) Yes, because the speaker of the quotation is an expert on travel to different locales, and readers will appreciate her wide base of knowledge

(D) No, because, according to her title, the speaker is not qualified to comment on the seasonal offerings at Waldorf Astoria Park City

(E) No, all readers will be familiar with Danielle Summers and her position at Waldorf Astoria Park City

336. The writer is considering adding the following sentence before sentence 12:

> <u>*Winter*</u> *is magical in Park City, with snowmobiling, sleigh rides, ice-skating, and cross-country skiing—making Park City a winter wonderland for people of all ages.*

Should the writer add the sentence before sentence 12?

(A) Yes, because winter in Park City is superior to summer, and this sentence clearly makes that claim

(B) Yes, because this sentence strongly refutes the claims made by Danielle Summers above

(C) Yes, because this sentence serves as a topic sentence for this paragraph and clarifies that this paragraph will focus on winter, while the last one focused on summer activities

(D) No, because the mention of skiing and snowboarding in sentence 12 makes this sentence redundant and unnecessary for both the paragraph and the passage

(E) No, because this sentence undermines the strong case for how great Park City is in the summer and serves to work against the writer's major claim

337. The writer is considering adding the underlined portion to sentence 13 (reproduced below):

> *If you have not yet purchased your Epic Pass, <u>which provides unlimited and unrestricted skiing access at the best resorts,</u> for this next season, here are two more reasons why you should: legendary deep, dry powder and exciting nightlife at après-ski venues.*

Should the writer add the underlined portion to sentence 13?

(A) Yes, because potential travelers to Park City are exclusively interested in skiing

(B) Yes, because potential visitors to Park City are all on tight budgets and are looking for the best value options

(C) Yes, because readers may not be familiar with the Epic Pass, and this additional information could be useful

(D) No, because all readers of this passage are already familiar with the Epic Pass and its offerings

(E) No, because readers of this passage are interested in the summertime offerings and not the available ski passes

338. The author wants to avoid expressing the claims in sentence 14 (reproduced below) in absolute terms that cannot be supported by fact.

> *Located at the base of the new Park City Mountain Resort, now the <u>largest</u> ski and snowboard resort in the country, Waldorf Astoria Park City offers prime access to a myriad of year-round outdoor activities.*

Which version of the underlined word best meets the writer's needs?

(A) as it is now

(B) best

(C) nicest

(D) fanciest

(E) prettiest

339. The writer is considering removing the underlined portion of sentence 15 (reproduced below):

> *"We are very excited about our partnership with Vail Resorts because similar to Waldorf Astoria, Vail Resorts is known for being the best in class in what they do," states Kerry Hing, general manager of the Waldorf Astoria Park City.*

Should the writer remove the underlined portion of the sentence?

(A) Yes, because Kerry Hing's role as general manager is irrelevant to whether readers are considering visiting the resort

(B) Yes, because it makes sentence 15 too long and disrupts the continuity between the quotations in sentences 15 and 16

(C) Yes, because the speaker is employed by the Waldorf Astoria and is not an expert on travel to different locales

(D) No, because it is helpful to readers to provide the titles and identifying information for speakers of quotations, who may be unfamiliar

(E) No, because readers are familiar with Kerry Hing and her role and will be glad to see her name and identifying information in print

340. The writer is considering replacing the underlined word in sentence 16 (reproduced below):

> *"Waldorf Astoria Park City is fortunate to be the only Forbes four-star luxury hotel located at the base of the resort, which makes for a very elite partnership that will afford both Vail Resorts and Waldorf Astoria great opportunity."*

Which version of the underlined word should the writer use?

(A) as it is now

(B) provide

(C) supply

(D) offer

(E) give

Passage 7e: Mary Rowlandson, *Narrative of the Captivity and Restoration of Mrs. Mary Rowlandson*

I can remember the time when I used to sleep quietly without workings in my thoughts, whole nights together, but now it is other ways with me. When all are fast about me, and no eye open, but His who ever waketh, my thoughts are upon things past, upon the awful dispensation of the Lord towards us, upon His wonderful power and might, in carrying of us through 5 so many difficulties, in returning us in safety, and suffering none to hurt us. I remember in the night season, how the other day I was in the midst of thousands of enemies, and nothing but death before me. It is then hard work to persuade myself, that ever I should be satisfied with bread again. But now we are fed with the finest of the wheat, and, as I may say, with 10 honey out of the rock. Instead of the husk, we have the fatted calf. The thoughts of these things in the particulars of them, and of the love and goodness of God towards us, make it true of me, what David said of himself, "I watered my Couch with my tears" (Psalm 6.6). Oh! the wonderful power of God that mine eyes have seen, affording matter enough for my thoughts 15 to run in, that when others are sleeping mine eyes are weeping.

I have seen the extreme vanity of this world: One hour I have been in health, and wealthy, wanting nothing. But the next hour in sickness and wounds, and death, having nothing but sorrow and affliction.

Before I knew what affliction meant, I was ready sometimes to wish for 20 it. When I lived in prosperity, having the comforts of the world about me, my relations by me, my heart cheerful, and taking little care for anything, and yet seeing many, whom I preferred before myself, under many trials and afflictions, in sickness, weakness, poverty, losses, crosses, and cares of the world, I should be sometimes jealous least I should have my portion 25 in this life, and that Scripture would come to my mind, "For whom the Lord loveth he chasteneth, and scourgeth every Son whom he receiveth" (Hebrews 12.6). But now I see the Lord had His time to scourge and chasten me. The portion of some is to have their afflictions by drops, now one drop and then another; but the dregs of the cup, the wine of astonishment, 30 like a sweeping rain that leaveth no food, did the Lord prepare to be my portion. Affliction I wanted, and affliction I had, full measure (I thought), pressed down and running over. Yet I see, when God calls a person to anything, and through never so many difficulties, yet He is fully able to carry them through and make them see, and say they have been gainers thereby. 35 And I hope I can say in some measure, as David did, "It is good for me that I have been afflicted." The Lord hath showed me the vanity of these outward things. That they are the vanity of vanities, and vexation of spirit, that they are but a shadow, a blast, a bubble, and things of no continuance. That we must rely on God Himself, and our whole dependance must be upon Him. 40 If trouble from smaller matters begin to arise in me, I have something at hand to check myself with, and say, why am I troubled? It was but the other day that if I had had the world, I would have given it for my freedom, or to have been a servant to a Christian. I have learned to look beyond present and smaller troubles, and to be quieted under them. As Moses said, "Stand 45 still and see the salvation of the Lord" (Exodus 14.13).

341. The occasion for the passage is:
 (A) the speaker's crisis of faith and her accompanying doubt
 (B) the speaker's release from captivity by Native Americans
 (C) the speaker's loss of her family and the pain she suffers as a result
 (D) the speaker's process of being ostracized from her community
 (E) the speaker's uncertainty about her choices in life

342. In lines 3–7, the speaker describes God as all of the following *except*:
 (A) powerful
 (B) protective
 (C) punishing
 (D) awe-inspiring
 (E) strong

343. In line 20, the word "affliction" most nearly means:
 (A) distress
 (B) wealth
 (C) wisdom
 (D) faith
 (E) maturity

344. The quotation, "For whom the Lord loveth he chasteneth, and scourgeth every Son whom he receiveth" (Hebrews 12.6) in lines 26–27 means:
 (A) God punishes those who do not make their love of Him known
 (B) God loves those who are obedient
 (C) God makes those that He does not love suffer
 (D) God does not love people that question Him
 (E) God tests those he loves through difficult trials

345. The function of the metaphor of the wine in the cup in the statement "The portion of some is to have their afflictions by drops, now one drop and then another; but the dregs of the cup, the wine of astonishment, like a sweeping rain that leaveth no food, did the Lord prepare to be my portion" in lines 29–32 is to:

(A) illustrate that some people have a little bit of suffering at a time while others have extreme suffering

(B) show that God provides food and wine to the faithful

(C) prove that all people suffer at the same rate, whether they see it that way or not

(D) make a connection between suffering and drunkenness, which should be avoided

(E) draw a comparison between suffering and starvation, which is a horrible fate

346. The word "vanity" in line 37 can best be defined as:

(A) egotism

(B) beauty

(C) worthlessness

(D) youth

(E) confusion

347. Outward things are described as "a shadow, a blast, a bubble, and things of no continuance" in line 39 to emphasize their:

(A) impressive nature

(B) ephemeral nature

(C) natural origins

(D) astonishing characteristics

(E) deceptive simplicity

348. The audience for this piece was most likely:

(A) Native Americans who should repent

(B) the Founding Fathers, who needed to be informed

(C) local American politicians who could enact change

(D) women and mothers who had similar trials

(E) fellow Christians who had similar belief systems

349. The overall purpose of the passage is to:
   (A) narrate the speaker's experience in captivity
   (B) expose the identities of her captors so that they would be punished
   (C) appeal to the authorities of her time to see that this type of suffering would not happen to anyone else
   (D) reflect on the speaker's time of difficulty and share what she learned and how she grew
   (E) express the speaker's self-reliance and strength through difficult times

350. The tone of the passage can be described as:
   (A) bitter and scorned
   (B) thankful and trepidatious
   (C) grateful and introspective
   (D) learned and didactic
   (E) confident and self-assertive

18th Century with Draft Passages

Passage 8a: Edward Gibbon, *The History of the Decline and Fall of the Roman Empire*

After a diligent inquiry, I can discern four principal causes of the ruin of Rome, which continued to operate in a period of more than a thousand years. I. The injuries of time and nature. II. The hostile attacks of the Barbarians and Christians. III. The use and abuse of the materials. And, IV. The domestic quarrels of the Romans.

  I. The art of man is able to construct monuments far more permanent than the narrow span of his own existence; yet these monuments, like himself, are perishable and frail; and in the boundless annals[1] of time, his life and his labors must equally be measured as a fleeting moment. Of a simple and solid edifice, it is not easy, however, to circumscribe the duration. As the wonders of ancient days, the pyramids[2] attracted the curiosity of the ancients: a hundred generations, the leaves of autumn, have dropped[3] into the grave; and after the fall of the Pharaohs and Ptolemies, the Cæsars and caliphs, the same pyramids stand erect and unshaken above the floods of the Nile. A complex figure of various and minute parts is more accessible to injury and decay; and the silent lapse of time is often accelerated by hurricanes and earthquakes, by fires and inundations[4]. The air and earth have doubtless been shaken; and the lofty turrets of Rome have tottered from their foundations; but the seven hills do not appear to be placed on the great cavities of the globe; nor has the city, in any age, been exposed to the

---

1. records of events by years

2. Gibbon's footnote: [The age of the pyramids is remote and unknown, since Diodorus Siculus (tom. i l. i. c. 44, p. 72) is unable to decide whether they were constructed 1000, or 3400, years before the clxxxth Olympiad. Sir John Marsham's contracted scale of the Egyptian dynasties would fix them about 2000 years before Christ, (Canon. *Chronicus*, p. 47.)]

3. Gibbon's footnote: [See the speech of Glaucus in the *Iliad*, (Z. 146.) This natural but melancholy image is peculiar to Homer.]

4. floods

convulsions of nature, which, in the climate of Antioch, Lisbon, or Lima, have crumbled in a few moments the works of ages into dust. Fire is the most powerful agent of life and death: the rapid mischief may be kindled and propagated by the industry or negligence of mankind; and every period of the Roman annals is marked by the repetition of similar calamities. A 25 memorable conflagration, the guilt or misfortune of Nero's reign, continued, though with unequal fury, either six or nine days[5]. Innumerable buildings, crowded in close and crooked streets, supplied perpetual fuel for the flames; and when they ceased, four only of the fourteen regions were left entire; three were totally destroyed, and seven were deformed by the relics of smoking 30 and lacerated edifices[6]. In the full meridian of empire, the metropolis arose with fresh beauty from her ashes; yet the memory of the old deplored their irreparable losses, the arts of Greece, the trophies of victory, the monuments of primitive or fabulous antiquity. In the days of distress and anarchy, every wound is mortal, every fall irretrievable; nor can the damage be restored 35 either by the public care of government, or the activity of private interest. Yet two causes may be alleged, which render the calamity of fire more destructive to a flourishing than a decayed city. 1. The more combustible materials of brick, timber, and metals, are first melted or consumed; but the flames may play without injury or effect on the naked walls, and massy arches, that have 40 been despoiled of their ornaments. 2. It is among the common and plebeian habitations, that a mischievous spark is most easily blown to a conflagration; but as soon as they are devoured, the greater edifices, which have resisted or escaped, are left as so many islands in a state of solitude and safety.

351. The first paragraph of the passage (lines 1–5) is structured by:

   (A) minor causes to major causes
   (B) chronological sequence
   (C) specific to general
   (D) general to specific
   (E) enumeration

---

5. Gibbon's footnote: [The learning and criticism of M. des Vignoles (*Histoire Critique de la République des Lettres*, tom. viii. p. 47–118, ix. p. 172–187) dates the fire of Rome from July 19, A.D. 64, and the subsequent persecution of the Christians from November 15 of the same year.]

6. Gibbon's footnote: [Quippe in regiones quatuordecim Roma dividitur, quarum quatuor integræ manebant, tres solo tenus dejectæ: septem reliquis pauca testorum vestigia supererant, lacera et semiusta. Among the old relics that were irreparably lost, Tacitus enumerates the temple of the moon of Servius Tullius; the fane and altar consecrated by Evander præsenti Herculi; the temple of Jupiter Stator, a vow of Romulus; the palace of Numa; the temple of Vesta cum Penatibus populi Romani. He then deplores the opes tot victoriis quæsitæ et Græcarum artium decora . . . multa quæ seniores meminerant, quæ reparari nequibant, (*Annal*. xv. 40, 41.)]

352. The paradox of the first sentence of paragraph two (lines 6–9) is that the art of man is:

(A) more permanent than his life span
(B) both more permanent and fleeting
(C) both perishable and frail
(D) measured as a fleeting moment
(E) like himself

353. The purpose of footnote 2 is to:

(A) elaborate on the unknown age of the pyramids
(B) cite Diodorus Siculus
(C) cite Sir John Marsham
(D) argue that the pyramids were constructed 1,000 or 3,400 years before the clxxxth Olympiad
(E) argue that the pyramids were constructed 2,000 years before Christ

354. The discussion of the pyramids is provided as an example of:

(A) permanent monuments
(B) perishable monuments
(C) unknown duration of edifices
(D) wonders of ancient days
(E) curiosity of the ancients

355. The purpose of footnote 3 is to:

(A) cite Glaucus's speech
(B) cite the *Iliad*
(C) cite Homer
(D) cite a direct quotation on page 146
(E) elaborate on the image of the leaves and its allusiveness

356. In context, the word "propagated" in line 24 most nearly means:

(A) spread
(B) caused to multiply
(C) bred
(D) transmitted
(E) made widely known

357. The purpose of footnote 5 is all of the following *except* to:

    (A) provide the date of the Roman fire as July 19, A.D. 64

    (B) provide the date of the Roman fire as November 15, A.D. 64

    (C) provide the author of *Histoire Critique de la République des Lettres* as M. des Vignoles

    (D) cite the page ranges of 47 to 118 and 172 to 187

    (E) provide the writer's source of information on the major fire during Nero's reign

358. The purpose of footnote 6 is all of the following *except* to:

    (A) provide in Latin the account of the devastation of the fire

    (B) list in English the old relics that were irreparably lost

    (C) cite passages from the *Annal*

    (D) cite passages from *Histoire Critique de la République des Lettres*

    (E) cite passages on pages 40 and 41

359. The speaker of the piece can best be described as:

    (A) pretentious

    (B) belligerent

    (C) mournful

    (D) learned

    (E) accusatory

360. The primary purpose of the passage as a whole is to:

    (A) narrate the story of the latter portion of the fall of Rome

    (B) describe the hostile attacks of the Barbarians and the Christians

    (C) analyze the causes of the fall of Rome

    (D) define monuments and explore their uses

    (E) classify the types of combustible materials

Passage 8b: *Grateful Dead Draft*

(1) The Grateful Dead was the most singularly unique popular American musical phenomenon of the 20th century. (2) I dub the Dead a "phenomenon" and not only a "band" for the many ways in which they influenced history and impacted the lives of their unconventional fanbase—not only played and recorded music. (3) Many "Deadheads," who make up what would traditionally be called the Grateful Dead's fanbase, consider themselves part of a "family" that incorporates the core musicians along with fans. (4) While it is widely known that the fanbase followed the touring band around the country from venue to venue, it is less known that 25 years after the death of Jerry Garcia (generally understood to be the band's leader), the loose structure of this friendly network continues to thrive.

(5) In 1995, the Dead community appeared to crash with Garcia's death, but what truly has followed (another 25 years on) is a continually pollinating national scene of musicians, craftspeople, and their fans that keep a passion for the Grateful Dead's music at the forefront of their culture. (6) In this scene, what might classically be called "cover" or "tribute" bands are elevated to the level of primary acts, should they be considered to carry the spirit of the original compositions and performers. (7) Some of these bands tour nationally and even partially perform their own compositions alongside "Dead music."

(8) Additionally, the Grateful Dead's famous iconography, such as the colorful Dancing Bears and the "Stealie"—a skull-with-lightning-bolt logo that resembles an American yin-yang—have taken on an almost mythical stature within this subculture. (9) Countless artisans continue to craft and sell these icons in wood, steel, and ceramic, while thousands of Deadheads adorn themselves with tattoos of the same imagery.

(10) A quick Google search reveals Grateful Dead yoga groups, as well as other spirituality and wellness connections like aromatherapy and meditation, and even sporting clubs for golf and "disc" golf. (11) Corporations like Nike, Igloo, and American Express have forged partnerships with the Grateful Dead "brand" and have produced products, services, and charities under the same banner.

361. Which sentence below can best be described as the writer's thesis?

(A) The Grateful Dead was the most singularly unique popular American musical phenomenon of the 20th century.

(B) I dub the Dead a "phenomenon" and not only a "band" for the many ways in which they influenced history and impacted the lives of their unconventional fanbase—not only played and recorded music.

(C) In fact, many "Deadheads," who make up what would traditionally be called the Grateful Dead's fanbase, consider themselves part of a "family" that incorporates the core musicians along with fans.

(D) While it is widely known that the fanbase followed the touring band around the country from venue to venue, it is less known that 25 years after the death of Jerry Garcia (generally understood to be the band's leader), the loose structure of this friendly network continues to thrive.

(E) In 1995, the Dead community appeared to crash with Garcia's death, but what truly has followed (another 25 years on) is a continually pollinating national scene of musicians, craftspeople, and their fans that keep a passion for the Grateful Dead's music at the forefront of their culture.

362. The writer is considering removing the word "singularly" from sentence 1 (reproduced below):

> *The Grateful Dead was the most singularly unique popular American musical phenomenon of the 20th century.*

Should the writer remove "singularly"?

(A) Yes, because readers may be unfamiliar with the term

(B) Yes, because it weakens the writer's argument

(C) Yes, because it is redundant when placed before "unique"

(D) No, because it helps clarify the writer's position

(E) No, because it develops the writer's voice and tone

363. The writer is considering removing the underlined portion of sentence 2 (reproduced below):

> *I dub the Dead a "phenomenon" and not only a "band" for the many ways in which they influenced history and impacted the lives of their unconventional fanbase—not only played and recorded music.*

Should the writer remove the underlined portion of sentence 2?

(A) Yes, because the Grateful Dead is mostly known for playing and recording music

(B) Yes, because the definition of "phenomenon" is made clear by the earlier part of the sentence

(C) Yes, because readers are already familiar with the definition of a "phenomenon" when describing a music group

(D) No, because it clarifies the definition of a "band" in order to argue how the Grateful Dead should be categorized as a "phenomenon"

(E) No, because it is crucial that the writer explains how well the Grateful Dead plays and records music

364. The writer is considering adding a transition to the beginning of sentence 3 (reproduced below):

> *Many "Deadheads," who make up what would traditionally be called the Grateful Dead's fanbase, consider themselves part of a "family" that incorporates the core musicians along with fans.*

Adjusting for punctuation and capitalization, which transition would best express the relationship between sentences 2 and 3?

(A) However,

(B) In fact,

(C) Nevertheless,

(D) Regardless,

(E) Nonetheless,

365. The writer is considering adding the underlined phrase to sentence 5 (reproduced below):

> In 1995, *after about 30 years of touring*, the Dead community appeared to crash with Garcia's death, but what truly has followed (another 25 years on) is a continually pollinating national scene of musicians, craftspeople, and their fans that keep a passion for the Grateful Dead's music at the forefront of their culture.

Should the writer add the underlined portion to sentence 5?

(A) Yes, because while 1995 provides the date, the added information helps to provide context and a timeline of the band and its life span

(B) Yes, because it provides the reason why the Dead community appeared to crash, mentioned in the next portion of the sentence

(C) Yes, because it expresses how long musicians, fans, and craftspeople have been contributing to the Dead subculture

(D) No, because the number of years that the Grateful Dead toured is irrelevant to their popularity

(E) No, because all readers know that the Grateful Dead starting touring in the 1960s

366. The writer wants to replace the underlined word in sentence 6 (reproduced below) to match the meaning and tone of the rest of the sentence and paragraph:

> In this scene, what might classically be called "cover" or "tribute" bands are *elevated* to the level of primary acts, should they be considered to carry the spirit of the original compositions and performers.

Which option below best captures the meaning and tone of the rest of the sentence and paragraph?

(A) as it is now

(B) relegated

(C) classified

(D) situated

(E) hoisted

367. The writer is considering removing the underlined portion of sentence 8 (reproduced below):

> *Additionally, the Grateful Dead's famous iconography, such as the colorful Dancing Bears and the "Stealie"—a skull-with-lightning-bolt logo that resembles an American yin-yang—have taken on an almost mythical stature within this subculture.*

Should the writer remove the underlined portion of sentence 8?

(A) Yes, because of the fame of the iconography, it is unnecessary to define the "Stealie"

(B) Yes, because some readers may be offended by the image of a skull

(C) Yes, because some readers may be unfamiliar with the image of a yin-ying

(D) No, because while some readers may be familiar with the iconography, some may not, and the description offers helpful information

(E) No, because while everyone has seen the Dancing Bears, some may have not seen the "Stealie"

368. The writer is considering adding the underlined phrase to sentence 9 (reproduced below):

> *Countless artisans continue to craft and sell these icons in wood, steel, and ceramic, while thousands of Deadheads adorn themselves with tattoos of the same imagery, indicating the deep connections of a tribal spirituality.*

Should the writer add the underlined phrase to sentence 9?

(A) Yes, because tattoos are of great importance to readers, and that should be clearly expressed

(B) Yes, because it communicates the significance of the examples provided in the first part of the sentence

(C) Yes, because readers may not agree with or understand the need for the continued artwork centered around the Grateful Dead

(D) No, it is unnecessary to communicate any significance behind the simple enjoyment of the artwork centered around the Grateful Dead

(E) No, because not all those who enjoy the artwork centered around the Grateful Dead are necessarily spiritual

369. The writer is considering adding the following sentence after sentence 10:

> *Disc golf, created in the 1900s, is a flying disc sport in which players throw a disc at a target and is played with similar rules to golf.*

Should the writer add this sentence after sentence 10?

(A) Yes, because while golf is popular, disc golf may be unfamiliar to readers
(B) Yes, because understanding the origins of disc golf is crucial to understanding Grateful Dead culture and pastimes
(C) Yes, because it is irresponsible for the writer to introduce disc golf in sentence 10 without a full explanation of the sport
(D) No, because this much information about disc golf is not necessary to the paragraph or the passage as a whole
(E) No, because disc golf is wholly familiar to readers, and this level of explanation is unnecessary

370. The writer would like to add a sentence after sentence 11 to conclude the passage by returning to the passage's opening and solidifying the major claim made there. Which of the following sentences best meets the writer's needs?

(A) No other band in history could say they have had this far of a reach into the lives of fans.
(B) In July 2020, Nike Grateful Dead sneakers sold out instantly.
(C) There even exists a vegan Grateful Dead deodorant!
(D) With so many musicians playing Grateful Dead music and music inspired by the Dead, you have plenty of opportunities to have a live Dead musical experience.
(E) It's wonderful to see how those who love the Dead have used their passion for philanthropy through charities that partner with the Grateful Dead.

Passage 8c: John Locke, *Second Treatise on Government*

Sect. 22. THE *natural liberty* of man is to be free from any superior power on earth, and not to be under the will or legislative authority of man, but to have only the law of nature for his rule. The liberty of man, in society, is to be under no other legislative power, but that established, by consent, in the commonwealth; nor under the dominion of any will, or restraint of 5 any law, but what that legislative shall enact, according to the trust put in

it. Freedom then is not what *Sir Robert Filmer* tells us, *Observations, A. 55. a liberty for every one to do what he lists, to live as he pleases, and not to be tied by any laws*: but *freedom of men under government* is, to have a standing rule to live by, common to every one of that society, and made by the legisla- 10
tive power erected in it; a liberty to follow my own will in all things, where the rule prescribes not; and not to be subject to the inconstant, uncertain, unknown, arbitrary will of another man: as *freedom of nature* is, to be under no other restraint but the law of nature.

Sect. 23. This *freedom* from absolute, arbitrary power, is so necessary 15
to, and closely joined with a man's preservation, that he cannot part with it, but by what forfeits his preservation and life together: for a man, not having the power of his own life, *cannot*, by compact, or his own consent, *enslave himself* to any one, nor put himself under the absolute, arbitrary power of another, to take away his life, when he pleases. No body can give 20
more power than he has himself; and he that cannot take away his own life, cannot give another power over it. Indeed, having by his fault forfeited his own life, by some act that deserves death; he, to whom he has forfeited it, may (when he has him in his power) delay to take it, and make use of him to his own service, and he does him no injury by it: for, whenever he finds 25
the hardship of his slavery outweigh the value of his life, it is in his power, by resisting the will of his master, to draw on himself the death he desires.

Sect. 24. This is the perfect condition of *slavery*, which is nothing else, but *the state of war continued, between a lawful conqueror and a captive*: for, if once *compact* enter between them, and make an agreement for a limited 30
power on the one side, and obedience on the other, the *state of war and slavery ceases*, as long as the compact endures: for, as has been said, no man can, by agreement, pass over to another that which he hath not in himself, a power over his own life.

371. The first paragraph of the passage (lines 1–14) defines all of the following terms *except*:
- (A) natural liberty
- (B) legislative authority
- (C) freedom
- (D) freedom of men under government
- (E) freedom of nature

372. Paragraph one (lines 1–14) relies on the following type of evidence:

    (A) anecdote

    (B) statistics

    (C) expert testimony

    (D) direct quotation

    (E) observation

373. The evidence provided in paragraph one (lines 1–14) is used as:

    (A) the major claim

    (B) an underlying assumption

    (C) a counterargument

    (D) a rebuttal

    (E) a qualification

374. The writer uses asyndeton, or the omission of conjunctions, in the line "and not to be subject to the inconstant, uncertain, unknown, arbitrary will of another man" (lines 12–13) to:

    (A) mirror the overwhelming will of another man on a man's freedom

    (B) confuse readers with multiple adjectives

    (C) demonstrate his ease with vocabulary

    (D) provide many synonyms for those who may be unfamiliar with some of the terms

    (E) offer words with disparate meanings to qualify "will"

375. In context, the first use of the word "arbitrary" in line 13 most nearly means:

    (A) belonging to an earlier time

    (B) determined by impulse

    (C) known to only a few

    (D) having the power to judge

    (E) strenuous and difficult

376. In context, the second and third uses of the word "arbitrary" in lines 15 and 19 most nearly mean:

    (A) inherited

    (B) usurped

    (C) without substance

    (D) not limited by law

    (E) fleeting

377. The following claim of paragraph two (lines 15–27) is ironic:

(A) a man without power cannot enslave himself to another

(B) a man who is frustrated with the hardship of slavery can bring about his own death

(C) a man who has the power of another man may delay taking his life

(D) a man's preservation is dependent upon his freedom

(E) a man cannot give more power than he has

378. Paragraph three (lines 28–34) defines the following term:

(A) slavery

(B) war

(C) conqueror

(D) captive

(E) compact

379. The primary purpose of the passage as a whole is to:

(A) provide examples of freedom of man

(B) justify the speaker's choices of structuring the passage by sections and numbers

(C) explore the meanings and states of freedom and slavery

(D) describe the conditions of slavery

(E) argue against those who define freedom differently than the speaker

380. The tone of the passage can best be described as:

(A) apologetic and contrite

(B) conciliatory and amiable

(C) forceful and confident

(D) mocking and derisive

(E) humorous and jocular

Passage 8d: *Spinach Quiche Recipe Draft*

(1) In order to make your two spinach quiches, you need to have two frozen pie shells, one softened 8-ounce foil pack of cream cheese, six eggs, one 10-ounce frozen package of chopped spinach, one 8-ounce bag of shredded cheddar cheese, one 8-ounce bag of shredded mozzarella cheese, and salt and pepper to taste. (2) To soften the cream cheese, leave it out on the counter for a while. (3) Since you just need it to be soft, not melted, don't microwave it, which may make it too runny. (4) Once you have all of your ingredients ready, preheat the oven to 350°F.

(5) Now you are ready to make your spinach quiches. (6) Next, poke a few holes in the bottom of the frozen shells with a fork and bake them empty for about 10 minutes. (7) After that, pull them out and set them aside to wait for the filling. (8) Next, defrost and drain the frozen spinach. (9) I try to push out as much water as I can with paper towels in the colander. (10) Then mix together the drained spinach, six eggs, cream cheese, cheddar, mozzarella, salt, and pepper. (11) Pour the mixture into the two pie shells. (12) Bake until golden. (13) (I guess around 30 minutes, but I usually keep an eye on it and look for it to get some nice color on top.) (14) Also, last night I used about 6 ounces of the bags of shredded cheese that come with 8 ounces of cheese. (15) Either way is fine. (16) I've used the whole bag or a bit less.

(17) In addition, there are some alternatives to the recipe: you could use any other meats, cheeses, or vegetables that you like. (18) You could sauté and add mushrooms, crisp and combine bacon, crumble and sprinkle in feta cheese, and so on. (19) The spinach is my mom's classic, but the recipe is easy to adapt for individual tastes. (20) It's good warm, at room temperature, or even straight from the fridge. (21) Make a salad with it, and it works for dinner too. (22) Enjoy!

381. The writer would like to add a sentence before sentence 1 that engages the reader and introduces the topic. Which sentence below would best meet the writer's needs?

(A) You'll have to go to the grocery store to get all of your ingredients.

(B) It's easy to make spinach quiche, a delicious and healthy vegetable and egg tart, which can be eaten for any meal!

(C) The first example of English usage of the word "quiche" was recorded in 1925.

(D) Quiche is a French dish, but the English made a similar egg-and-cream-in-pastry dish as early as the 14th century.

(E) The most popular quiche is quiche Lorraine, which includes bacon.

382. The writer is considering removing the underlined portion of sentence 1 (reproduced below):

> *In order to make spinach quiche, you need <u>to have</u> a frozen pie shell, one softened foil pack of cream cheese, six eggs, one frozen package of chopped spinach, one bag of shredded cheddar cheese, one bag of shredded mozzarella cheese, and salt and pepper.*

Should the writer remove the underlined portion of sentence 1?

(A) Yes, because it is redundant when placed after "you need"
(B) Yes, because it creates a forceful rather than inviting tone
(C) Yes, because it should be replaced with "to buy"
(D) No, because the ingredients list is unclear without that phrase
(E) No, because it makes clear the directive nature of the passage

383. The writer is considering removing sentence 5 (reproduced below):

> *Now you are ready to make your spinach quiches.*

Should the writer remove sentence 5?

(A) Yes, because readers may not be ready to start cooking at this point
(B) Yes, because the construction of the quiches began in the first paragraph
(C) Yes, because some readers may not be following the recipe but rather just reading
(D) No, because it helps the reader transition from the preparing stage to the cooking stage and serves as a topic sentence for paragraph 2
(E) No, because this passage is meant to be understood as an explanation of how quiche is made, not as directions to be followed

384. The writer is considering replacing the transition used to begin sentence 6 (reproduced below):

> *Next, poke a few holes in the bottom of the frozen shells with a fork and bake them empty for about 10 minutes.*

Which is the best transition to begin sentence 6?

(A) as it is now
(B) Thus,
(C) Moreover,
(D) However,
(E) First,

385. The writer is considering revising the use of pronouns in sentence 9 (reproduced below):

> *I try to push out as much water as I can with paper towels in the colander.*

Should the writer use the proposed revised sentence 9 below?

> *Try to push out as much water as you can with paper towels in a colander.*

(A) Yes, because the switch to "you" contributes to consistency between this sentence and the rest of the passage
(B) Yes, because the reader does not expect the writer to have personal experience with following the recipe
(C) Yes, because it changes the tone from helpful and informative to demanding and pedantic
(D) No, because it offers a personal experience that can help readers relate to the writer
(E) No, because readers may be confused by the use of "you" in this context

386. The writer would like to combine sentences 10 and 11 (reproduced below):

> *Then mix the drained spinach, six eggs, cream cheese, cheddar, mozzarella, salt, and pepper. Pour the mixture into the two pie shells.*

Which of the following options is the best combination of sentences 10 and 11?

(A) Then mix the drained spinach, six eggs, cream cheese, cheddar, mozzarella, salt, and pepper, but pour the mixture into the two pie shells.

(B) Then mix the drained spinach, six eggs, cream cheese, cheddar, mozzarella, salt, and pepper, so pour the mixture into the two pie shells.

(C) Then mix the drained spinach, six eggs, cream cheese, cheddar, mozzarella, salt, and pepper, and pour the mixture into the two pie shells.

(D) Then mix the drained spinach, six eggs, cream cheese, cheddar, mozzarella, salt, and pepper, yet pour the mixture into the two pie shells.

(E) Then mix the drained spinach, six eggs, cream cheese, cheddar, mozzarella, salt, and pepper; moreover, pour the mixture into the two pie shells.

387. The writer would like to combine sentences 12 and 13 (reproduced below):

> *Bake until golden. (I guess around 30 minutes, but I usually keep an eye on it and look for it to get some nice color on top.)*

Which version below is the simplest and clearest combination of sentences 12 and 13?

(A) Bake until golden, which I guess is around 30 minutes, but I usually keep an eye on it and look for it to get some nice color on top.

(B) Bake until golden, which is around 30 minutes, but I usually keep an eye on it and look for it to get some nice color on top.

(C) Bake until golden, for around 30 minutes, but I usually keep an eye on it and look for it to get some nice color on top.

(D) Bake until golden on top, around 30 minutes, but check on it sporadically.

(E) Bake until golden, which is around 30 minutes, but keep an eye on it and look for it to get some nice color on top.

388. The writer is considering removing sentences 14 through 16 (reproduced below):

> *Also, last night I used about 6 ounces of the bags of shredded cheese that come with 8 ounces of cheese. Either way is fine. I've used the whole bag or a bit less.*

Should the writer remove sentences 14 through 16?

(A) Yes, because recipes should always be followed exactly according to the directions

(B) Yes, because the information does not seem crucial to understanding the process of making spinach quiche

(C) Yes, because readers should always try to cut down on how much of an ingredient they add for health and spending concerns

(D) No, because readers want to know how to make spinach quiche with as little of the ingredients as possible

(E) No, because these sentences add a personal experience and voice to the passage that help the writer's credibility

389. The writer is considering adding a transition to the beginning of sentence 18 (reproduced below):

> *You could sauté and add mushrooms, crisp and combine bacon, crumble and sprinkle in feta cheese, and so on.*

Adjusting for capitalization and punctuation, which of the following transitions would be best placed at the beginning of sentence 18?

(A) Next,

(B) Thus,

(C) Therefore,

(D) For example,

(E) Moreover,

390. The writer is considering removing sentence 19 (reproduced below):

> *The spinach is my mom's classic, but the recipe is easy to adapt for individual tastes.*

Should the writer remove sentence 19?

(A) Yes, because it is inappropriate to mention family members in a passage of this type
(B) Yes, because readers will already know about the recipe's adaptability based on their prior knowledge
(C) Yes, because it changes the tone and focus of the passage too dramatically
(D) No, because readers will be wondering about the source of the recipe
(E) No, because it adds a personal touch that is appropriate for a recipe and makes the claim that the recipe is easy to adapt

Passage 8e: Richard Steele, *The Tatler*

A gentleman has writ to me out of the country a very civil letter, and said things which I suppress with great violence to my vanity. There are many terms in my narratives which he complains want explaining, and has therefore desired, that, for the benefit of my country readers, I would let him know what I mean by a Gentleman, a Pretty Fellow, a Toast, a Coquette, a   5
Critic, a Wit, and all other appellations in the gayer world, who are in present possession of these several characters; together with an account of those who unfortunately pretend to them. I shall begin with him we usually call a Gentleman, or man of conversation.

It is generally thought, that warmth of imagination, quick relish of   10
pleasure, and a manner of becoming it, are the most essential qualities for forming this sort of man. But any one that is much in company will observe, that the height of good breeding is shown rather in never giving offence, than in doing obliging things. Thus, he that never shocks you, though he is seldom entertaining, is more likely to keep your favour, than he who often   15
entertains, and sometimes displeases you. The most necessary talent therefore in a man of conversation, which is what we ordinarily intend by a fine gentleman, is a good judgment. He that has this in perfection, is master of his companion, without letting him see it; and has the same advantage over men of any other qualifications whatsoever, as one that can see would have   20
over a blind man of ten times his strength.

This is what makes Sophronius the darling of all who converse with him, and the most powerful with his acquaintance of any man in town. By the light of this faculty, he acts with great ease and freedom among the men of pleasure, and acquits himself with skill and despatch among the men of 25 business. This he performs with so much success, that, with as much discretion in life as any man ever had, he neither is, nor appears, cunning. But as he does a good office, if he ever does it, with readiness and alacrity; so he denies what he does not care to engage in, in a manner that convinces you, that you ought not to have asked it. His judgment is so good and unerr- 30 ing, and accompanied with so cheerful a spirit, that his conversation is a continual feast, at which he helps some, and is helped by others, in such a manner, that the equality of society is perfectly kept up, and every man obliges as much as he is obliged: for it is the greatest and justest skill in a man of superior understanding, to know how to be on a level with his com- 35 panions. This sweet disposition runs through all the actions of Sophronius, and makes his company desired by women, without being envied by men. Sophronius would be as just as he is, if there were no law; and would be as discreet as he is, if there were no such thing as calumny.

In imitation of this agreeable being, is made that animal we call a Pretty 40 Fellow; who being just able to find out, that what makes Sophronius accept- able, is a natural behaviour; in order to the same reputation, makes his own an artificial one. Jack Dimple is his perfect mimic, whereby he is of course the most unlike him of all men living. Sophronius just now passed into the inner room directly forward: Jack comes as fast after as he can for the right 45 and left looking-glass, in which he had but just approved himself by a nod at each, and marched on. He will meditate within for half an hour, till he thinks he is not careless enough in his air, and come back to the mirror to recollect his forgetfulness.

391. The occasion of the passage is:

(A) a public outcry for clarification

(B) a letter written by a reader asking for explanation of terms used by the writer

(C) a letter written by a reader praising the writer of the passage

(D) a public notice in a competing paper arguing against the writer's views

(E) a request by the publisher for the writer to be clearer in his writing

392. The intended audience for the passage is:

(A) country readers

(B) city readers

(C) critics

(D) gentlemen

(E) pretty fellows

393. In context, the word "appellations" in line 6 most nearly means:

(A) identifying names

(B) nicknames

(C) careers

(D) types of men

(E) country personalities

394. According to the second paragraph (lines 10–21), the most important characteristic of a gentleman is:

(A) being consistently entertaining

(B) being inoffensive

(C) being strong

(D) being imaginative

(E) being of good breeding

395. Sophronius is provided in the passage as an example of:

(A) a poor substitute for a Gentleman

(B) a Gentleman

(C) a Pretty Fellow

(D) a Critic

(E) a Wit

396. In context, the word "office" in line 28 most nearly means:

(A) a building in which business is carried out
(B) a building in which medicine is practiced
(C) a function or duty assumed by someone
(D) a public position
(E) a position of authority given to someone

397. Jack Dimple is provided in the passage as an example of:

(A) a Gentleman
(B) a Pretty Fellow
(C) a Toast
(D) a Critic
(E) a Wit

398. The Gentleman is also referred to as all of the following *except*:

(A) a man of conversation
(B) a man of pleasure
(C) a master of his companion
(D) a man of superior understanding
(E) an agreeable being

399. The primary purpose of the passage is to:

(A) criticize those who try to imitate the gentleman
(B) argue that to always avoid conflict makes the gentleman well-liked
(C) praise the gentleman's breeding and judgment
(D) define the gentleman
(E) indirectly shame his readers who do not know his city terminology

400. The tone of the passage can best be described as:

(A) condescending and patronizing
(B) poignant and provocative
(C) sarcastic and mocking
(D) objective and aloof
(E) informative and playful

CHAPTER 9

19th Century with Draft Passages

Passage 9a: Samuel Taylor Coleridge, *Biographia Literaria*

My own conclusions on the nature of poetry, in the strictest use of the word, have been in part anticipated in some of the remarks on the Fancy and Imagination in the early part of this work. What is poetry?—is so nearly the same question with, what is a poet?—that the answer to the one is involved in the solution of the other. For it is a distinction resulting from the poetic 5
genius itself, which sustains and modifies the images, thoughts, and emotions of the poet's own mind.

    The poet, described in ideal perfection, brings the whole soul of man into activity, with the subordination of its faculties to each other according to their relative worth and dignity. He diffuses a tone and spirit of unity, 10
that blends, and (as it were) fuses, each into each, by that synthetic and magical power, to which I would exclusively appropriate the name of Imagination. This power, first put in action by the will and understanding, and retained under their irremissive, though gentle and unnoticed, control, *laxis effertur habenis*[1], reveals "itself in the balance or reconcilement of opposite 15
or discordant" qualities: of sameness, with difference; of the general with the concrete; the idea with the image; the individual with the representative; the sense of novelty and freshness with old and familiar objects; a more than usual state of emotion with more than usual order; judgment ever awake and steady self-possession with enthusiasm and feeling profound or vehe- 20
ment; and while it blends and harmonizes the natural and the artificial, still subordinates art to nature; the manner to the matter; and our admiration of the poet to our sympathy with the poetry. Doubtless, as Sir John Davies observes of the soul—(and his words may with slight alteration be applied, and even more appropriately, to the poetic Imagination)— 25

    Doubtless this could not be, but that she turns
    Bodies to spirit by sublimation strange,

---

1. Latin for "it is carried onwards with loose reins"

As fire converts to fire the things it burns,
As we our food into our nature change.

From their gross matter she abstracts their forms,   30
And draws a kind of quintessence from things;
Which to her proper nature she transforms
To bear them light on her celestial wings.

Thus does she, when from individual states
She doth abstract the universal kinds;   35
Which then re-clothed in divers names and fates
Steal access through the senses to our minds.

Finally, Good Sense is the Body of poetic genius, Fancy its Drapery,
Motion its Life, and Imagination the Soul that is everywhere, and in each;
and forms all into one graceful and intelligent whole.   40

401. The primary purpose of the passage is to:

    (A) argue for the importance of poetry

    (B) describe the different types of poetry

    (C) analyze the effects of poetry on the life of the poet

    (D) define poetry, the poet, and imagination

    (E) analyze the poet's process of constructing poetry

402. In context, the word "subordination" in line 9 most nearly means:

    (A) the treatment of something as less valuable or important

    (B) the treatment of something as more valuable or important

    (C) the treatment of something as unnecessary or redundant

    (D) the treatment of something as exceeding expectations

    (E) the treatment of something as equal with another thing

403. "Its" in line 9 refers to:

    (A) poet

    (B) ideal perfection

    (C) the whole soul of man

    (D) man

    (E) activity

404. According to lines 8–13, the poet does all of the following *except*:

(A) brings the soul to life

(B) separates the different abilities of the soul

(C) brings together the different abilities of the soul

(D) creates Imagination

(E) transforms his own mind

405. Imagination is defined as:

(A) ideal perfection

(B) a tone and spirit of unity

(C) synthetic and magical power

(D) will and understanding

(E) the balance or reconcilement of opposite or discordant qualities

406. All of the following pairs are represented as opposites in lines 16–19 *except*:

(A) sameness and difference

(B) the general and the concrete

(C) the idea and the image

(D) the individual and the representative

(E) novelty and freshness

407. As presented in lines 21–23, which of the following is more valued than its counterpart?

(A) art

(B) nature

(C) manner

(D) admiration of the poet

(E) the soul

408. The writer of the passage uses the poem to:

(A) define the nature of poetry

(B) characterize imagination

(C) display the poet's perfection

(D) describe the difference between fancy and imagination

(E) explore the soul

409. The last paragraph of the passage (lines 38–40) relies on the following rhetorical technique to make its claims about poetic genius:

(A) figurative language
(B) syllogism, or deductive reasoning
(C) allusion
(D) varied sentence structure
(E) colloquial diction

410. The author regards poetry with:

(A) distrust
(B) puzzlement
(C) indifference
(D) admonition
(E) awe

Passage 9b: *Lemon Chicken Recipe Draft*

(1) In order to make lemon chicken, you need one pound of chicken cutlets, two lemons, three shallots (finely chopped), two cups of chicken broth, one egg (beaten), some flour, three tablespoons of butter, and olive oil. (2) First, wash the chicken thoroughly and cut it into bite-sized pieces. (3) Then dredge the chicken in egg, throw it into a large Ziploc bag with flour, and shake it up. (4) Coat the chicken with flour.

(5) Heat three tablespoons of butter with some olive oil in a sauté pan. (6) Then add the chopped shallots and begin to sauté on low/medium heat. (7) After the shallots start to cook, add the chicken. (8) Cook the chicken for a few minutes on each side. (9) Add a little pepper to the chicken.

(10) Once the chicken is mostly cooked, add the lemon juice. (11) Cook for about one minute. (12) Add the chicken broth, turn down the heat, and cover. (13) Cook for 15 minutes and serve. (14) Your lemon chicken should be ready to be eaten after approximately 15 minutes. (15) I always enjoy it with some rice and broccoli.

411. The writer would like to add a sentence before sentence 1 that engages the reader and introduces the topic. Which sentence below would best meet the writer's needs?

(A) Get ready to make lemon chicken!

(B) Lemon chicken can be found in several cuisines around the world, ranging from Chinese to Italian.

(C) Lemon chicken is a widely enjoyed dish that is easy to make following this simple recipe.

(D) French lemon chicken usually includes Dijon mustard.

(E) In Spain, lemon chicken includes pine nuts, rosemary, and ham.

412. The writer is considering removing "some" before the word "flour" in sentence 1 (reproduced below):

In order to make lemon chicken, you need one pound of chicken cutlets, two lemons, three shallots (finely chopped), two cups of chicken broth, one egg (beaten), <u>some</u> flour, three tablespoons of butter, and olive oil.

Should the writer remove "some"?

(A) Yes, because "some" is an inexact amount, and adding it as a descriptor before "flour" does not provide any useful information

(B) Yes, because readers already know that "some" means two cups

(C) Yes, because the writer should replace "some" with "a lot of"

(D) No, because all ingredients need a description before them

(E) No, because the list would be too short if it were removed

413. The writer is considering adding the underlined phrase to sentence 3 (reproduced below):

> *Then dredge the chicken in egg, throw it into a large <u>(at least quart-sized)</u> Ziploc bag with flour, and shake it up.*

Should the writer add the underlined portion to sentence 3?

(A) Yes, because a gallon-sized bag would be entirely too large
(B) Yes, because "large" is a vague description, and the underlined phrase adds more specific information for those seeing it
(C) Yes, because readers will assume they should buy snack-size bags, the smallest of all Ziploc bags
(D) No, because "at least quart-sized" is no more specific than "large," and adding this phrase will not serve to clarify what the reader will need to use
(E) No, because this additional phrase may confuse readers who are novice cooks

414. The writer would like to combine sentences 3 and 4 (reproduced below):

> *Then dredge the chicken in egg, throw it into a large Ziploc bag with flour, and shake it up. Coat the chicken with flour.*

Which of the following options is the best combination of sentences 3 and 4?

(A) Then dredge the chicken in egg, throw it into a large Ziploc bag with flour, and shake it up, but coat the chicken with flour.
(B) Then dredge the chicken in egg, throw it into a large Ziploc bag with flour, and shake it up, and coat the chicken with flour.
(C) Then dredge the chicken in egg, throw it into a large Ziploc bag with flour, and shake it up, so coat the chicken with flour.
(D) Then dredge the chicken in egg, throw it into a large Ziploc bag with flour, and shake it up to coat it.
(E) Then dredge the chicken in egg, throw it into a large Ziploc bag with flour, and shake it up; then coat the chicken with flour.

415. The writer is considering adding a transition to the beginning of sentence 5 (reproduced below):

Heat three tablespoons of butter with some olive oil in a sauté pan.

Adjusting for capitalization and punctuation, which of the following transitions would be best placed at the beginning of sentence 5?

(A) Next,
(B) Thus,
(C) Therefore,
(D) For example,
(E) Moreover,

416. The writer is considering removing the underlined portion of sentence 6 (reproduced below):

Then add the chopped shallots and <u>begin to</u> sauté on low/medium heat.

Should the writer remove the underlined portion of sentence 6?

(A) Yes, because giving instructions to "begin to sauté" and "sauté" are essentially the same directive
(B) Yes, because readers are ending the sauté phase at this point in the recipe
(C) Yes, because readers may be unfamiliar with how to sauté and may need further definition
(D) No, because readers will not know that this is the point at which they should begin to sauté
(E) No, because removing "begin to" is detracting from the writer's voice and style

417. The writer would like to combine sentences 8 and 9 (reproduced below):

> *Cook the chicken for a few minutes on each side. Add a little pepper to the chicken.*

Which of the following options is the best combination of sentences 8 and 9?

(A) Cook the chicken for a few minutes on each side, and add a little pepper to the chicken.
(B) Cook the chicken for a few minutes on each side; add a little pepper to the chicken.
(C) Cook the chicken for a few minutes on each side, and then you should add a little pepper to the chicken.
(D) Cook the chicken for a few minutes on each side, and add a little pepper.
(E) Cook the chicken for a few minutes on each side, and make sure you add a little pepper to the chicken.

418. The writer is considering adding a transition to the beginning of sentence 12 (reproduced below):

> *Add the chicken broth, turn down the heat, and cover.*

Adjusting for capitalization and punctuation, which of the following transitions would be best placed at the beginning of sentence 12?

(A) First,
(B) Second,
(C) Third,
(D) Then
(E) Finally,

419. The writer is considering removing sentence 14 (reproduced below):

> *Your lemon chicken should be ready to be eaten after approximately 15 minutes.*

Should the writer remove sentence 14?

(A) Yes, because it is more important to tell readers when they can serve the dish than when they can eat it
(B) Yes, because this sentence repeats what was said in sentence 13 and is redundant as a result
(C) Yes, because not all readers will be cooking and eating this recipe; some will just be reading the passage
(D) No, because although the chicken can be served after 15 minutes, this does not mean it is ready to be eaten
(E) No, because this paragraph would be too short if it were removed

420. The writer would like a final sentence after sentence 15 to conclude the passage by commenting on the recipe's versatility. Which of the following sentences would best meet the writer's needs?

(A) Lemon chicken is a staple in cuisines around the world.
(B) Bon appetit!
(C) Lemon chicken can be served at brunch, lunch, or dinner to small groups or large crowds.
(D) You'll be making this delicious dish for years to come!
(E) Your family will be asking you to make this tasty dish at every holiday.

Passage 9c: Francis Parkman, *The Oregon Trail: Sketches of Prairie and Rocky-Mountain Life*

Last spring, 1846, was a busy season in the City of St. Louis. Not only were emigrants from every part of the country preparing for the journey to Oregon and California, but an unusual number of traders were making ready their wagons and outfits for Santa Fe. Many of the emigrants, especially of those bound for California, were persons of wealth and standing. The 5
hotels were crowded, and the gunsmiths and saddlers were kept constantly at work in providing arms and equipments for the different parties of travelers. Almost every day steamboats were leaving the levee and passing up the Missouri, crowded with passengers on their way to the frontier.

In one of these, the *Radnor*, since snagged and lost, my friend and rela- 10
tive, Quincy A. Shaw, and myself, left St. Louis on the 28th of April, on a
tour of curiosity and amusement to the Rocky Mountains. The boat was
loaded until the water broke alternately over her guards. Her upper deck
was covered with large weapons of a peculiar form, for the Santa Fe trade,
and her hold was crammed with goods for the same destination. There 15
were also the equipments and provisions of a party of Oregon emigrants, a
band of mules and horses, piles of saddles and harness, and a multitude of
nondescript articles, indispensable on the prairies. Almost hidden in this
medley one might have seen a small French cart, of the sort very appropriately called a "mule-killer" beyond the frontiers, and not far distant a tent, 20
together with a miscellaneous assortment of boxes and barrels. The whole
equipage was far from prepossessing in its appearance; yet, such as it was, it
was destined to a long and arduous journey, on which the persevering reader
will accompany it.

The passengers on board the *Radnor* corresponded with her freight. In 25
her cabin were Santa Fe traders, gamblers, speculators, and adventurers of
various descriptions, and her steerage was crowded with Oregon emigrants,
"mountain men," negroes, and a party of Kansas Indians, who had been on
a visit to St. Louis.

Thus laden, the boat struggled upward for seven or eight days against the 30
rapid current of the Missouri, grating upon snags, and hanging for two or
three hours at a time upon sand-bars. We entered the mouth of the Missouri
in a drizzling rain, but the weather soon became clear, and showed distinctly
the broad and turbid river, with its eddies, its sand-bars, its ragged islands, and
forest-covered shores. The Missouri is constantly changing its course; wearing 35
away its banks on one side, while it forms new ones on the other. Its channel is
shifting continually. Islands are formed, and then washed away; and while the
old forests on one side are undermined and swept off, a young growth springs
up from the new soil upon the other. With all these changes, the water is so
charged with mud and sand that it is perfectly opaque, and in a few minutes 40
deposits a sediment an inch thick in the bottom of a tumbler. The river was
now high; but when we descended in the autumn it was fallen very low, and
all the secrets of its treacherous shallows were exposed to view. It was frightful
to see the dead and broken trees, thick-set as a military abatis, firmly imbed-
ded in the sand, and all pointing down stream, ready to impale any unhappy 45
steamboat that at high water should pass over that dangerous ground.

421. The rhetorical function of the first sentence of the passage (line 1) is to:

(A) provide the major claim
(B) establish the setting
(C) introduce the narrator
(D) present the point of view
(E) establish the tone

422. In context, the word "outfits" in line 4 most nearly means:

(A) sets of clothing
(B) associations of people
(C) the acts of equipping
(D) sets of equipment with a specific purpose
(E) shipments of goods

423. In the first sentence of paragraph two (lines 10–12), the pronoun "these" refers to:

(A) steamboats
(B) passengers and travelers
(C) hotels
(D) gunsmiths and saddlers
(E) arms and equipments

424. The purpose of the personification of the boat in paragraph two (lines 10–24) is to:

(A) give it magical powers
(B) give it comprehension
(C) give it life
(D) give it agency
(E) give it sympathy

425. The rhetorical function of the statement "The whole equipage was far from prepossessing in its appearance; yet, such as it was, it was destined to a long and arduous journey, on which the persevering reader will accompany it" (lines 21–24) is primarily to:

(A) appeal to the reader's religious beliefs
(B) appeal to the reader's patriotism
(C) appeal to the reader's apprehension
(D) appeal to the reader's sense of adventure
(E) appeal to the reader's distrust of the narrator

426. In detailing all of the things and people on the *Radnor* (lines 10–29), the writer primarily relies on:

(A) sensory description
(B) sparse language
(C) accumulation of detail
(D) technical language
(E) figurative language

427. The primary function of paragraph four (lines 30–46) is to:

(A) narrate the tale of a traveler
(B) describe the Missouri River
(C) define the perfect conditions for travel
(D) analyze the effects of a hard journey on the travelers
(E) classify the types of travelers

428. The tone of paragraph four (lines 30–46) can best be described as:

(A) awed
(B) contemptuous
(C) ominous
(D) detached
(E) morose

429. In context, the word "treacherous" in line 43 most nearly means:

(A) providing insecure support
(B) marked by hidden dangers
(C) likely to betray trust
(D) given with assurance
(E) true to the standard

430. The overall tone of the passage can best be described as:

(A) informative and enthusiastic
(B) critical and judgmental
(C) incredulous and disbelieving
(D) sorrowful and mournful
(E) discontent and frustrated

Passage 9d: *Course Contract Draft*

(1) The AP® English Language and Composition Course offers students opportunities to learn to read and write as writers, with an awareness of purpose and audience. (2) We work in the beginning of the year on developing close-reading skills to be able to identify and then emulate the techniques that writers use to persuade their readers. (3) We begin by labeling rhetorical devices and appeals and by reading examples of the different rhetorical modes, which continues all year. (4) The course is designed to help students think about all of the choices of effective writers, ranging from choosing precise vocabulary to choosing credible sources for supporting evidence. (5) Students should then bring that level of careful decision making to the development of their own written arguments.

(6) We will be reading works of American literature during this semester, classic and contemporary essays from *50 Essays,* and some American models of effective rhetoric. (7) Therefore, we will read Martin Luther King Jr.'s "Letter from Birmingham Jail," Thomas Jefferson's Declaration of Independence, and Abraham Lincoln's Gettysburg Address.

(8) Work is due on the due date. (9) Ten points will be deducted each day for work submitted late for the next three days. (10) When you miss a quiz or an exam (due to an excused absence), come to schedule a make-up assessment as soon as possible. (11) Bring a note on the day of your return. (12) Any work that you miss due to lateness cannot be made up, so make every effort to be on time every day. (13) Refer to the school website for additional information on discipline and academic integrity.

431. The writer would like to add a sentence before sentence 1 that serves to engage readers by providing a warm and inviting greeting. Which of the following sentences best meets the writer's needs?

   (A) The College Board, based in New York City, has run the Advanced Placement Program since 1955.

   (B) The most widely taken AP® exam is AP English Language and Composition.

   (C) Welcome to AP® English Language and Composition, where we will sharpen our reading and writing skills in a supportive and open classroom environment.

   (D) AP® English Language and English Literature were separated into two distinct courses in 1980.

   (E) AP® English Language and Composition focuses on rhetoric, analysis, and nonfiction.

432. The writer is considering removing the underlined portion of sentence 1 (reproduced below):

> The AP® English Language and Composition Course offers students opportunities to learn to read and write as writers, <u>with an awareness of purpose and audience.</u>

Should the writer remove the underlined portion of sentence 1?

(A) Yes, because it is unclear whether the underlined portion is describing students or writers

(B) Yes, because it is obvious that writers have an awareness of purpose and audience

(C) Yes, because what is meant by "purpose" and "audience" is unclear in this underlined phrase

(D) No, because it clarifies what it means to read and write as writers

(E) No, because the first part of the sentence is grammatically incomplete without the underlined portion

433. The writer is considering removing the underlined portion of sentence 2 (reproduced below):

> We work in the beginning of the year on developing close-reading skills to <u>be able to</u> identify and then emulate the techniques that writers use to persuade their readers.

Should the writer remove the underlined portion of sentence 2?

(A) Yes, because "be able to" is redundant and can be removed without changing the meaning of the sentence

(B) Yes; just because this skill will be taught, it is not guaranteed that all students will "be able to" identify and use the techniques discussed

(C) Yes, because identifying and emulating, or imitating, are different skills

(D) No, because the removal of this phrase would dramatically change the meaning of the sentence

(E) No, because the rhythm of the sentence would be drastically altered, resulting in a less pleasing sentence

434. The writer would like to combine sentences 4 and 5 (reproduced below):

> *The course is designed to help students think about all of the choices of effective writers, ranging from choosing precise vocabulary to choosing credible sources for supporting evidence. Students should then bring that level of careful decision making to the development of their own written arguments.*

Which of the following options is the best combination of sentences 4 and 5?

(A) The course is designed to help students think about all of the choices of effective writers, ranging from choosing precise vocabulary to choosing credible sources for supporting evidence, and students should then work hard to bring that level of careful decision making to the development of their own written arguments.

(B) The course is designed to help students think about all of the choices of effective writers, ranging from choosing precise vocabulary to choosing credible sources for supporting evidence, and bring that level of careful decision making to the development of their own written arguments.

(C) The course is designed to help students think about all of the choices of effective writers, ranging from choosing precise vocabulary to choosing credible sources for supporting evidence, and students should bring that level of careful decision making to the development of their own written arguments.

(D) The course is designed to help students think about all of the choices of effective writers, ranging from choosing precise vocabulary to choosing credible sources for supporting evidence, and students who have learned these skills should bring that level of careful decision making to the development of their own written arguments.

(E) The course is designed to help students think about all of the choices of effective writers, ranging from choosing precise vocabulary to choosing credible sources for supporting evidence, and then students write while bringing that level of careful decision making to the development of their own written arguments.

435. The writer is considering replacing the transition used to begin sentence 7 (reproduced below):

> *Therefore, we will read Martin Luther King Jr.'s "Letter from Birmingham Jail," Thomas Jefferson's Declaration of Independence, and Abraham Lincoln's Gettysburg Address.*

Which is the best version of the underlined transition to start sentence 7?

(A) as it is now
(B) However,
(C) Nevertheless,
(D) For example,
(E) Thus,

436. The writer is considering adding the following sentence after sentence 7:

> *Some other possible texts include Truman Capote's* In Cold Blood, *Ta-Nehisi Coates's* Between the World and Me, *and Upton Sinclair's* The Jungle.

Should the writer include this sentence after sentence 7?

(A) Yes, because readers of this type of passage will be interested in possible text options for the course
(B) Yes, because readers are ready to plan for their reading and writing assignments based on the proposed schedule
(C) Yes, because readers of this passage will expect these particular texts to be included
(D) No, because readers of this type of passage are not interested in learning of texts that may be read
(E) No, because some of the readers may have already read these texts and will be discouraged and disappointed to hear them mentioned

437. The writer would like to combine sentences 8 and 9 (reproduced below):

> *Work is due on the due date. Ten points will be deducted each day for work submitted late for the next three days.*

Which of the following options is the best combination of sentences 8 and 9?

(A) Work is due on the due date, but 10 points will be deducted each day for work submitted late for the next three days.

(B) Work is due on the due date, yet 10 points will be deducted each day for work submitted late for the next three days.

(C) Work is due on the due date, and 10 points will be deducted each day for work submitted late for the next three days.

(D) Work is due on the due date, so 10 points will be deducted each day for work submitted late for the next three days.

(E) Work is due on the due date, for 10 points will be deducted each day for work submitted late for the next three days.

438. The writer is considering revising sentence 10 by replacing "you" with "we" (reproduced below):

> *When you miss a quiz or an exam (due to an excused absence), come to schedule a make-up assessment as soon as possible.*

Should the writer replace the underlined "you" with "we"?

(A) Yes, because "we" has been used throughout, and the revision would keep the passage consistent

(B) Yes, because it would help maintain a welcoming and inclusive tone

(C) Yes, because the writer hopes to connect with the readers by using "we" throughout the passage

(D) No, because although "we" was appropriate for the sentences about shared reading, it doesn't make sense for this sentence because the writer will not be missing assignments

(E) No, because the writer is hoping to create an intimidating and authoritative tone for the concluding parts of the passage

439. The writer is considering revising the underlined portion of sentence 12 to be certain that it matches the established tone and formality of the rest of the passage:

> *Any work that you miss <u>due to lateness</u> cannot be made up, so make every effort to be on time every day.*

Which version of the underlined portion of sentence 12 best meets the writer's needs?

(A) as it is now
(B) because you have walked in whenever you want
(C) when you stroll in late
(D) because you can't be bothered to make it to class on time
(E) due to wasting time on your way to class

440. The writer would like to add a sentence after sentence 13 that ends the passage on a note of excitement and enthusiasm for the course being described. Which sentence below best meets the writer's needs?

(A) Be sure to read the section marked "Plagiarism" carefully.
(B) Information on the AP® English Language and Composition exam will be covered throughout the year.
(C) I look forward to our time working and learning together!
(D) Course materials will also be posted on the school website.
(E) More information about the course can be found on the College Board's website.

Passage 9e: Oscar Wilde, *De Profundis*

Suffering is one very long moment. We cannot divide it by seasons. We can only record its moods, and chronicle their return. With us time itself does not progress. It revolves. It seems to circle round one centre of pain. The paralyzing immobility of a life every circumstance of which is regulated after an unchangeable pattern, so that we eat and drink and lie down and pray, or 5 kneel at least for prayer, according to the inflexible laws of an iron formula: this immobile quality, that makes each dreadful day in the very minutest detail like its brother, seems to communicate itself to those external forces the very essence of whose existence is ceaseless change. Of seed-time or harvest, of the reapers bending over the corn, or the grape gatherers threading 10 through the vines, of the grass in the orchard made white with broken blossoms or strewn with fallen fruit: of these we know nothing and can know nothing.

For us there is only one season, the season of sorrow. The very sun and moon seem taken from us. Outside, the day may be blue and gold, but the light that creeps down through the thickly-muffled glass of the small iron-barred window beneath which one sits is grey and niggard[1]. It is always twilight in one's cell, as it is always twilight in one's heart. And in the sphere of thought, no less than in the sphere of time, motion is no more. The thing that you personally have long ago forgotten, or can easily forget, is happening to me now, and will happen to me again to-morrow. Remember this, and you will be able to understand a little of why I am writing, and in this manner writing. . . .

A week later, I am transferred here. Three more months go over and my mother dies. No one knew how deeply I loved and honoured her. Her death was terrible to me; but I, once a lord of language, have no words in which to express my anguish and my shame. She and my father had bequeathed me a name they had made noble and honoured, not merely in literature, art, archaeology, and science, but in the public history of my own country, in its evolution as a nation. I had disgraced that name eternally. I had made it a low by-word among low people. I had dragged it through the very mire. I had given it to brutes that they might make it brutal, and to fools that they might turn it into a synonym for folly. What I suffered then, and still suffer, is not for pen to write or paper to record. My wife, always kind and gentle to me, rather than that I should hear the news from indifferent lips, travelled, ill as she was, all the way from Genoa to England to break to me herself the tidings of so irreparable, so irremediable, a loss. Messages of sympathy reached me from all who had still affection for me. Even people who had not known me personally, hearing that a new sorrow had broken into my life, wrote to ask that some expression of their condolence should be conveyed to me. . . .

Three months go over. The calendar of my daily conduct and labour that hangs on the outside of my cell door, with my name and sentence written upon it, tells me that it is May. . . .

Prosperity, pleasure and success, may be rough of grain and common in fibre, but sorrow is the most sensitive of all created things. There is nothing that stirs in the whole world of thought to which sorrow does not vibrate in terrible and exquisite pulsation. The thin beaten-out leaf of tremulous gold that chronicles the direction of forces the eye cannot see is in comparison coarse. It is a wound that bleeds when any hand but that of love touches it, and even then must bleed again, though not in pain.

---

1. stingy or ungenerous

441. The speaker opens the passage with a series of simple sentences (in lines 1–3) in order to define and describe sorrow with:

(A) sensitivity and compassion
(B) comprehension and complexity
(C) depth and directness
(D) cynicism and skepticism
(E) disbelief and criticism

442. According to the first paragraph (lines 1–13), sorrow:

(A) makes us incapable of ordinary life
(B) seems to stop the passage of time
(C) feels impossible to live through
(D) forces us to pay attention to the small details of life
(E) asks us to appreciate what we have

443. The primary purpose of paragraph two (lines 14–23) is to:

(A) narrate the speaker's tale of woe
(B) describe the speaker's experience of sorrow
(C) present to the reader the speaker's causes of sorrow
(D) argue that sorrow is incomprehensible
(E) analyze the process of the speaker's slow recovery from sorrow

444. Line 24, "A week later, I am transferred here," primarily transitions from:

(A) theory on mourning to practice
(B) specific claims to general ideas
(C) reflections on sorrow to personal experience
(D) refutations of others' claims to original argument
(E) narrative structure to descriptive language

445. The use of the pronoun "it" in line 31 refers to:

(A) the writer's anguish
(B) the writer's shame
(C) the writer's name
(D) the writer's mother's death
(E) the writer's country

446. The writer of the passage identifies himself as all of the following *except*:

(A) a husband
(B) a prisoner
(C) a writer
(D) a son
(E) a father

447. In context, the word "tremulous" in line 48 most nearly means:

(A) exceedingly sensitive
(B) timid
(C) hesitant
(D) having little substance
(E) uncertain

448. The language of the last paragraph (lines 45–51) can be characterized as:

(A) specialized and technical
(B) colloquial and informal
(C) descriptive and figurative
(D) nuanced and obsolete
(E) concrete and archaic

449. The major claim of the passage is expressed in all of the following lines *except*:

(A) "Suffering is one very long moment." (line 1)
(B) "For us there is only one season, the season of sorrow." (line 14)
(C) "Messages of sympathy reached me from all who had still affection for me." (lines 37–38)
(D) "Prosperity, pleasure and success, may be rough of grain and common in fibre, but sorrow is the most sensitive of all created things." (lines 45–46)
(E) "There is nothing that stirs in the whole world of thought to which sorrow does not vibrate in terrible and exquisite pulsation." (lines 46–48)

450. The tone of the passage as a whole can best be described as:

(A) plaintive
(B) mirthful
(C) sanguine
(D) indignant
(E) belligerent

CHAPTER 10

20th Century with Draft Passages

Passage 10a: Willa Cather, *On the Art of Fiction*

One is sometimes asked about the "obstacles" that confront young writers who are trying to do good work. I should say the greatest obstacles that writers today have to get over, are the dazzling journalistic successes of twenty years ago, stories that surprised and delighted by their sharp photographic detail and that were really nothing more than lively pieces of reporting. The whole aim of that school of writing was novelty—never a very important thing in art. They gave us, altogether, poor standards—taught us to multiply our ideas instead of to condense them. They tried to make a story out of every theme that occurred to them and to get returns on every situation that suggested itself. They got returns, of a kind. But their work, when one looks back on it, now that the novelty upon which they counted so much is gone, is journalistic and thin. The especial merit of a good reportorial story is that it shall be intensely interesting and pertinent today and shall have lost its point by tomorrow.

Art, it seems to me, should simplify. That, indeed, is very nearly the whole of the higher artistic process; finding what conventions of form and what detail one can do without and yet preserve the spirit of the whole— so that all that one has suppressed and cut away is there to the reader's consciousness as much as if it were in type on the page. Millet had done hundreds of sketches of peasants sowing grain, some of them very complicated and interesting, but when he came to paint the spirit of them all into one picture, *The Sower*, the composition is so simple that it seems inevitable. All the discarded sketches that went before made the picture what it finally became, and the process was all the time one of simplifying, of sacrificing many conceptions good in themselves for one that was better and more universal.

Any first rate novel or story must have in it the strength of a dozen fairly good stories that have been sacrificed to it. A good workman can't be a cheap workman; he can't be stingy about wasting material, and he

cannot compromise. Writing ought either to be the manufacture of stories 30
for which there is a market demand—a business as safe and commendable
as making soap or breakfast foods—or it should be an art, which is always
a search for something for which there is no market demand, something
new and untried, where the values are intrinsic and have nothing to do with
standardized values. The courage to go on without compromise does not 35
come to a writer all at once—nor, for that matter, does the ability. Both are
phases of natural development. In the beginning the artist, like his public,
is wedded to old forms, old ideals, and his vision is blurred by the memory
of old delights he would like to recapture.

451. The writer of the passage most values writing that is:

(A) simple
(B) detailed
(C) novel
(D) interesting
(E) complicated

452. The journalistic successes described in paragraph one (lines 1–14)
serve as _____ of the definition of good writing explored
by the speaker throughout the passage.

(A) examples
(B) cautionary tales
(C) a historical basis
(D) counterexamples
(E) predecessors

453. In context, the word "novelty" in lines 6 and 11 most nearly means:

(A) newness
(B) fiction
(C) nonfiction
(D) realism
(E) marketability

454. In line 7, the pronoun "they" refers to:

(A) young writers
(B) obstacles
(C) successes
(D) standards
(E) ideas

455. In the first paragraph (lines 1–14), the author uses dashes in order to:

(A) provide definitions
(B) offer refutations to the previous point
(C) set apart important conclusions
(D) supply the sources of information
(E) highlight inaccuracies

456. The tone of the last sentence of the first paragraph, "The especial merit of a good reportorial story is that it shall be intensely interesting and pertinent today and shall have lost its point by tomorrow," (lines 12–14) can best be described as:

(A) objectively detached
(B) ironically disparaging
(C) sentimentally poignant
(D) indignantly irate
(E) mournfully sad

457. The line "Art, it seems to me, should simplify" (15) expresses the idea that revision should:

(A) choose the proper materials for the art form
(B) make sure the form and the content are matched
(C) add the most important details
(D) focus on improving the minor imperfections
(E) remove what is not essential

458. The purpose of mentioning Jean François Millet's *The Sower* in the second paragraph is to:

(A) provide an example of journalistic success
(B) provide an example of a good reportorial story
(C) provide an example of conventions of form
(D) provide an example of simplicity
(E) provide an example of a first-rate story

459. In its treatment of writing, the third paragraph (lines 26–39) relies primarily on the mode of:

(A) narration
(B) description
(C) classification
(D) definition
(E) process analysis

460. The passage as a whole can best be described as:

(A) a lively narrative
(B) a detailed description
(C) a thoughtful argument
(D) a balanced comparison
(E) a clear classification

Passage 10b: *Education Reflection Draft*

(1) My most important goal as an educator is to teach students how to think. (2) I hope to train them to think with criticism about what they hear, see, and read; to think persuasively and openly as they speak their truths and listen to their peers; and to think clearly as they communicate their ideas in writing. (3) I once believed that I had to tell them all I knew about a text or topic, but I have learned through reflection and experience that it is my job and my joy to teach them how to think through and about the material they encounter in school and in their lives.

(4) I believe that all students are capable of this type of thinking and the growth that accompanies it. (5) Children are naturally curious and have so many questions about the world and its inhabitants. (6) If I help students refine their questions (to move from "what?" to "how?" and "why?") and push them to probe more deeply, they amaze me with their capacity to engage and think. (7) When I step out of the center of the classroom, the students have the room to explore ideas with one another, and the result is magic.

(8) Thinking is not predictable, and the teacher must be open to what will emerge in the classroom. (9) To that end, it is my belief that I must create a positive classroom environment in which students feel safe enough to ask questions and to work through difficult issues together. (10) This kind of work can be messy. (11) As John Dewey wrote in *Experience and Nature*, "Every thinker puts some portion of an apparently stable world in peril and no one can wholly predict what will emerge in its place." (12) It is my role to

create a secure place for students to question what we know, and I must be comfortable with letting things unfold and flexible enough to go to places that may be unexpected.

461. Which sentence below can best be described as the writer's thesis?

(A) My most important goal as an educator is to teach students how to think.

(B) I hope to train them to think critically about what they hear, see, and read; to think persuasively and openly as they speak their truths and listen to their peers; and to think clearly as they communicate their ideas in writing.

(C) I once believed that I had to tell them all I knew about a text or topic, but I have learned through reflection and experience that it is my job and my joy to teach them how to think through and about the material they encounter in school and in their lives.

(D) I believe that all students are capable of this type of thinking and the growth that accompanies it.

(E) Children are naturally curious and have so many questions about the world and its inhabitants.

462. The writer would like to revise the underlined portion of sentence 2 (reproduced below):

> *I hope to train them to think <u>with criticism</u> about what they hear, see, and read; to think persuasively and openly as they speak their truths and listen to their peers; and to think clearly as they communicate their ideas in writing.*

What is the best version of the underlined portion of sentence 2?

(A) as it is now

(B) critically

(C) in a critically minded way

(D) with critical attributes

(E) with a goal of critical mindedness

463. The writer is considering removing sentence 3 (reproduced below):

> *I once believed that I had to tell them all I knew about a text or topic, but I have learned through reflection and experience that it is my job and my joy to teach them how to think through and about the material they encounter in school and in their lives.*

Should the writer remove sentence 3?

(A) Yes, because the writer's personal experience and reflection are inappropriate and irrelevant for this type of passage

(B) Yes, because it shows the writer's original inexperience and ignorance, which may cause readers to lose trust in the writer's expertise on the subject

(C) Yes, because readers are not concerned with the writer's beliefs and are reading the passage for helpful teaching strategies

(D) No, because many readers may still believe that it is their job to share all of their knowledge and information on a topic with students

(E) No, because this passage is a statement of an educational philosophy and the writer's shift in perspective is appropriate and helpful for understanding the writer's current outlook

464. The writer is considering removing the underlined portion of sentence 6 (reproduced below):

> *If I help students refine their questions (<u>to move from "what?" to "how?" and "why?"</u>) and push them to probe more deeply, they amaze me with their capacity to engage and think.*

Should the writer remove the underlined portion of the sentence?

(A) Yes, because parenthetical statements are not appropriate for a passage of this type and tone

(B) Yes, because readers already understand what it means for students to "refine their questions"

(C) Yes, because it is unclear how a movement to "why" and "how" questions serves as a refinement

(D) No, because it offers a specific example of how students can refine their questions to think more deeply

(E) No, because the quotations from outside sources should remain in the parenthetical statement

465. The writer is considering adding the underlined phrase to sentence 7 (reproduced below):

> When I step out of the center of the classroom, _both literally and figuratively_, the students have the room to explore ideas with one another, and the result is magic.

Should the writer make this addition to sentence 7?

(A) Yes, because it offers a helpful elaboration of what the writer means by "step out of the center of the classroom"

(B) Yes, because readers would only imagine a figurative version if it were not clarified

(C) Yes, because readers do not know what "literally" and "figuratively" mean, and they need the proposed definitions

(D) No, because readers are not concerned with whether the writer meant for the action in the sentence to be read figuratively or literally

(E) No, because the writer should separate "figuratively" and "literally" into two different sentences

466. The writer is considering adding the following sentence before sentence 8:

> This type of instruction involves risk on the part of the educator and the students.

Should the writer include the proposed sentence?

(A) Yes, because it differentiates the different types of instruction available to students and teachers

(B) Yes, because it warns of the dangers and risks of this type of education

(C) Yes, because it serves as an effective transition between paragraphs 2 and 3 and as a topic sentence to unify the ideas that follow

(D) No, because the risks of this type of educational approach were covered in the last paragraph

(E) No, because this sentence serves as a rebuttal to the major claim

467. The writer would like to combine sentences 9 and 10 (reproduced below):

> *To that end, it is my belief that I must create a positive classroom environment in which students feel safe enough to ask questions and to work through difficult issues together. This kind of work can be messy.*

Which of the following sentences is the best combination of sentences 9 and 10?

(A) To that end, it is my belief that I must create a positive classroom environment in which students feel safe enough to ask questions and to work through difficult issues together; this kind of work can be messy.

(B) To that end, it is my belief that I must create a positive classroom environment in which students feel safe enough to ask questions and to work through difficult issues together, but this kind of work can be messy.

(C) To that end, it is my belief that I must create a positive classroom environment in which students feel safe enough to ask questions and to work through difficult issues together, and this kind of work can be messy.

(D) To that end, it is my belief that I must create a positive classroom environment in which students feel safe enough to ask questions and to work through difficult issues together because this kind of work can be messy.

(E) To that end, it is my belief that I must create a positive classroom environment in which students feel safe enough to ask questions and to work through difficult issues together, for this kind of work can be messy.

468. The writer would like to include a brief description of John Dewey after his name in sentence 11 (reproduced below):

> *As John Dewey wrote in Experience and Nature, "Every thinker puts some portion of an apparently stable world in peril and no one can wholly predict what will emerge in its place."*

Adjusting for punctuation, which descriptive phrase below, if placed after his name, would be best for introducing John Dewey to readers who may be unfamiliar with him?

(A) born in 1859
(B) from Burlington, Vermont
(C) of modest means
(D) an American philosopher and educational reformer
(E) once a professor at the University of Chicago

469. The quotation in sentence 11 (reproduced below) is most useful as support for which of the writer's claims?

> *As John Dewey wrote in Experience and Nature, "Every thinker puts some portion of an apparently stable world in peril and no one can wholly predict what will emerge in its place."*

(A) I once believed that I had to tell them all I knew about a text or topic, but I have learned through reflection and experience that it is my job and my joy to teach them how to think through and about the material they encounter in school and in their lives.
(B) I believe that all students are capable of this type of thinking and the growth that accompanies it.
(C) Children are naturally curious and have so many questions about the world and its inhabitants.
(D) When I step out of the center of the classroom, the students have the room to explore ideas with one another and the result is magic.
(E) Thinking is not predictable, and the teacher must be open to what will emerge in the classroom.

470. The writer is considering removing sentence 12 (reproduced below):

> *It is my role to create a secure place for students to question what we know, and I must be comfortable with letting things unfold and flexible enough to go to places that may be unexpected.*

Should the writer remove the sentence?

(A) Yes, because it assumes that the reader needs a definition of the writer's role

(B) Yes, because all educators serve the same purpose and share the same perspective

(C) Yes, because sentence 8 already made this point for readers

(D) No, because it concludes the paragraph by summarizing the passage's perspective on the writer's role as an educator

(E) No, because it is inappropriate to end a passage with a quotation from another writer

Passage 10c: Charlotte Perkins Gilman, *The Man-Made World; or, Our Androcentric Culture*

When we are offered a "woman's" paper, page, or column, we find it filled with matter supposed to appeal to women as a sex or class; the writer mainly dwelling upon the Kaiser's four K's—Kuchen, Kinder, Kirche, Kleider. They iterate and reiterate endlessly the discussion of cookery, old and new; of the care of children; of the overwhelming subject of clothing; and of moral 5 instruction. All this is recognized as "feminine" literature, and it must have some appeal else the women would not read it. What parallel have we in "masculine" literature?

"None!" is the proud reply. "Men are people! Women, being 'the sex,' have their limited feminine interests, their feminine point of view, which 10 must be provided for. Men, however, are not restricted—to them belongs the world's literature!"

Yes, it has belonged to them—ever since there was any. They have written it and they have read it. It is only lately that women, generally speaking, have been taught to read; still more lately that they have been allowed to 15 write. It is but a little while since Harriet Martineau[1] concealed her writing beneath her sewing when visitors came in—writing was "masculine"—sewing "feminine."

---

1. Harriet Martineau (1802–1876) was a British social theorist and Whig writer, often cited as the first female sociologist.

We have not, it is true, confined men to a narrowly construed "masculine sphere," and composed a special literature suited to it. Their effect on literature has been far wider than that, monopolizing this form of art with special favor. It was suited above all others to the dominant impulse of self-expression; and being, as we have seen essentially and continually "the sex;" they have impressed that sex upon this art overwhelmingly; they have given the world a masculized literature. 20 25

It is hard for us to realize this. We can readily see, that if women had always written the books, no men either writing or reading them, that would have surely "feminized" our literature; but we have not in our minds the concept, much less the word, for an overmasculized influence.

Men having been accepted as humanity, women but a side-issue; (most literally if we accept the Hebrew legend!), whatever men did or said was human—and not to be criticized. In no department of life is it easier to contravert this old belief; to show how the male sex as such differs from the human type; and how this maleness has monopolized and disfigured a great social function. 30 35

Human life is a very large affair; and literature is its chief art. We live, humanly, only through our power of communication. Speech gives us this power laterally, as it were, in immediate personal contact. For permanent use speech becomes oral tradition—a poor dependence. Literature gives not only an infinite multiplication to the lateral spread of communion but adds the vertical reach. Through it we know the past, govern the present, and influence the future. In its servicable common forms it is the indispensable daily servant of our lives; in its nobler flights as a great art no means of human inter-change goes so far. 40

In these brief limits we can touch but lightly on some phases of so great a subject; and will rest the case mainly on the effect of an exclusively masculine handling of the two fields of history and fiction. In poetry and the drama the same influence is easily traced, but in the first two it is so baldly prominent as to defy objection. 45

471. The primary function of paragraph one (lines 1–8) is:
   (A) to narrate an anecdote about female readers to prepare the audience for the speaker's claim
   (B) to argue for another type of women's literature to add to the list of four presented
   (C) to classify the types of "feminine" literature in order to introduce the speaker's major claim
   (D) to celebrate the variety of women's literature available to women
   (E) to refute the claims made by the speaker's critics before launching into her own argument

472. The second paragraph of the passage (lines 9–12) functions as:

(A) claim
(B) underlying assumption, or warrant
(C) data, or evidence
(D) counterargument
(E) modification, or revision

473. The tone of paragraph two (lines 9–12) can best be described as:

(A) saddened
(B) overwhelmed
(C) exasperated
(D) relieved
(E) resigned

474. In line 14, the phrase "generally speaking" is included to:

(A) refute that women had only recently been taught to read
(B) support that women had only recently been taught to read
(C) qualify that women had only recently been taught to read
(D) illustrate that women had only recently been taught to read
(E) analyze that women had only recently been taught to read

475. The words "masculine" and "feminine" at the end of paragraph three (lines 17 and 18) are in quotation marks because:

(A) the writer disagrees with the sentiment
(B) someone else is speaking
(C) she is quoting another work of literature
(D) she wants to make clear her major claim
(E) she spoke this line to Harriet Martineau

476. In context, the word "construed" in line 19 most nearly means:

(A) analyzed
(B) structured
(C) labored
(D) expressed
(E) understood

477. What does the speaker mean when she refers to women as "the sex" in lines 9 and 23?

(A) that women are considered the weaker sex
(B) that men are considered the stronger sex
(C) that only women are considered gendered and that men are considered just human
(D) that women are defined by their sexuality
(E) that men have dominated culture

478. The first sentence of paragraph six, "Men having been accepted as humanity, women but a side-issue; (most literally if we accept the Hebrew legend!), whatever men did or said was human—and not to be criticized," (lines 30–32) uses allusion to:

(A) bring a religious perspective to the speaker's argument
(B) ask women to question their traditional beliefs
(C) make the claim that men are considered the dominant sex
(D) appeal to male readers
(E) pacify religious experts and clergymen

479. In line 41, the phrase "vertical reach" refers to the reach of literature:

(A) across nations
(B) through the ages
(C) across continents
(D) through classes
(E) through the sexes

480. The purpose of the last paragraph (lines 45–49) is to:

(A) address those who would argue against the writer's claims
(B) describe the type of material in feminine literature
(C) introduce the examples to follow of masculine literature
(D) define masculine literature and its genres
(E) argue against the proliferation of feminine literature

Passage 10d: *New York City Travel Blog Draft*

(1) You will be swept off your feet in a New York minute by the dramatic views of Gotham's iconic skyline and the East River from the new Millennium Hilton New York One UN Plaza. (2) The property has recently undergone a 68-million-dollar renovation and is now managed by Hilton. (3) The renovation has resulted in expansive rooms and stunning suites, and in a city where location is everything, this hotel is close to many of the major New York City attractions and transportation hubs.

(4) This landmark hotel is situated alongside the United Nations headquarters and has long welcomed visitors—including many of the world's most esteemed leaders, diplomats, and heads of state. (5) The hotel's 439 guest rooms and suites; meetings and event spaces; and public areas and restaurant have all been updated. (6) The renovation has fortunately preserved the distinctive architecture and layout of the original Kevin Roche–designed building.

(7) The hotel is within walking distance (or a short Citi Bike ride) of Grand Central Terminal, the Empire State Building, Fifth Avenue, Times Square, and the Broadway theater district, all making this a perfect location for both business travelers and tourists coming to New York City. (8) With its 24-hour fitness center and a year-round tennis court, everyone must find time in their schedule to stick to an exercise routine. (9) Tip: If you are planning to travel to Manhattan in July, make sure to reserve your room well in advance as you will have the best seats in town from your room for the Macy's Fourth of July fireworks.

(10) Hotel guests can enjoy a variety of dining options without needing to leave the property. (11) The Skyline Club is an executive's retreat on the 30th floor and is the perfect place for breakfast or an after-work bite. (12) The Ambassador Grill is a modern, all-day dining destination that offers fresh, globally inspired fare, including classic dishes and all-time favorites. (13) The Ambassador Lounge is set within the hotel's signature restaurant and is a wonderful place for guests to unwind in a chic and casual setting. (14) The UN Café is perfect for the guest "on the go" by serving freshly brewed coffee complemented by a wide selection of pastries, salads, and sandwiches. (15) The hotel also offers six adaptable meeting, function, and exhibit spaces with panoramic views of New York City, including the hotel's stunning ballroom, which can accommodate up to 300 guests.

481. The writer is considering removing the underlined portion of sentence 4 (reproduced below):

> *This landmark hotel is situated alongside the United Nations head-quarters and has long welcomed visitors—<u>including many of the world's most esteemed leaders, diplomats, and heads of state</u>.*

Should the writer remove the underlined portion of sentence 4?

(A) Yes, because this list of distinguished guests may be intimidating to readers

(B) Yes, because potential visitors may not feel welcome when they read this list of previous guests

(C) Yes, because this categorization of welcomed visitors may feel noninclusive to readers who do not belong to any of these groups

(D) No, because this portion of the sentence provides examples of guests based on the hotel's location

(E) No, because readers should be aware of the type of visitor the hotel is seeking

482. The writer would like to add a description of the building's style to the end of sentence 6 (reproduced below):

> *The renovation has fortunately preserved the distinctive architecture and layout of the original Kevin Roche–designed building, _____.*

Which option below would best meet the writer's needs?

(A) who passed away in March 2019

(B) an Irish-born American architect

(C) winner of the Pritzker Prize

(D) retaining its sleek and minimalist modernism

(E) born in Dublin in 1922

483. The writer is considering removing the word "all" from sentence 7 (reproduced below):

> *The hotel is within walking distance (or a short Citi Bike ride) of Grand Central Terminal, the Empire State Building, Fifth Avenue, Times Square, and the Broadway theater district, <u>all</u> making this a perfect location for both business travelers and tourists coming to New York City.*

Should the writer remove "all" from sentence 7?

(A) Yes, because "making this a perfect location" is describing that the hotel is within walking distance, not "all" of the destinations

(B) Yes, because while some examples of destinations are offered, this sentence doesn't provide all of the possible sights to see

(C) Yes, because the writer wants to avoid making absolute claims

(D) No, because it expresses how many options are available for tourists to see

(E) No, because it clarifies the opportunities present for business travelers

484. The writer is considering revising the underlined portion of sentence 8 (reproduced below) to create an inviting tone:

> *With its 24-hour fitness center and a year-round tennis court, <u>everyone must</u> find time in their schedule to stick to an exercise routine.*

Which version of the underlined portion of this sentence best meets the writer's needs?

(A) as it is now

(B) it is important to

(C) you must

(D) it is crucial to

(E) guests may want to

485. The writer is considering removing sentence 9 (reproduced below):

> *Tip: If you are planning to travel to Manhattan in July, make sure to reserve your room well in advance as you will have the best seats in town from your room for the Macy's Fourth of July fireworks.*

Should the writer remove sentence 9?

(A) Yes, because very few business travelers will be going to New York City in July
(B) Yes, because tourists are more likely to visit beach towns rather than cities in July
(C) Yes, because potential hotel visitors will not be able to get reservations during the busy summer months
(D) No, because this is a useful tip for potential travelers who may be reading this passage
(E) No, because all visitors are looking to stay in New York City for the July 4 holiday

486. The writer is considering adding a transition at the beginning of sentence 11 (reproduced below):

> *The Skyline Club is an executive's retreat on the 30th floor and is the perfect place for breakfast or an after-work bite.*

Adjusting for capitalization and punctuation, which of the following transitions would work best at the beginning of sentence 11?

(A) Therefore,
(B) Next,
(C) For example,
(D) In contrast,
(E) Thus,

487. The writer is considering adding a transition at the beginning of sentence 12 (reproduced below):

> *The Ambassador Grill is a modern, all-day dining destination that offers fresh, globally inspired fare, including classic dishes and all-time favorites.*

Adjusting for capitalization and punctuation, which of the following transitions would work best at the beginning of sentence 12?

(A) First,
(B) Second,
(C) Third,
(D) Fourth,
(E) Finally,

488. The writer is considering adding a transition at the beginning of sentence 13 (reproduced below):

> *The Ambassador Lounge is set within the hotel's signature restaurant and features an extensive menu for guests to unwind in a chic and casual setting.*

Adjusting for capitalization and punctuation, which of the following transitions would work best at the beginning of sentence 13?

(A) Regardless,
(B) Similarly,
(C) Nevertheless,
(D) In addition,
(E) Thus,

489. The writer is considering adding a transition at the beginning of sentence 14 (reproduced below):

> *The UN Café is perfect for the guest "on the go" by serving freshly brewed coffee complemented by a wide selection of pastries, salads, and sandwiches.*

Adjusting for capitalization and punctuation, which of the following transitions would work best at the beginning of sentence 14?

(A) Furthermore,
(B) Moreover,
(C) Finally,
(D) Thus,
(E) Therefore,

490. The writer would like to add a sentence after sentence 15 that concludes the passage by returning to its opening claims and making a general statement about the property. Which of the following sentences best meets the writer's needs?

(A) The ballroom at the Millennium Hilton New York One UN Plaza is a stunning location for your wedding or other major event.
(B) Your meetings and conventions will have the best views in New York City!
(C) The Millennium Hilton New York One UN Plaza, with its dazzling views, well-appointed rooms, delicious dining options, and close proximity to many exciting sites, is a wonderful place to stay, whatever your personal and business traveling needs.
(D) With all of its dining options, you can eat well all day without ever leaving the Millennium Hilton New York One UN Plaza.
(E) Don't forget to book your Independence Day trip early to have an incredible view of the fireworks!

Passage 10e: Olive Schreiner, *Woman and Labour*

In that clamour which has arisen in the modern world, where now this, and then that, is demanded for and by large bodies of modern women, he who listens carefully may detect as a keynote, beneath all the clamour, a demand which may be embodied in such a cry as this: Give us labour and the training which fits for labour! We demand this, not for ourselves alone, but for the race. 5

If this demand be logically expanded, it will take such form as this: Give us labour! For countless ages, for thousands, millions it may be, we have laboured. When first man wandered, the naked, newly-erected savage, and hunted and fought, we wandered with him: each step of his was 10 ours. Within our bodies we bore the race, on our shoulders we carried it; we sought the roots and plants for its food; and, when man's barbed arrow or hook brought the game, our hands dressed it. Side by side, the savage man and the savage woman, we wandered free together and laboured free together. And we were contented! 15

Then a change came.

We ceased from our wanderings, and, camping upon one spot of earth, again the labours of life were divided between us. While man went forth to hunt, or to battle with the foe who would have dispossessed us of all, we laboured on the land. We hoed the earth, we reaped the grain, we shaped 20 the dwellings, we wove the clothing, we modelled the earthen vessels and drew the lines upon them, which were humanity's first attempt at domestic art; we studied the properties and uses of plants, and our old women were the first physicians of the race, as, often, its first priests and prophets.

We fed the race at our breast, we bore it on our shoulders; through us 25 it was shaped, fed, and clothed. Labour more toilsome and unending than that of man was ours; yet did we never cry out that it was too heavy for us. While savage man lay in the sunshine on his skins, resting, that he might be fitted for war or the chase, or while he shaped his weapons of death, he ate and drank that which our hands had provided for him; and while we knelt 30 over our grindstone, or hoed in the fields, with one child in our womb, perhaps, and one on our back, toiling till the young body was old before its time—did we ever cry out that the labour allotted to us was too hard for us? Did we not know that the woman who threw down her burden was as a man who cast away his shield in battle—a coward and a traitor to his race? 35 Man fought—that was his work; we fed and nurtured the race—that was ours. We knew that upon our labours, even as upon man's, depended the life and well-being of the people whom we bore. We endured our toil, as man bore his wounds, silently; and we were content.

Then again a change came. 40

Ages passed, and time was when it was no longer necessary that all men should go to the hunt or the field of war; and when only one in five, or one in ten, or but one in twenty, was needed continually for these labours. Then our fellow-man, having no longer full occupation in his old fields of labour, began to take his share in ours. He too began to cultivate the field, 45 to build the house, to grind the corn (or make his male slaves do it); and the hoe, and the potter's tools, and the thatching-needle, and at last even the grindstones which we first had picked up and smoothed to grind the food for our children, began to pass from our hands into his. The old, sweet life of the open fields was ours no more; we moved within the gates, where the 50 time passes more slowly and the world is sadder than in the air outside; but we had our own work still, and were content.

If, indeed, we might no longer grow the food for our people, we were still its dressers; if we did not always plant and prepare the flax and hemp, we still wove the garments for our race; if we did no longer raise the house 55 walls, the tapestries that covered them were the work of our hands; we brewed the ale, and the simples which were used as medicines we distilled and prescribed; and, close about our feet, from birth to manhood, grew up the children whom we had borne; their voices were always in our ears. At the doors of our houses we sat with our spinning-wheels, and we looked 60 out across the fields that were once ours to labour in—and were contented. Lord's wife, peasant's, or burgher's, we all still had our work to do!

491. The purpose of the passage as a whole is to:

    (A) define what a woman's labor and training are
    (B) tell the story of how women's work has changed over time
    (C) describe a woman's labor and training in the modern world
    (D) analyze the causes of men's taking over the role women once played
    (E) argue that men are to blame for the diminishing role of women over time

492. In context, the word "clamour" in line 3 most nearly means:

    (A) loud continuous noise
    (B) assertion
    (C) something unavoidable
    (D) ignorance
    (E) fear

493. The tone of the statement "Give us labour and the training which fits for labour!" (lines 4–5) is:

   (A) pleading and petulant
   (B) lamenting and sorrowful
   (C) insistent and forceful
   (D) questioning and querulous
   (E) aloof and detached

494. The sentence "We hoed the earth, we reaped the grain, we shaped the dwellings, we wove the clothing, we modelled the earthen vessels and drew the lines upon them, which were humanity's first attempt at domestic art; we studied the properties and uses of plants, and our old women were the first physicians of the race, as, often, its first priests and prophets" (lines 20–24) uses repetition of "we" to show the _____ of women.

   (A) artistic skill
   (B) domestic skill
   (C) varied roles and talents
   (D) physical strength
   (E) intelligence

495. The statement "While savage man lay in the sunshine on his skins, resting, that he might be fitted for war or the chase, or while he shaped his weapons of death, he ate and drank that which our hands had provided for him; and while we knelt over our grindstone, or hoed in the fields, with one child in our womb, perhaps, and one on our back, toiling till the young body was old before its time—did we ever cry out that the labour allotted to us was too hard for us?" (lines 28–34) uses repetition and rhetorical questioning to show all of the following about women *except*:

   (A) strength
   (B) resiliency
   (C) constancy
   (D) capacity
   (E) impatience

496. The biggest shift in the passage occurs at:

    (A) line 7: "If this demand . . . "
    (B) line 16: "Then a change came."
    (C) line 25: "We fed the race . . . "
    (D) line 40: "Then again a change came."
    (E) line 53: "If, indeed, we might . . . "

497. The purpose of the final sentence of the passage, "Lord's wife, peasant's, or burgher's, we all still had our work to do!" (line 62) is to express that:

    (A) women of privilege had it easier than poor women
    (B) poor women had less work to do in the home
    (C) women's husbands controlled them
    (D) the constancy of women's labor was not reliant on class
    (E) women's labor is dependent on their husbands' positions in society

498. The tone of the last paragraph (lines 53–62) can best be described as:

    (A) resilient
    (B) derisive
    (C) facetious
    (D) mirthful
    (E) irate

499. The structure of the passage as a whole can best be described as:

    (A) moving from specific to general
    (B) moving from general to specific
    (C) enumerative
    (D) providing flashbacks
    (E) chronological

500. The passage relies most heavily on the following mode of composition to construct its argument:

    (A) narration
    (B) description
    (C) definition
    (D) classification
    (E) comparison

ANSWERS

Chapter 1

Passage 1a

1. (A) In the third line of the passage, the writer states that he trusts his autobiography will be "useful and instructive," showing that according to him, the purpose of his autobiography is to teach, or instruct.

2. (B) Throughout the first paragraph, the author discusses his hesitation and anxiety about sharing information that is so indecent and often not shared by English people. Although he at last concludes that he will write his autobiography, he uses this paragraph to tell the reader about his reservations. This paragraph serves to introduce his narrative, but not an argument. While he discusses that French literature includes more sordid details about people's lives than English literature, he does not criticize it. The opening is not an anecdote or short story, and since the work has not been read by the public before, he is not apologizing to those who have already read this piece.

3. (D) The words "infirmities" (meaning diseases or weaknesses), "ulcers," "scars," and "frailty" (again meaning weakness) can all be used to describe physical ailments and illness. The word "indulgence" is an act for pleasure or comfort and does not refer to illness in any way.

4. (A) "Decent drapery" uses the metaphor of drapes, or curtains, to compare the hiding of "moral ulcers or scars" to the use of drapery to block the vision of outsiders with a thick fabric. The phrase is figurative and is not offering sensory details of drapery, but just using drapery as a metaphor for hiding. In addition, the author presents time as something that hides, rather than reveals. The comparison is not indirect and drapery is not being compared to human frailty. Lastly, the drapery is a metaphor for hiding things that would disgust the English, but the drapery does not symbolize disgust.

5. (E) The pronoun "our," if traced to its antecedent, refers to the English. This can be seen in that the writer is discussing English feelings and uses "our" in the earlier part of that sentence to refer to "our notice," also referring to the English.

6. (B) The word "propriety," used in the line "I have for many months hesitated about the propriety of allowing this or any part of my narrative to come before the public eye until after my death," can best be understood as a synonym for "decency," in that the writer doubted the decency of publishing an autobiography that showed his self-indulgence and moral failings.

7. (C) Guilt and misery are given the human actions of shrinking, courting, and sequestering; and they are also given the human characteristic of having instinct, but the word "notice" is used in the phrase "public notice," something outside of guilt and misery. In other words, "notice" does not describe guilt and misery.

8. (A) In the line before the one quoted in the question, the writer provides a conditional claim, considering a situation in which his self-accusation did constitute a confession of guilt. In the line quoted, he makes clear that his admitting that he was both sick and in pain does not mean that he's accepting guilt; therefore, he's refuting the conditional, or hypothetical, claim made in the line before.

9. (B) In the final portion of the passage, the writer looks on his past with ambivalence as he uses positive words, such as "accomplished" and "self-conquest," along with negative words, such as "accursed" and "self-indulgence." The writer discusses the counterbalance between the positive and negative, showing his ambivalence.

10. (B) Because the writer discusses his self-indulgence openly after acknowledging his uncertainty about sharing such private and improper behavior, the tone can best be characterized as forthright, or frank.

Passage 1b

11. (B) The most appropriate sentence to capture the audience's interest and provide the most effective introduction to the topic is "Although most people believe 'cologne' is for men and 'perfume' is for women, these terms are actually used to describe the amount of perfume oil present in each bottle of fragrance" because this sentence both brings up a misconception, which can capture the audience's attention, and introduces the topic of explaining the different types of fragrance based on oil concentration.

12. (D) The sentence, "Perfume, or fragrance, oils can be naturally or synthetically derived and are added to water and/or alcohol to make the bottle of perfume that can then be sprayed and enjoyed" should be kept because it offers a definition of fragrance oil that aids in the classification of perfume types by fragrance oil concentration per bottle.

13. (A) The sentence "All together, there are five perfume concentrations, which range from approximately 1–40 percent of perfume oil per bottle" is the best option as a thesis statement because it provides the main idea of the passage, which is an explanation of the classification of types of perfumes. This sentence clearly summarizes that classification.

14. (D) "Additionally" is the best transition because this sentence is adding another type of perfume to those already listed. "Next" is more appropriate for time sequencing, introducing an event that follows the one listed previously. "However" and "nevertheless" are used to change direction, and this sentence provides another type of perfume, not a thought that contradicts the one before.

15. (B) Only this sentence mentions that there will be three types of perfumes discussed in this paragraph: "'Eau de toilette,' the middle point in terms of strength and longevity and the least potent of the next three types of perfume described, has a fragrance concentration between 5 and 15 percent." As a result, this is the best sentence for previewing what will be covered in the paragraph.

16. (A) Saying that eau de toilette is a "popular" choice is more factual and objective than the other terms, which all imply a value judgment of the choice. Calling the choice "ill-informed," "superior," "the only," or "the best" all evaluate the choice as good or bad, while "popular" just means that many people choose it, which is a neutral statement.

17. (B) The word "finally" communicates that this fragrance type is the last one of the list. "Fifthly" could mean that more options will follow this type. Also, the other transitions are used to communicate a change in direction or an effect from a cause. "Finally" simply communicates that this type is the last one discussed.

18. (C) The quote from expert Sue Phillips that reads, "So the word 'perfume' is now becoming more generic. It doesn't apply to feminine anymore" helps rebut the claim that perfume is only for women and cologne is only for men by stating that the term is generic, meaning it can be used to describe a broader category of fragrances. The other quotations provided maintain the distinction between male and female scents, or between cologne and perfume.

19. (D) Choice D is meant to elicit an emotional reaction from readers by asking them to reflect on their own scent memories and experiences. Choices A through C are specific to the writer's individual experiences, and choice E is an objective statement, not meant to draw forth an emotional response from readers.

20. (E) Choice E lays out the options and considerations for those choosing a perfume type, while the other options state or recommend what option is best. Only choice E maintains an objective tone, laying out choices without evaluating which are better or worse.

Passage 1c

21. (B) The writer of the passage describes in detail his planned process of "arriving at moral perfection." Although he does define the virtues he needs to practice (he doesn't classify) and define moral perfection, these are steps along the way of him describing the process. He does not argue in this passage, nor does he analyze the effects, as he just discusses the plan.

22. (C) In context, "rectitude" most nearly means "morally correct behavior," which refers to earlier in the sentence when he writes about being "completely virtuous" (line 10). While he uses "uniform" to describe "rectitude," "rectitude" itself does not mean "consistent," "continuous," or "ingrained."

23. (D) As Franklin composes his list of virtues, he reads others' lists, or enumerations, he provides the example of "temperance" as a virtue that has been both widely and narrowly defined. He uses this definition to show how others have defined the term, to provide those different meanings, to show his process of writing his own list, and to be clear about his decision-making process in creating his list of thirteen virtues. He never argues against the definition of "temperance" provided by other writers.

24. (D) Because the writer calls what follows each virtue a precept, it can be seen that precept most nearly means a particular course of action to follow each virtue. What follow each virtue, the precepts, are specific directions, such as "eat not to dullness; drink not to elevation." The imperative sentence shows that these precepts are commands.

25. (C) Franklin discusses the ordering of his list being the most effective possible order to mastering each virtue on the list. It is a logical sequence, in his view, to begin with temperance and to end with humility, as each virtue builds upon the practicing of the one before it.

26. (A) Franklin begins his piece by proclaiming his goal of arriving at moral perfection, and through his early trial and error, he discovers that to achieve his goal "the contrary habits must be broken, and good ones acquired and established" (lines 10–11). In other words, vices cannot just be removed; they must be replaced with good habits, or virtues. He doesn't believe the task easy and he does not argue that religion is necessary for each virtue. This is an independent task, but one that he does see as possible with time and practice.

27. (B) Because of his enumeration and process analysis, the writer can be characterized as someone who is methodical, meaning that he is characterized as having systematic behavior or habits. Both the style and content are orderly and mirror the writer's nature.

28. (D) He refers to the Golden Verses of Pythagoras as a model of daily examination, which requires reflection on one's practice and habits.

29. (C) His style and organization can best be described as systematic with his use of chronological process analysis and his listing and numbering of the virtues.

30. (B) The writer's tone can best be described as resolved, as he is committed to his process of arriving at moral perfection. He has made a firm decision and is trying to achieve his goal.

Passage 1d

31. (A) While choices B through E all provide evidence to support a major claim or detailed examples, only choice A, "John Carpenter is widely considered to be one of the greatest horror-movie directors of all time," provides a major claim to be supported throughout the paragraph and passage.

32. (D) Choice D, which turns "widely considered to be one of the greatest horror-movie directors of all time" into a description of John Carpenter between two commas and uses "is" as the main verb of the sentence in the predicate—"is best known for the landmark slasher film Halloween"—is the simplest combination of the two sentences. It avoids the unnecessary use of the pronoun "he" to rename Carpenter and keeps the descriptions of Carpenter and the film *Halloween* close to the nouns they are describing.

33. (E) This portion of the sentence should be deleted because it does not offer any new or necessary information to the reading. "Enduring chillers" may be a new phrase to readers, but it can hopefully be understood through context clues and is not difficult or technical enough to require a definition in the middle of the sentence.

34. (E) The proposed sentence repeats in new language what was already stated in sentence 4. Because it does not add any new information, it would be better left out because it makes the paragraph more cluttered and redundant.

35. (A) Only choice A provides the various types of sources, ranging from original stories to classic horror films to movie versions of novels, including sequels to his own films. The other choices provide details, but they focus on one type of example, either classic horror, books, sequels, or original stories.

36. (D) The use of "however" is the most appropriate transition because this sentence is changing direction as a means to shift from the first paragraph into the second. The first paragraph focuses on Carpenter's success as a horror-movie director, but the second discusses his successes in other areas, not just films. Because of the change in direction and the phrase "beyond simply"—a transition that marks a change in direction—"however" is the most appropriate transition to begin this sentence.

37. (A) While this sentence makes the claim that Carpenter is successful in many fields beyond just directing horror movies, it is the only one of the options that *does not* serve as a specific example that provides details in support of this major claim.

38. (C) The writer uses this series of transitions to open these sentences to provide an organized list of examples to support Carpenter's successes. While these words can be used for sequencing, the writer is not providing a narrative in this paragraph but is instead providing illustrations to support a claim.

39. (A) Choice A retains an informative and somewhat conversational tone when describing Carpenter starring in his own movies. The language is direct and objective, not looking to pass judgment or treat the subject with more respect or mockery than it deserves.

40. (D) Choice D retains the argument that Carpenter is widely considered to be one of the best horror-movie directors while not taking away the specificity that he did create popular and well-acclaimed horror movies. Choices A through C take away specificity, while choice E adds to the absolute nature of the argument.

Passage 1e

41. (D) Newman uses this portion of his book to prepare to answer the charges of untruthfulness leveled at him by Charles Kingsley. While he does extoll truth, it is not the purpose of this passage; in addition, he mentions his critic as raising these charges, but he does not spend the passage criticizing him. And while he does discuss the English, he doesn't argue that they're more truthful or praise them for valuing truth.

42. (B) "Imputation" means "accusation" and Newman is referring to the accusation of being untruthful that his critic makes of him. While "insult" is close, an accusation is more serious and formal. The two words differ in tone.

43. (C) Newman says the charges will fall in their season, meaning when it's the right or appropriate time for them to fall. That time is not necessarily in old age, autumn, extended, or recurrent.

44. (D) Newman argues that truthfulness is in, not out of, the jurisdiction of mankind to judge, unlike faith, hope, and charity, which he claims are outside of humans' ability to judge. He describe truthfulness as open to human judgement, a natural virtue, capable of becoming supernatural, and difficult to ascertain, or make certain.

45. (A) Newman uses the analogy to give a comparison of how it is as difficult to judge a case out of its nation as it is to ascertain the truth of something outside of its context. It's about the ability, not the right, and he does not argue that it is paradoxical, impossible, or illegal.

46. (D) Newman says the English are suspicious, touchy, unreasonable, and unjust, but he's also proud to be English and calls them generous, hasty, burly, and repentant. Because the list of adjectives and descriptions is so disparate, it's most accurate to say that he regards the English with ambivalence, or mixed or contradictory feelings.

47. (B) It is ironic that Newman is grateful for not being able to make the decision of when and how he answers the charges against him, when one would imagine that someone would be upset or bothered by losing control over those decisions.

48. (C) In preparing to respond to the charges of untruthfulness that have been made about him, Newman writes confidently. He calls himself confident, says he will be content when he faces the challenge, and says that he will be acquitted of the charges in time. Overall, he is confident, rather than trying to make peace, overly angry, nervous, or joyful.

49. (A) Overall, the footnotes serve to provide different information that is useful to the reader, including translations and background information on people and an old form of English government. The footnotes do not refute, cite, or try to persuade. Choice E does not include the translations, so it does not cover the purpose of all of the footnotes.

50. (D) The footnotes show that Newman is learned, or well-read, and worldly, as he can refer to other places and nationalities when discussing his topic. He is also bilingual, as he includes Latin, which he would know from his religious studies. "Litigious" means that a person is overly concerned with lawsuits, but Newman is answering accusations, not raising them.

Chapter 2

Passage 2a

51. (E) The sentence provided in choice E defends the writer's choice to include as many details and particulars as possible when writing Johnson's biography. The other statements are generally about the genre of biography but do not say anything specific about the writer's claims about Johnson's biography.

52. (A) The first sentence of the second paragraph contains an admission that the writer is fully aware of the objections (i.e., counterargument) which may be made to "the minuteness on some occasions of [his] detail of Johnson's conversation." The writer acknowledges that some may think that he included too much detail, but he disagrees.

53. (B) "It" refers to "minuteness" in the sentence "I am fully aware of the objections which may be made to the minuteness on some occasions of my detail of Johnson's conversation, and how happily it is adapted for the petty exercise of ridicule, by men of superficial understanding and ludicrous fancy; but I remain firm and confident in my opinion, that minute particulars are frequently characteristick, and always amusing, when they relate to a distinguished man." It could be restated as " . . . how happily minuteness is adapted for the petty exercise of ridicule."

54. (D) The writer argues that some biographers believe themselves to be writing good biographies when they are showing a chronological series of actions, but one of the claims of the passage is that good biographies include personal details, such as minute particulars, idle talk, table talk, and anecdotes.

55. (D) "Superfluous" means "extra," "unnecessary," or "redundant." "Superficial" uses the same prefix but is different in meaning.

56. (C) The tone can be described as confident because the writer speaks with certainty when defending his choice to write Johnson's biography. His confidence is in part due to his special relationship with Johnson, which provides him with access to the intimate details that would make a strong biography. He confidently aligns himself with Julius Caesar, whom he refers to as "the greatest man of any age."

57. (E) Boswell argues that what brings to life the subject of a biography are the intimate details of the person's life, including the things that the person says off-record and informally.

58. (E) The passage as a whole uses argument. The writer makes claims defending his writing of Johnson's biography, he acknowledges and refutes counterargument, he uses expert testimony as evidence, and he uses a confident tone.

59. (A) The style is complex and reasoned because of his use of complicated syntax, evidence, and argument skills. He creates a reasoned argument with complicated syntax.

60. (C) The passage relies heavily on quotes, beginning with a block quote from Johnson, continuing with a block quote from Secker, and ending with an embedded quote from Francis Bacon about Julius Caesar. All of this expert testimony is meant to justify the writer's choices in writing Johnson's biography.

Passage 2b

61. (D) The sentence should not be added because it does not offer any new information to advance the writer's purpose of defining and explaining *Dia de Muertos*. It simply repeats what was previously stated and is therefore redundant.

62. (C) Choice C combines the two sentences in a way that keeps the meaning intact, is grammatically correct, and is the shortest and simplest possible version. Choices D and E each add a transitional word that is not fitting for the relationship between the two sentences.

63. (E) This portion of the sentence should be deleted because it does not offer any new or necessary information to the reading. *Dia de Muertos* has been sufficiently defined and introduced in the opening paragraph before this sentence occurs.

64. (D) Although "1,000 or 2,000 years ago" is not an exact number of years, it is the most precise span of time provided as an option. While "a few millennia" is close in meaning, it is not as exact as "1,000 or 2,000 years ago."

65. (A) Choice A makes clear that *Dia de Muertos* is one of many pagan traditions appropriated by Roman Catholic colonizers. The other possible introductory phrases either limit the meaning to argue that this tradition is unique or include them all, which is an overstatement.

66. (C) The sentence should be added because it serves as a topic sentence for the paragraph, which compares and contrasts Halloween and *Dia de Muertos*. Without it, readers may be a bit unready for the discussion of Halloween that follows.

67. (B) "Even some" as an opening to describe Mexican celebrants avoids making the argument in absolute terms. Words like "all," "no," and "never" overstate the argument by saying no or all Mexican celebrants dress in this way. The word "some" must be included before "Mexican" to be clear that this statement only relates to a select few Mexican celebrants and to avoid putting the claim in absolute terms.

68. (C) This sentence should be included because the Pyramid of the Sun and the Avenue of the Dead both support the claim made in the topic sentence about a death-centered religion, which includes sacrificial sites. These illustrations are helpful new evidence to advance the writer's argument.

69. (E) The adjective "central" is the best adjective to place before "element" to express the importance of the construction of household altars to modern-day *Dia de Muertos* because "central" means that the element is at the center, and hence crucial, to the celebrations. The other options add value judgment or unnecessary opinions on this tradition.

70. (B) While the other phrases given may describe the bread or add additional details to the description, only choice B, "*pan de muerto*," provides the Spanish name, or correct terminology, for the bread baked for the ancestors during *Dia de Muertos*.

Passage 2c

71. (D) The passage as a whole is being used to ask the audience to think critically about the Conservative Party on the occasion of the upcoming election. Churchill discusses their abuses of power and their lack of proposed social programs to get the audience to see that they are not the right choice for the nation.

72. (B) The opening line of the passage is meant to galvanize, or excite the audience to act, by expressing the seriousness and urgency of the situation for those who value the Liberal cause. He hopes they will be both informed and persuaded to act by what follows.

73. (A) Churchill lists synonyms for both "weapons" and "harass" to express how varied and far-reaching the abuses have been. By offering many words with similar meanings, he makes the list more comprehensive and exhaustive, which also serves to overwhelm the reader with this list of unacceptable behaviors on the part of the Conservative Party.

74. (C) All of the listed options are opposites, except "lucky vs. unfair," because "lucky" describes those who are also wealthy, happy, and strong. "Unfair" modifies "advantages," not the "weak and poor."

75. (C) Churchill offers a collection of examples of previous social reforms proposed and carried out by the Conservative Party. These examples serve to highlight how unacceptable their lack of current proposed reforms is.

76. (A) After listing the social reforms offered in the past by the Conservative party in the last paragraph, Churchill crafts a rhetorical question in lines 34–35 to ask the audience to consider for themselves the current lack of any social reforms being offered by the Conservatives. While this passage does show Churchill's knowledge of the matter, the question is asked so that the audience will ask themselves this question and will hopefully vote against the Conservative Party after they draw their own conclusions.

77. (C) "Repugnant" most nearly means "offensive" in this statement. It is a much harsher word than "incompatible," which seems to be a close fit. The church is described as offensive to the conscience of the Welsh people.

78. (E) The writer is scorning and critical of the Conservative Party in the last paragraph and his tone is clear in the following line, between two dashes, "if you can call them leaders." His tone is harsh and full of contempt and judgment. This is also clear in his diction, with choices such as "monopolised" and "coercion" to describe the Conservative Party.

79. (E) Churchill uses lots of repetition, namely epistrophe (or repetition at the end of successive phrases or clauses), to great effect in the last paragraph. He repeats: "no policy whatever" to keep the audience focused on the lack of social reform being presented in the platform of the Conservative Party for the upcoming election.

80. (B) The speaker can be described as passionate and informed. He offers a lot of information to persuade his audience and seems to be deeply tied to it in his use of provocative language. He is passionate in making his case against the Conservatives.

Passage 2d

81. (A) The writer's opening sentence is the major claim of the passage that the rise of photography changed visual art. The other sentences provide history, amplification, and examples, but the first line most clearly provides the writer's thesis.

82. (E) The adjective "primary" is the best adjective to place before "focus" to express how, before the camera, the most important goal of art was to capture realistic representations of people, places, and things. "Primary," meaning first, expresses how—while there may have been other more minor goals—capturing reality was the first and most important goal of art. The other options add value judgments or unnecessary opinions on this focus.

83. (D) The sentence should remain, because while earlier in the passage, the major claim is made that the camera replaced painting and sculpture as the main way to capture realistic representations, this sentence provides the three reasons why that replacement took place. The camera was quicker, easier, and cheaper than the earlier alternatives of painting and sculpture.

84. (A) Choice A provides contextual information about other movements of the time by listing some of the modern philosophies taking shape during the emergence of modern art. The other options define "phenomenon" or comment on "this phenomenon" without offering the context for the general audience that the writer is hoping to include.

85. (B) The writer should add the proposed sentence because it supports the claim that modern art was dismissed by some because of how different it was from preceding styles. It is a useful and specific illustration of the claim made in sentence 6.

86. (C) Only choice C provides an amplification, or additional information, that states *how* these new forms of art could possibly be even more realistic than earlier forms of representative art. The ways this could be accomplished are through expressing an interior reality, or inner life, and capturing changes over time. The other choices either comment on "simple representative art" or provide commentary on the opinion expressed in the opening of the sentence.

87. (D) The writer should not remove sentence 8 because it provides relevant information and examples that shed light on the sources, styles, and practitioners of modern art. The sources here are modern ideas on psychology and dreams, and the practitioners, or those who practiced this type of art, are Dali and Magritte.

88. (C) "Supposed" before "rationalism" brings up questions about the nature of what was generally accepted as the truth as art was shifting to reveal more truth through ingenious new techniques and perspectives. The other options provide comment on the word "rationalism" whether casting doubt or skepticism on it.

89. (B) The writer compares and contrasts traditional and modern art in this final paragraph, using Andy Warhol's *Brillo Boxes* as an example of the latter. All of the words or phrases provided, except "artisanal," meaning characterized by a skilled trade, are used to refer to modern art.

90. (A) "For example" is the best choice for the transition between sentences 10 and 11 because Andy Warhol's *Brillo Boxes* are provided as an illustration of pop art, a form of modern art that is more intellectual, theoretical, and philosophical than more traditional and representational art forms. The other choices express a final step in a sequence, a result, or a change in direction, which are all inappropriate choices to link these two sentences.

Passage 2e

91. (A) The overall purpose of the passage is for the writer to justify his writing of Macaulay's biography. He describes the era and then defends his choices in writing this biography, for which he has personal knowledge.

92. (B) The claim of the passage is that the taste of the age allows for biographies that provide little to no personal information about the subject. The writer makes this claim about the time to prepare his audience for the defense of his own biography of Lord Macaulay.

93. (D) In context, the word "apology" most nearly means "justification," in that the writer who wants to publish a memoir is justified in wanting to do so due to the popularity of the genre at the time.

94. (D) In the first paragraph of the essay the writer speaks generally about the subject of biographies in his era and the next paragraph shifts to a specific discussion of Macaulay as not being known through his works, much like Shakespeare, in contrast to Dickens and Thackeray, whose works reflected more of their lives and personal qualities.

95. (C) The line is an analogy that compares getting an idea of Macaulay from his works to getting an idea of who Shakespeare is from his plays. The point is that it is difficult to know the writer from his body of work without his personal conversations, letters, etc.

96. (E) The primary audience for this passage would be those who were familiar with and interested in Macaulay's work and as a result would want to know more of his personal life and could do so by reading his biography, as written by the writer of the passage.

97. (C) In the last paragraph, the writer characterizes himself as not having the skill necessary to write this biography. He is trying to make himself humble in the eyes of the reader.

98. (D) The word "affectation" is used to mean "artificiality," and is used to describe Macaulay by saying he was incapable of being artificial or concealing himself in his private letters.

99. (D) The speaker regards Macaulay with considerate admiration. He is considerate, or kind, in that he's thinking about "what he has the heart to publish," and he clearly admires Macaulay by praising him throughout the passage, discussing his "eminence and ability."

100. (B) In discussing Macaulay as a good subject for a biography, the speaker remarks that he has written so much, but has revealed so little of his personal life. It is this combination of being "prolific and private" that makes Macaulay such an ideal subject for a biographer.

Chapter 3

Passage 3a

101. (B) Overall, the writer is arguing for the necessity of criticism in a time when there is not a "national glow of life." This is seen in the line "In the England of the first quarter of this century there was neither a national glow of life and thought, such as we had in the age of Elizabeth, nor yet a culture and a force of learning and criticism such as were to be found in Germany." The other answer choices are inaccurate.

102. (A) In context, sanguine means "optimistic," as it is used to describe the hopes that the literature of this time period would last longer than the literature of the time periods before it.

103. (C) The writer refers to the poetry of the first quarter of the century as having creative force, but not having data, which he defines as materials, a current of ideas, fresh thought, and a national glow of life.

104. (E) In context, "wanting" is used to mean "lacking" or "missing." Arnold is saying that the one thing lacking for Wordsworth as a poet was that he could have been more well-read.

105. (D) The statement presented acknowledges and refutes the possible counter-argument that books and reading were missing from the poets of the first quarter of the 19th century.

106. (B) "A current of ideas" is a metaphor in which a collection of ideas is compared to a part of a body of water that has a definite and powerful force, something that could take over.

107. (C) Arnold discusses Goethe's era in Germany and refers to the strength of the criticism several times: "the long and widely combined critical effort of Germany" and "a culture and a force of learning and criticism such as were to be found in Germany."

108. (B) With its provocative statements and self-praise on the role of criticism, the tone of the passage can best be described as confident and polemical, meaning disputatious and controversial.

109. (E) Each footnote provides all of the following information: the author's full name, life span, nationality, and occupation. Some of the footnotes contain the titles of written works, but not all.

110. (E) The information from the footnotes confirms that all of the people mentioned are poets. Some are Greek, and one is German, so they are not all English. The Greek writers are well before the 17th Century. Since even the dramatists write in verse, they are all poets.

Passage 3b

111. (C) Choice C—which uses a comma and "and"—is the best option to combine the two sentences because it presents them as connected and coordinated ideas. The other transition words either show a change in direction or a consequence, neither of which fits the relationship between the two ideas. Choice D combines the two sentences without communicating a relationship between them.

112. (B) Adding "nearly" before "impossible" tempers the claim, making it less absolute by saying it was not fully impossible. Choices A and C both communicate that it was fully impossible to find characters of color not depicted in the listed ways, while choices D and E change the meaning of the sentence by claiming that it was possible to find these characters.

113. (D) The writer has to consider whether or not to include a parenthetical clause that defines the civil rights movement based on what basic knowledge is expected of the audience. Since the clause simply defines the movement, the author may not need it if the audience is expected to have a basic knowledge of its existence.

114. (D) The sentence should not be removed because it provides specific detailed examples that support the claim made in sentence 7, and the rest of the paragraph refers back to the texts mentioned in this sentence.

115. (E) While the example of *Corduroy* responds to all of the sentences about the need for diverse characters in children's books, the details of the black mother with a full purse most clearly serves as a counterexample of characters of color being depicted in relation to poverty, crime, or struggle.

116. (B) Sentence 16 expresses that the shift began to include more diverse characters during the 1960s, and the previous paragraphs communicate that this was a long-awaited shift. "Finally" as a transition communicates that information in one word. The other options are not appropriate because they seem to say that the shift was a result of the previous sentence(s) or are a "surprising" advance, which changes the meaning.

117. (D) The word "beautiful" should not be removed because the word is not a departure from the tone and perspective of the passage. The passage laments the lack of diversity in earlier children's books and celebrates the arrival of many children's books with characters of varying backgrounds. Positive language is used throughout and is appropriate here as well.

118. (C) This final paragraph moves from the 1960s to today, and this example serves as a useful illustration of a current book with diverse characters. Providing this example supports the writer's claim that there is an abundance of books with diverse characters available today.

119. (C) The use of "countless" is not doing any new work in the sentence since the writer describes the books as "so abundant" later in the sentence. It is clear that there are many books with diverse characters to choose from without the use of "countless" before "books."

120. (A) The use of "celebrating" is a positive term to communicate the way these books are providing examples of diversity from various cultures. The other options are synonyms and are neutral rather than positive words.

Passage 3c

121. (B) Above all else, the writer is exploring what poetry is, and while he explores the inspirations for poetry and surprising places that poetry exists, he doesn't explore forms or types of poetry and poets.

122. (E) The author argues that any subject that one is eager to communicate on is a fit subject for poetry, meaning that it is appropriate to have poetry about it. He does not say that poetry is not a fit subject, but he does say that poetry is not all of the other options in choices A through D.

123. (C) Although the words "deep" and "wide" are both used in the sentence, they do not encompass all that the word "grave" connotes. Although "somber" is a synonym for "grave," the writer isn't arguing that poetry is dark. "Momentous" is also a synonym for grave, as in a grave decision, but that doesn't fit its use here. Overall, the writer is arguing that poetry is "serious" in that it requires serious thought and has both breadth and depth.

124. (A) In defining poetry in this line, the author uses repetition and listing, specifically epistrophe and enumeration, to list many emotions, returning most directly to the opening line's claim that "poetry is the language of the imagination and the passions." The emotions listed can also be called passions.

125. (A) Although slaves and tyrants could be considered opposites, there is no textual evidence to make them opposites here. All of the other pairs are set up in the same parallel structure and this form asks us to see them all as pairs of opposites.

126. (A) The last sentence of the passage states that poets are not the only ones who have keen insight, wild imagination, and an understanding beyond what rationality can offer. In other words, poets are not the only sources of poetry in the world.

127. (E) The author alludes to other literature, quotes throughout, provides many and varied examples of what poetry is, and uses figurative language throughout to make his claim clear to the reader. At no point does the writer tell a short story or personal narrative.

128. (D) The packed style and structure most communicates the variation of poetry. The writer gives many examples of what poetry is and these examples show lots of range, which returns to the first big definition of poetry as being "the language of the imagination and the passions," which is quite broad.

129. (C) The many examples listed in the passage present situations that the writer calls poetry. All show powerful and beautiful moments in life. His main claim is that poetry is not confined to the works of poets; poetry is all of the most poignant of human emotions and experiences.

130. (B) Because of the writer's long and enumerative sentences, long paragraph length, figurative language, and thorough exploration of the definition of poetry, his tone can be described as effusive. In other words, the style and content of the passage leads to the belief that the writer has great enthusiasm and emotion for his subject, poetry.

Passage 3d

131. (C) Choice C is the best combination of the two sentences because it uses "but" to show the change in direction between the two sentences. The first sentence provides Gödel's birthplace, but the second provides the information that his birthplace is no longer considered to be in Austria-Hungary due to new political borders.

132. (A) Choice A provides contextual information about Gödel that helps us to understand the sequence of his life. Choices B, C, and D are about the time period, but not about Gödel. While choice E is about Gödel, it provides very little context about his life and instead discusses his thought process before moving.

133. (C) Because "became a member of" is the most formal phrase used to describe Gödel's involvement with the Institute of Advanced Study, it maintains the formal and informative tone of the passage.

134. (B) Of the sentences provided, choice B can best be described as the thesis of this passage because it is the main idea about the subject. Choice A is about Gödel but is just a detail about his life and not a main idea. The other options are larger ideas but are not about Gödel.

135. (D) The addition of "closely" before "related" will help the writer further define the connectedness of these two subjects, which makes clear how Gödel and others like him were considered both mathematicians and philosophers. The other options all lessen the connection between the two subjects, which weakens the points made in the surrounding sentences.

136. (E) Choice E makes clear, through its use of "consequently," that the information provided in sentence 9 is a consequence, or result, of the information provided in sentence 8. Godel and others like him are considered philosophers and mathematicians because the mathematical concepts he studied are closely related to philosophy.

137. (A) Choice A best serves as a topic sentence for paragraph 3 because it states that Gödel's largest contribution was the two theorems that are then named and described in more detail in the following sentences of the paragraph.

138. (D) This sentence serves to clarify the theorem introduced in the preceding sentence and uses plain language to explain a mathematical concept. Therefore, the language is not meant to be overly technical or understood only by mathematicians.

139. (E) The portion of the sentence should not be removed because it is consistent with the rest of the paragraph. The other theorem is explained for a general audience and so should this one for both a clear discussion of Gödel's work and for the unity of the paragraph. It would be unbalanced without this portion of the sentence.

140. (A) Choice A makes the claim that Gödel's work influenced proof theory without expressing it in absolute terms. The other versions of the sentence include words like "most," "completely," and "solely" that overstate the influence and express it in absolute terms.

Passage 3e

141. (D) The writer would most agree that feelings make us irrational, which is what causes writers to produce and readers to accept a lack of truth in our impression of external things.

142. (E) The passage as a whole makes an argument while relying on illustrative quotations to show and discuss examples of the pathetic fallacy in poetry.

143. (D) The meaning of the passage relies heavily on Ruskin's defining of the term "pathetic fallacy" throughout. He is exploring this poetic term, its types, and who uses it.

144. (E) The author uses classification throughout the passage, categorizing true vs. false appearances, types of the pathetic fallacy, types of poetry, and types of poets. However, grief is described as one of the violent feelings; it is not set up in opposition to violent feelings.

145. (A) When the writer defines "pathetic fallacy," he is using a definition of "pathetic" that is "caused by the feelings," because the fallacy that he is discussing is a "falseness in all our impressions of external things" caused by strong feelings.

146. (D) The tone of the passage can best be described as didactic, as the passage is intended to instruct. The writer aims to make his topic clear to readers by defining, classifying, and ultimately making a claim about who uses the pathetic fallacy in their poetry.

147. (C) The last line of the passage states the major claim "But I believe, if we look well into the matter, that we shall find the greatest poets do not often admit this kind of falseness,—that it is only the second order of poets who much delight in it.[55]" Understanding what the writer means by the "second order of poets" requires you to read footnote 55 for his definition.

148. (A) Holmes. The writer's name being quoted is Oliver Wendell Holmes. Footnote 53 provides the name of the author being quoted and his first and middle name in parentheses. It would be incorrect to provide a first name to cite a quote, so it's clear that the author leads with the last name in the footnote.

149. (B) Kingsley. Footnote 54 more clearly provides the author's last name and the title of the work that is being quoted. The title of the work is *Alton Locke*, and these lines are taken from chapter 26 of that work.

150. (C) The writer looks down on "young pseudo-poets" and writes that "all inferior poetry is an injury to the good." Because of his judgments and lack of patience with those who write bad poetry, his tone can best be described as condescending.

Chapter 4

Passage 4a

151. (D) The passage seeks to answer the question "what is humor?" The first paragraph primarily enumerates what humor is not, the third paragraph provides an allegory to help define humor and its sources, and the fourth and final paragraph classifies true and false humor to further clarify the definition of humor.

152. (B) The first sentence of the passage claims that authors are most likely to fail when writing humor because it is the kind of writing in which they are most ambitious to excel.

153. (E) The first four answer choices state what humor is not. After providing what humor is not, the writer states that humor "should always lie under the check of reason."

154. (D) When the writer uses the word "barbarous," he is referring to his inability to enjoy false humor and, as such, the word is used to mean "uncivilized." He suggests that the false humor is beneath him in terms of his level of sophistication and culture.

155. (D) The writer provides an allegory in which Truth is the father of Good Sense, who is the father of Wit, who marries Mirth, with whom Wit fathered a child named Humor. Allegory uses symbolic fictional actions and figures to reveal truths.

156. (B) The second "him" refers to Humor, while the first "him" in that sentence refers to "an impostor." We are told the impostor would try to pass for "him" in this world, which lets us know that the "him" is Humor.

157. (A) "Spurious" is here being used to mean "counterfeit." While "deceptive" is close, the context states that the reader should be looking for signs of a lack of authenticity. Readers are told to look for "an impostor," in other words, a fake or a counterfeit.

158. (A) The tone is self-assured in that the writer feels certain of his convictions about humor and in his expertise. For example, the writer sees himself as qualified to judge the skill of an author in the sentence "For my part, when I read the delirious mirth of an unskilful author, I cannot be so barbarous as to divert myself with it, but am rather apt to pity the man, than to laugh at anything he writes."

159. (B) There are two references to the claim that the writer of humor should not be the amused party and that while the reader should laugh, "False Humour is always laughing whilst everybody about him looks serious."

160. (C) The footnotes provide information about two common nouns alluded to in the passage, Bedlam (a place) and Cowley (a person). Some of the other responses address one of the footnotes, but not both.

Passage 4b

161. (C) Choice C can best be described as the writer's major thesis, naming the location and making the statement that Koh Samui exceeded his or her expectations. All of the other details in the passage contribute to this dominant impression of the visited location.

162. (D) Choice D, which brings together the two ideas with the use of "and" best combines these two sentences because the second sentence does not follow as a conclusion or change direction, as the other options express.

163. (A) Yes, the writer should remove "over." "Exceeded" already means surpassed, or to be greater or beyond, so the inclusion of "over" is unnecessary and does not do any new work for the meaning of the sentence.

164. (B) "Recovered from" is the best option for maintaining a tone that is not overly formal but is also not purely conversational. "Recovered from" is more formal than "got over," "beat," and "destroyed," but less so than "dramatically and precipitously reduced," which sounds too formal for a travel blog and personal narrative of a trip.

165. (C) Yes, the writer should include it because a narrative begins in the first sentence of this paragraph, and this sentence completes that narrative, neatly concluding the recounting of the first day of the trip.

166. (A) The writer should include the sentence because it serves as a topic sentence and provides the main idea that connects the range of supporting details that follow, which are descriptions of the offerings best suited to different types of travelers.

167. (D) The sentence describing some of the menu offerings at the restaurant should not be removed because it adds to the totality of the experience being described on the trip and is typical of travel blogs that discuss activities, food, lodging, and so on.

168. (A) As it is now, the sentence makes the claim that Koh Samui has a lot to offer guests without overstating its offerings in comparison to other locations. It avoids expressing the claim by using the phrase "a lot to offer" and by avoiding absolute terms, such as "everything," "best," "all," or "most."

169. (D) The writer should not remove the underlined portion of the sentence because people reading a travel blog are considering the types of experiences offered at the location and how appropriate it is for their particular tastes and needs. Information about the age and experience level is appropriate and relevant for this type of text.

170. (E) While choices A through D all provide additional information, choice E gives information that can help readers know what to expect if they visit Buddha's magic garden. Because of the type of information it provides, choice E best meets the writer's needs.

Passage 4c

171. (A) Although he does explain why people worship babies, the writer's primary purpose in the passage is to defend the practice of worshipping babies. He explains why it happens and why it makes perfect sense. His goal is not to persuade people to worship babies, although that may be a side effect. The primary purpose is to defend baby-worship.

172. (A) The fact that babies are serious is stated as a reason that we are drawn to them in the first sentence, but their seriousness is not alone in why we worship them. The rest of the sentence makes it clear that their seriousness is a cause of their happiness, which is a reason to worship them. They are completely happy because of their seriousness, and that is worthy of worship.

173. (C) The claim that jolliness in babies is a result of their humorlessness is a paradox in that one would expect jolliness to be a result of humor, but according to the writer, the truth is that their seriousness contributes to their happiness.

174. (A) The metaphor of the human mushroom comes right after the speaker discusses the enormity of babies' heads in proportion to their bodies. This metaphor is used as a comparison to clarify their physical dimensions.

175. (D) The sentence provided uses anaphora (by repeating "new" at the beginning of the successive phrases) to show the wonder of the newness of the universe from a baby's perspective. The items on the lists are both naturally occurring and man-made, so answers that specify one or the other don't work.

176. (D) The sentence claims that we believe that if we could destroy custom and see the stars as a child seems them, it would be revolutionary. In this sense, "custom" is used as a routine that we follow without thinking about it, and the context that if we could destroy that monotonous routine we would see the world anew makes that particular meaning clear.

177. (C) The sentence uses irony in its use of "trifling." "Trifling" means lacking in significance or worth, and so the writer's modifying the "effort of remaking heaven and earth" is verbally ironic or sarcastic in that this effort is the opposite of meaningless and insignificant.

178. (E) The passage defends the worship of babies by explaining how they provide for us a deeper appreciation of what we would normally ignore or treat as ordinary. Their astonishment at the world around them makes us pause to take notice as well.

179. (B) The references to clay go back to the mention of creation in the first paragraph and the fact that in the Book of Genesis, it is said that Adam is created from the earth. These mentions of clay work as allusions.

180. (E) The tone is jocular and thoughtful in that the writer is playful with his description of babies as "human mushrooms" and his ironic use of "trifling." But, besides being playful and joking, the writer is thoughtful in that he is musing on big concepts throughout the passage, such as creation, apocalypse, maturity, appreciation, and so on.

Passage 4d

181. (C) Choice C is the simplest combination of the two sentences because it retains the meaning while using the fewest words.

182. (E) Choices A through D pose a problem and work through a solution, but the solution is not offered until sentence 13. Sentence 13 makes the major claim of the passage, which is that there is a 70.6% chance that, in a group of 30 people, at least two of them share a birthday.

183. (B) Choice B keeps with the approachable tone used throughout the passage without sliding into the slang presented in choice E. The tone throughout has been breezy but informed, which choice B represents with its diction and syntax.

184. (A) "First" is the best transitional word for this sentence because it begins a process of several steps that take the reader through understanding how the probability of sharing a birthday is determined.

185. (D) The writer should not remove this example because it serves as an illustration that clarifies the process of solving this problem. While revealing the birthday of every student in the class, the examples of Students #1 and #2 clarify the steps taken to solve this problem.

186. (B) This sentence is expressing a conclusion drawn from the sentences above, so "therefore" is the best transition. This sentence is not an addition or a change in direction from what preceded it.

187. (D) In this sentence, the writer is looking to signal a change in direction. The last sentence was about the probability of not sharing a birthday, but this sentence is looking to explore the probability of sharing a birthday.

188. (A) The definition of probability, or the synonym "likelihood," is the most helpful addition for an audience that is unfamiliar with the concept of probability. While the other options offer information about probability and its founding, only the definition in choice A helps to clarify the concept.

189. (C) The term "intuitions," meaning "the ability to understand something immediately, without the need for conscious reasoning" (https://www.lexico.com/en/definition/intuition) is a more precise word choice than the other options provided, which could be interpreted in more varied ways.

190. (E) The statement made in sentence 14 is an important conclusion that moves the meaning of this passage to a broader understanding that can be applied in similar situations.

Passage 4e

191. (D) The overall purpose of the passage is to support the practice of punishing cowardice through a range of examples. While the speaker acknowledges and accepts some of the counterclaims, he ultimately argues in favor of punishing cowardice.

192. (E) The speaker classifies faults as proceeding from infirmity or malice in order to acknowledge and accept the counterclaim that faults from infirmity are more pardonable because they proceed from our human nature. While he accepts this claim, he still maintains that cowardice should be punished.

193. (A) The sentence provided is an acknowledgment of the counterargument because the writer does believe that cowardice should be punished when it is extreme enough. He agrees that there is reason to differentiate between faults, but ultimately his claim is against the claim stated at the beginning of the passage.

194. (E) The definition of "questionable" as used in this sentence is obsolete. In context it means capable of being inquired of or capable of being questioned. The statement reads that we are not capable of being questioned for anything not committed against our consciences.

195. (B) The only answer choice that contains a description of cowardice is B, a product of frailty, or infirmity. All of the other descriptions are used to describe faults proceeding from treachery and malice.

196. (A) The quote is an adage that can be translated to "it is better to shame a man than kill him." The context before the quote provided makes it clear that it is better to shame a man because it is possible to awake his courage through his shame. If the man were killed, there would be no possibility of redemption.

197. (C) The writer qualifies the first claim presented. In the last line of the passage, he writes, "Notwithstanding, in case of such a manifest ignorance or cowardice as exceeds all ordinary example, 'tis but reason to take it for a sufficient proof of treachery and malice, and for such to be punished," meaning that if the example of cowardice is not within the realm of the ordinary, it should be treated as evil and should be punished as such. He is qualifying the original claim, stating that if the example is bad enough, it should be punished as if it were treachery or malice.

198. (E) The first set of brackets provides both amplification (that this surrender referred to was to Henry VIII) and the date. The second set provides a translation. The third set provides a citation, and the fourth and fifth sets provide dates. None provide personal commentary.

199. (D) The speaker relies on historical examples to build his argument, using Greece, Rome, and France through the ages.

200. (C) Although the writer is not indifferent, his tone is objective throughout the passage as he is not personally involved or subjective. The writer provides an objective account of the issue of the punishing of cowardice and then provides historical examples. Not until the final sentence of the passage does the writer make clear his opinion on the subject.

Chapter 5

Passage 5a

201. (D) The writer sees the ideal beauty of the wood-cutters' lives in spite of the slovenly nature of their huts. In the next paragraph, she speaks of the job of the poet, which is to add beauty to the normal lives and jobs of people and to leave out the dirt. As such, the writer's mentioning of their slovenly huts is an example of the dirt that would be left out.

202. (E) The last choice, "Men who must be at the full expense in describing their position," describes poets of the present time (when the passage was written), while the other choices describe men with the three listed positions that lived in slower times, etc.

203. (A) The first answer choice is the only option that speaks generally of poets. All of the other choices use the first person to describe the particular feelings of the writer. Also, the other choices are not direct results of the rapid growth.

204. (C) The second paragraph analyzes the effects of more rapid growth on the lives and jobs of poets. Because of rapid growth, the poet must describe the lives of workers, since workers don't have the time to find the moral and meaning of their lives.

205. (D) "Mushroom" is used metaphorically to say that the growth is fast. Mushrooms are rapidly growing fungi. To say something is mushrooming is to say it is growing rapidly.

206. (B) In context, the writer is saying that she will not be so open to the West as to confuse ugliness with beauty and discord with harmony, or to praise and be happy with everything she sees.

207. (D) Irony is expressed in the line "The march of peaceful is scarce less wanton than that of warlike invasion." One would not expect the march of the peaceful to have the same disastrous results as warlike invasion. It's ironic because one would expect the opposites of war and peace to have opposite effects, but according to the writer, they have the same results.

208. (E) The footnotes provide clarification for the allusions presented, namely Hamadryads, Midas, Macbeth, and Medea. These allusions are a combination of mythological and literary and help the writer to develop her piece.

209. (C) The passage relies heavily on natural description and alludes to Shakespeare, mythology, history, etc. It begins with the description of a place and carries through its argument using descriptive imagery and allusions.

210. (A) The tone of the passage can best be described as bittersweet, because the writer does seem to mourn a simpler time and regret the effects of the rapid growth of the present; however, she ends on a hopeful note, saying that she will be a part of a new body of poetry, a new intellectual growth.

Passage 5b

211. (C) The statement made in choice C is the main claim around which all the other examples and supporting claims revolve. It is the teacher's responsibility to be sure the students learn. What comes before this statement sets up this major claim, and supporting examples follow.

212. (A) The best combination of the sentences uses the coordinating conjunction "for" because the second sentence is supplementing the observation that not all students share the teacher's love of math. It says why the teacher must accept this—because ("for") the opposite is often the case. It does not change direction as stated in this explanation.. The other options communicate a different relationship between the sentences, including a change in direction, which does not fit the relationship of the two sentences.

213. (E) "Regardless" is the best transitional word to communicate the relationship between sentence 3 and the two sentences that came before it. In sentences 1 and 2, the writer discusses students' feelings about math, but this sentence communicates that, regardless of students' feelings toward the subject, it is the teacher's responsibility to make sure they learn the material.

214. (E) Sentence 5 should not be removed because it offers a useful example of the claim made in sentence 4, which is that the teacher has a set of techniques to reach students. Sentence 5 offers an example of one technique, which is using a real-world example to clarify a topic by increasing student interest.

215. (D) The definition of "lecture" should not be included in sentence 6 because, based on the tone and information included in the passage, it seems that the audience would be familiar with the term. In addition, the second half of the sentence provides clues of what lecture is not, further helping the reader to understand what a lecture is.

216. (E) Only choice E communicates a contrast, or shift in direction, between sentence 7 and what came before it. All of the other options can be used to add more information, which is what sentence 7 is providing.

217. (B) The additional information should be included in the sentence because it makes clear why the writer is using these technologies and serves as a supporting detail to the passage's major claim, which is that the writer's primary responsibility is to ensure that all students learn.

218. (D) Choice D uses "but" to combine the two sentences, which changes the relationship between them and does not work as a method to combine them.

219. (A) "Finally" is the clearest transition to begin this last sentence, as the writer is seeking to conclude the passage with this final thought. Choices B and C are communicating that this sentence is a conclusion from something it followed; choice D would be used to add more information; and choice E changes direction. A is the best choice for this point in the passage.

220. (D) The debate about grading based on accuracy or effort is not a necessary topic for the writer to cover, and it is certainly not a good idea to raise a new topic in the final sentence when the passage should be concluding.

Passage 5c

221. (D) The writer points out the logical fallacies and shortcomings in the arguments of the naturalists. He writes about how these writers lack discussions of coadaptation and how this field of study must use the existing knowledge of variation under domestication.

222. (E) "Affinities" most nearly means "resemblances in structure" in the context of the phrase "reflecting on the mutual affinities of organic beings." While the other options are synonymous with "affinities," only E is the scientific (biological) definition being used here.

223. (B) The conclusion is problematic because it is a hasty generalization, meaning that it is concluding something without sufficient evidence. Begging the question assumes something true in the writer's thesis that has yet to be proven. Ad hominem is attacking the person making the argument rather than the argument. Post hoc is a fallacy in which an event before something happened is assumed to be a cause; it mistakes following in time for having a causal relationship. Non sequitur means that the conclusion does not follow as a logical conclusion from the evidence presented.

224. (A) The writer provides the counterargument, which is the belief of the naturalists he refers to. He provides their view as possible but then provides an example that shows the limitations of their argument. A warrant is a shared assumption, a rebuttal is a response disagreeing with an argument, data is the evidence used in making an argument, and a claim is the thesis of the argument.

225. (C) The writer is in awe of the woodpecker and the misseltoe, which can be seen in his diction; for example, his use of the phrase "so admirably" to describe the adaptation of the feet, tail, beak, and tongue of the woodpecker for catching insects.

226. (D) The main clause of the sentence is "it is equally preposterous to account for the structure of this parasite with its relations to several distinct organic beings, by the effects of external conditions, or of habit, or of the volition of the plant itself." Therefore the subject and predicate are "it" and "is" in this complex sentence.

227. (A) In the last paragraph, the writer paves the way to present his findings. He explains reasonably that his studies involved domesticated animals and cultivated plants, and that although the knowledge gained is imperfect, he believes these studies to have afforded valuable information.

228. (C) In context, the problem is mysterious in that the answers are unknown. The other synonyms for "obscure" are more physical ("dark," "faint," and "remote") or a mismatch in terms of connotation. "Ambiguous" means that it can have more than one interpretation, which is not a good fit for this sentence.

229. (D) "Coadaptation" refers to the changes in a species that result from the species' relationship with other species and its life. The examples of the woodpecker and the misseltoe are presented to prove that their modifications must be a result of how they interact with other species. The other options are seen as limited by the writer.

230. (A) The writer is forthright, or straightforward and honest, in the last paragraph of the passage. He admits that it "seemed to [him] probable . . . " and that the knowledge he has gained is not perfect. He admits that his process is not perfect and that he is not completely certain. He's being honest.

Passage 5d

231. (D) The writer should not remove the phrase from the sentence because it helps to locate the Boca Raton Resort & Club in Florida to readers unfamiliar with the location of Boca Raton, and defining it as a "hotspot" is relevant for this type of passage.

232. (A) Yes, the writer should remove "over." "Exceeded" already means surpassed, or to be greater or beyond, so the inclusion of "over" is unnecessary and does not do any new work for the meaning of the sentence.

233. (A) Choice A can best be described as the writer's major thesis, naming the location and making the statement that Boca Raton Resort & Club will exceed the reader's expectations. All of the other details in the passage contribute to this dominant impression of the visited location.

234. (E) This sentence should not be removed because this type of information is relevant for a passage about a vacation locale. Readers of travel blogs are potential travelers, and this information is relevant for them when considering and planning to visit resorts.

235. (A) "Conveniently" is the best option for the context of the sentence, because while choices B through E all communicate the proximity of the rooms to the pool and beach, only A makes the connection that the closeness is a convenience for travelers with children.

236. (B) This description of Serendipity 3 should be added because it is not clear from the name what this eatery offers. The rest of the sentence makes clear what type of food Morimoto and Lucca offer, so this addition helps to complete the sentence.

237. (C) Choice C gives the spa a compliment by telling readers that it is award-winning, without using any superlatives. All of the other options communicate that the spa is the best, rather than just claiming that is highly regarded.

238. (A) Yes, this sentence should be added because all of the supporting details in the paragraph are about the offerings for children and families, and a topic sentence would help readers understand the focus of the paragraph.

239. (E) Choice E is the best version because it communicates that the property is kid-friendly *even when* the DJ is at the pools, which is geared for adults but only happens on the weekends. The other options communicate that there is always a DJ at the pools, but that the resort is still kid-friendly.

240. (B) The sentence should be added because it serves to conclude this paragraph on the property's suitability as a resort for families, while it also concludes the passage as a whole by claiming that the resort is highly recommended due to its ease and elegance.

Passage 5e

241. (C) The first paragraph is defining "geology" and does so in part by using etymology, looking at "ge" and "logos" as meaning a discourse on the earth. It also provides two questions that help define the subject of geology.

242. (A) The paragraph's claim is that the mineral kingdom was previously thought of as the subject of geology but that further study shows that changes in the earth, including those involving animals and plants, are also part of the subject of geology.

243. (D) The sentence works to clear up the common misconception that the solid parts of the earth have always been and remain in the same state in which we see them currently. The list is not exhaustive, which we can see from the author's use of "such as," meaning that there are other examples as well.

244. (E) The sentence is a cumulative sentence that has the main independent clause ("he can show that they have acquired their actual configuration and condition gradually") in the beginning of the sentence and additional details accumulated afterward.

245. (A) "Artificial" is used to mean "made by humans rather than nature" when describing excavations. This means that the miner finds things that are not revealed by natural forces but, rather, that are dug up.

246. (D) The meaning of "just" when used to describe the remark is "accurate." The writer is saying that although the remark is accurate, that the earth's crust is small, it is also big and in fact huge in relation to man.

247. (C) The last paragraph defines "earth's crust." It provides denotation, boundaries of the definition, and measurements. The last portion of the paragraph ruminates on the scope of the definition, reacting to both its enormity and its relative smallness. The author does not offer a personal, or subjective, definition of "earth's crust" within the paragraph.

248. (B) Because of both the enormity and relative smallness of the earth, the geologist views it with awe (at its hugeness) and humility (at its smallness in comparison to the universe).

249. (B) The passage as a whole can be described as logical in its systematic definition of the study of geology. The language and its claims are objective and straightforward. He does not use lyrical language, he is concrete in his terms and ideas, and his piece is not meant to provoke readers or be controversial.

250. (A) The primary purpose of the passage is to inform the reader about the study of geology. The writer seeks to clear up some misconceptions about the field. It defines geology, which is further evidence of its intention to inform.

Chapter 6

Passage 6a

251. (A) The first paragraph of this state of the union address is meant to inform the listeners of the present situation in foreign relations, especially with Spain. While Jefferson does try to persuade his listeners later to stay within the law, this paragraph is meant to inform.

252. (C) Jefferson is disappointed that he's not able to tell the nation that the problems of foreign relations have been settled. While he worked to achieve that end, it has not happened yet.

253. (B) The second sentence explains the efforts taken on the part of Jefferson to reach the intended outcome of an end to the foreign relations problems. However, despite Jefferson's best efforts, the conflict is not settled at the time of the address.

254. (B) The root of the word "promptitude" is prompt, which should help readers figure out that the word is used to describe the quickness with which the citizens responded.

255. (C) The sentence uses the emotions and values of honor, accomplishment or entitlement, confidence, camaraderie, strength, and determination. It relies on the appeal to pathos to persuade the listeners that these volunteers are outstanding citizens and that they are worthy of our help and protection.

256. (E) The first sentence of paragraph three transitions from praising the volunteer forces, who acted legally, to admonishing the citizens who organized illegally to fight the Spanish.

257. (C) "Efficaciously" most nearly means "effectively" in both of these sentences. "Expeditiously" is describing something done effectively, but with quickness, which is not mentioned in these contexts.

258. (E) The last paragraph's primary purpose is to defend the writer's choice to disarm the people who were taking matters into their own hands in terms of fighting the Spanish.

259. (A) The tone of the last paragraph can best be described as "fervent," meaning that the writer is showing intensity. This can be seen in the closing line, especially "should be promptly and efficaciously suppressed," which expresses the writer's intensity.

260. (A) The speaker can best be described as authoritative and decisive. Jefferson has the power and authority to punish those who acted outside of the law and he is decisive in his belief that those men should be disarmed. He is certain and strong in his opinions and actions.

Passage 6b

261. (B) Choice B provides both the topic and the time frame, which is the best option for engaging the reader, providing context, and preparing the reader for the information that follows. The other options are too focused on Thomas Young or engage the reader without providing context.

262. (C) The writer should add the sentence because it explains what is stated in sentence 1 and offers further information, or amplification, of the point made in that sentence. While not an example or a rebuttal, it is a useful explanation. The transitional phrase "That is" helps the reader to know that what follows is an explanation of what was previously stated.

263. (A) "However" serves as the best transition between sentences 1 and 2 because there is a change in direction from what was originally thought to what was thought after Einstein's discovery. The other transitions would be appropriate for introducing an example, sequencing events, or providing a conclusion.

264. (D) The writer should not include the underlined portion of the sentence because the phrase "In 1924, the physicist" before his name communicates the timing of the discovery and the primary field of study of Louis de Brogie. The additional information is redundant.

265. (A) Using the word "famous" to describe the experiment allows the writer to avoid expressing the claim in absolute terms. "Famous" communicates that it is well-known without saying that it is the most influential, most important, best known, or world's most prominent, which are all superlatives.

266. (D) The phrase should not be removed because it provides useful examples of what wave properties are, which is helpful for readers who may not be familiar with these properties.

267. (E) Of the options provided, "strange" has the most neutral connotation of simply meaning "unusual," and the tone is objective and formal, reporting the surprising results without becoming too informal and subjective.

268. (D) Because beams of subatomic matter are not people or animals with agency and choice, the writer uses quotation marks to signal the figurative use of the term.

269. (E) "However" serves as the best transition between sentences 8 and 9 because there is a change in direction from quantum physics dethroning classical physics to the continued struggle to interpret the results of the experiments. The other transitions would be appropriate for introducing an example, sequencing events, or providing a conclusion.

270. (D) The sentence should not be removed because it is a successful way to conclude both the paragraph and the passage. The passage begins with a discussion of how we used to understand how light functioned and ends with our current understanding of quantum physics, underlining just how shocking it is by including a quotation that succinctly makes that point.

Passage 6c

271. (D) The writers that the speaker is responding to have not made the necessary distinctions between society and government.

272. (C) In context, "confounded" means confused in that some writers have confused society with government and as a result have not seen any distinctions between the two.

273. (D) "Encourages and creates" are used to show the actions of society and government, but they are not opposites. They both mean "to bring about."

274. (E) Society is personified as a patron, while government is personified as a punisher. They are provided human actions and attributes.

275. (B) The line "for when we suffer, or are exposed to the same miseries BY A GOVERNMENT, which we might expect in a country WITHOUT GOVERNMENT, our calamity is heightened by reflecting that we furnish the means by which we suffer" makes the claim that causing our own suffering makes it worse.

276. (A) The sentence is a biblical allusion to the Garden of Eden, a paradise. When Adam and Eve eat from the Tree of the Knowledge of Good and Evil, they realize their nakedness and have the capacity for shame, or a loss of innocence. The allusion shows man fallible in that he can make mistakes and bad judgments; he is human and thus he fails.

277. (D) The mode of composition of paragraphs one and two is primarily definition, as the main purpose of those paragraphs is to define society and government. There are many constructions that are variations of "society is . . . " and "government is . . . ". Both are defining.

278. (D) The transition moves from all of the following pairs except from confirming to refuting. Overall, the shift moves from defining and discussing the difference between society and government to a concrete illustration of the principles.

279. (E) The third paragraph is developed by examples in order to illustrate what men can do together and their need for each other to survive. It illustrates the positivity of society.

280. (A) Government is necessary because men are inherently bad. Once their needs are met by society, they will turn on one another. So while government is bad, it is a necessary evil to provide men security.

Passage 6d

281. (E) Choice E, which is sentence 7, can best be described as the writer's thesis because it makes an arguable claim. The other sentences build up to the writer's thesis.

282. (A) The writer should remove the underlined portion because remembering and recalling are essentially the same thing, and it is redundant to list them as separate activities.

283. (B) Because this issue of summative assessments is not discussed elsewhere in this paragraph or the rest of the passage, sentence 2 should be removed because it does not advance the passage and its claims.

284. (D) The writer should not include the definition because the second part of the sentence provides sufficient contextual clues for readers to get an idea of what the word means.

285. (A) The coordinating conjunction "and" is the best option for combining sentences 4 and 5. While the other options work grammatically, they do not accurately communicate the relationship between the two sentences.

286. (D) Choice D provides examples of the types of assessments described in sentence 7 by naming "essays, projects, and assessments that provide choices" as assessments that are meaningful and account for different learning styles. The other sentences make claims about assessment but do not provide examples.

287. (C) The sentence should be included because the topic shifts between the paragraphs, and this sentence can help readers recognize that shift and connect all of the sentences that follow to that sentence.

288. (E) The best option to begin sentence 9 is "Now," because sentence 8 discusses the writer's old way of thinking, and sentence 9 shows the present line of thinking about what to teach students.

289. (A) "Define" is the best option for the underlined word in sentence 10 because this sentence is about being precise in the development, or definition, of what the writer hopes to achieve through instruction. Choices B through D are about the expression of that goal, not its development. Choice E addresses proving its validity, which again, doesn't fit the writer's needs.

290. (A) Yes, the writer should remove this underlined portion because when "by teaching" is included in the sentence, it is clear that it is through the writer's classes, making the underlined phrase redundant and unnecessary.

Passage 6e

291. (E) All of the provided statements are true, except the last, according to the first sentence of the passage. The writer refers to "sorrowful indignation," which points to both sadness and anger as a result of the difference between people that is either a result of nature or of their unequal treatment by civilization.

292. (A) In context, "solicitude" most nearly means "attention." The writer refers to herself as watching the world with "anxious solicitude," meaning that she is watching the world events with an anxious, concerned attention.

293. (D) According to the writer, "the neglected education of my fellow creatures is the grand source of the misery I deplore." The rest of the passage discusses the problems of women as a result of flaws in their education.

294. (B) The sentence develops an analogy between women's minds and flowers that are planted in too rich a soil. The comparison helps clarify that women are educated to be pleasing and that this flawed approach to their education proves detrimental. The analogy is used to elucidate the effects of a limited education on women.

295. (C) The writer does not point to the education of women as being inflicted by women on themselves. It points to the writings and prejudices of men in not treating women as equals.

296. (A) One of the surprising facts about this passage is that the writer, a woman fighting for the improvement of women's education, discusses what she believes to be the natural inferiority of women in comparison to men. This may be considered ironic by current-day readers, who would expect the opposite from this writer.

297. (E) The last word of the passage is "society," and it most nearly means "company or companionship" in that the claim is that women do not seek to be friends with the fellow creatures (men) when in their company.

298. (C) The writer's purpose is to persuade readers that women's education needs reform and that this education should not be limited to the goal of making women more alluring. It should instead seek to make women respectable.

299. (D) The speaker can best be described as reasonable and observant. She opens the piece by sharing her observations of both history and the present and proceeds through a reasonable argument that acknowledges truths, as she sees them, and makes concessions. While she is upset about the situation, she remains reasonable throughout her approach to persuading her audience.

300. (A) The tone can best be described as measured indignation because the writer is angry about the education of women. However, she expresses this anger in a limited amount. She is frustrated and angry, but she does admit that she sees women as inferior, which limits her anger.

Chapter 7

Passage 7a

301. (B) Ironically, the only way that being liberal can be positive for the prince is if it is enacted with dishonesty. It must be done in a way to secure a reputation for liberality without the true honesty that liberality should be characterized by.

302. (C) The purpose of the first paragraph is to analyze the effects of being liberal as a prince. The paragraph begins with the cause of exercising liberality and displays all of the effects and results of doing so.

303. (A) Ironically, being liberal leads to being poor, despised, and in danger, and to having a reputation for being miserly. Although liberality is synonymous with generosity, according to the writer, it does not lead to being loved.

304. (D) "Odious" most nearly means "detestable" in that being liberal will soon make the prince run out of money and he will have to spend the money of his subjects, arousing their hate and displeasure.

305. (E) The reputation for generosity would not be fleeting, but, rather, it would be long-lasting and something that takes time to develop. The reputation for meanness would fade over time and the reputation for generosity would develop later and remain.

306. (E) This paragraph is developed by example. After developing his major claims about the disastrous results of being liberal and the conclusion stating princes should therefore not fear a reputation for meanness, the writer uses paragraph three to provide historical examples to prove the validity of his argument.

307. (A) Paragraph four is developed by counterargument. The writer provides possible objections, or counterarguments, and then refutes them. He begins with the counterclaim that Caesar obtained empire by liberality and then argues that actually, if Caesar would have not moderated his expenses, he would have destroyed his government.

308. (B) The major claim of this passage is effective and paradoxical—it is seemingly contradictory that liberality would make a prince hated, but, according to the writer's reasoning, it is true nonetheless.

309. (B) The speaker is practical, meaning that his advice is meant to be realistic, not idealistic.

310. (C) Above all else, the writer's tone is forthright in that he is being completely honest about the realities of being a prince. He reveals the truth behind doing good things for reputation's sake and divulges how a prince can use this information to his benefit.

Passage 7b

311. (A) The major claim of the passage is presented in the first sentence and makes the argument that this Tim Burton exhibit should be seen by "everyone interested in pop culture." The rest of the passage goes on to support why this exhibit should be seen.

312. (B) The writer expects the audience to have a basic working knowledge and interest in art, which can be seen through the mention of surrealism, multimedia art, and NYC's Museum of Modern Art. These three things are mentioned without further definition or explanation, illustrating the writer's expectations of the audience's knowledge.

313. (D) Sentence 4 should not be removed because it provides specific examples of Burton's gift with ink and paper, which is mentioned in the previous sentence. This sentence offers vivid illustrations of the minor claim in sentence 3, and it offers support for the passage's major claim that this exhibit should be visited.

314. (B) Yes, the underlined portion should be included because regardless of the audience's opinion and knowledge of these three figures, they do serve as useful examples of recognizable personalities featured in Tim Burton's drawings.

315. (E) Choice E uses "and" to combine the two sentences, which is the best conjunction for the relationship between them. The other options communicate a change in direction ("however," "but," and "yet") or a conclusion drawn ("so").

316. (B) Option B offers examples of the range of artworks on display, as mentioned in sentence 11. These include concept drawings for the characters in his movies, recognizable iconic mannequins, costumes, and statuettes. The other options each mention one form of art, rather than the range introduced in sentence 11.

317. (B) "Hovers" is the best word to replace the underlined portion of sentence 12 because it contributes to the effect of the Jack O'Lantern's menacing nature and the "otherworldliness" mentioned later in the paragraph.

318. (E) The word "additionally" should be placed at the beginning of sentence 13 to communicate that this "crude ape head" is an additional large piece in the exhibit that contributes to a strange effect for visitors.

319. (A) "Exploring" is the best option to ensure that the connotation of the word is appropriate for the sentence because it conjures up images of looking into these liminal spaces between fun and fear in a way that can be both playful and arduous, or exhaustive. The other options are more technical in their connotations and seem to miss the playfulness of Burton's work.

320. (B) Choice B is specific in that it offers what the exhibit tells us through its displays. The other options may recommend or provide information about the exhibit, but only B is specific about what viewers can expect.

Passage 7c

321. (A) The passage relies on informing readers why men can't live sociably with one another (in contrast with certain living creatures that can). This can be seen in part by the fact that the writer claims men may desire to know why men can't do the same (live sociably with one another). He is not arguing or refuting; he is just informing those who may desire to know, not those who are arguing otherwise.

322. (C) The passage begins with a faulty comparison between political creatures and men, because while it is assumed that men can live sociably with each other, like bees and ants, man's ability to to reason, speak, and be jealous keeps him from that fate.

323. (A) The end of the paragraph, stating that mankind cannot "do the same," refers back to the beginning claim about certain creatures, which is that certain creatures live sociably with one another.

324. (D) The statement says that creatures "want that art of words," meaning that they lack the ability to speak.

325. (E) The first "their" refers to others and the second "their" refers to men, because the statement is that men say things about the appearance versus reality of good and evil to others, and in so doing, men trouble the peace of others for their own pleasure.

326. (B) The statement made is ironic in that it is the opposite of what one would expect. One would expect man to be least troublesome when he is at ease, not most troublesome. This is an example of situational irony, not verbal irony.

327. (B) The creatures are not ambitious because they have no differentiation between private and public good and, as such, always do what's best for the group.

328. (B) The structure of the passage is accomplished by enumeration, or listing, complete with a numbering of examples. This can be seen in the beginning of each paragraph, except the first, which presents the claim of the passage.

329. (B) The numbered listing, or enumeration, and the mode of carefully comparing and contrasting men and the creatures capable of living sociably together, contribute to a systematic style. The writer is relying on a logical structure and logical mode to make his points.

330. (E) The tone can best be described as learned, in that the writer is knowledgeable and informative about nature, Aristotle, human nature, politics, etc.

Passage 7d

331. **(D)** Choice D makes the major claim that the Waldorf Astoria Park City is a great vacation spot. The other sentences provide background information or begin to provide supporting details about what to do when visiting Park City.

332. **(D)** Sentence 5 should not be removed because it serves as a topic sentence for the second paragraph, which focuses on the summertime offerings of Park City. This sentence announces the topic and unifies the sentences that come after it.

333. **(A)** The writer should keep the term "must-do" as it best matches the tone of the sentence, paragraph, and passage as a whole. The other options are similar in denotation but carry much more serious connotations, turning this recommendation into an order or demand.

334. **(D)** "Strenuous" is the best word for the underlined portion of the sentence as it is precise and neutral. The writer wants to offer activities that are equally pleasing but less physical for those who want something relaxing. It's important that both types of activities are presented as good options for potential visitors to the area.

335. **(B)** Since Danielle Summers is most likely an unfamiliar person to most readers, it is helpful to provide her title. This information helps her credibility because readers will understand the basis for her expertise on the topic from her title.

336. **(C)** The paragraph that follows focuses on the winter offerings, and this sentence should be added because it serves as a helpful topic sentence to unify the sentences that follow.

337. **(C)** The underlined portion should be added because it defines the Epic Pass for those readers who may be unfamiliar with and possibly interested in what the pass offers.

338. **(A)** Leaving "largest" as a modifier for the ski and snowboard resort best meets the writer's needs because while it is an absolute claim, it can be supported by fact through measurements, whereas the other options are subjective and cannot be supported.

339. **(D)** Since Kerry Hing is most likely an unfamiliar name to readers, it is helpful to provide both her name and her title when quoting her for this piece on what Waldorf Astoria Park City and the surrounding area has to offer visitors.

340. **(A)** The writer should leave the word "afford" as is, because the other options are synonymous and similar in their tone and connotation. All else being equal, the writer should not make changes to a quotation that was provided verbatim from the speaker.

Passage 7e

341. (B) The speaker has just been released from captivity by Native Americans, which she describes as being "in the midst of thousands of enemies." She is reflecting on her experience and the power of God to deliver her from that danger.

342. (C) God is described as having an "awful dispensation" toward the speaker, but the archaic meaning of "awful" is awe-inspiring. She also describes God as having "wonderful power and might" and recounts how He returned them to safety without the captives being hurt. As a result, it can be said that the speaker calls God powerful, protective, awe-inspiring, and strong. She does not refer to God as punishing anyone.

343. (A) Although the speaker says that she used to wish for it before her captivity, "affliction" means distress or suffering. There is a context clue in line 16, in which affliction and sorrow are coupled as near synonyms.

344. (E) The quotation says that those the Lord loves He chastens or scourges. In other words, He makes those He loves receive discipline through hard trials.

345. (A) Some have afflictions drop by drop, or a little at a time, while some have the dregs of the cup, or the worst part there is. According to the speaker, her experience was so harrowing that she considers her suffering very extreme and not a bit at a time.

346. (C) The line is expressing that outward things have been revealed to be worthless, or futile, to the speaker by the Lord. Real suffering has shown her what is important in life, and the outward things are not important.

347. (B) All of the items on the list are used to express the ephemeral nature of outward things. In other words, the speaker is expressing that outward things are fleeting, while matters of the spirit are everlasting.

348. (E) As she is a woman speaking in the 1600s, the main audience would be Christians who would understand her faith through such a difficult trial. This intended audience is made clear through her references to David and her use of scripture as a way to view her captivity and its lessons in her life.

349. (D) Overall, the speaker is using the passage to reflect on her experience and share how it helped her grow in her faith. The identities of the captors are not revealed, and the speaker is thankful to God, not herself, for getting her through the ordeal.

350. (C) The speaker is reflecting on her experience, her spiritual growth, and her gratitude towards God for seeing her through the trial of her captivity. She is not trepidatious or fearful, at this point. The speaker presents this subject through her thankfulness that she is okay and by giving us insight into her thought process and feelings.

Chapter 8

Passage 8a

351. (E) The passage is structured by enumeration. It is listing, with the use of Roman numerals, the causes of the ruin of Rome.

352. (B) The paradox is that the art of man is described as both permanent and fleeting, which are opposites. This is true in a relative sense. The art of man is more permanent than his life and fleeting when measured against all of time.

353. (A) The footnote is elaborating on the claim that the pyramids' age is unknown. It provides two different theories on how old the pyramids are.

354. (C) The pyramids are used as an example of a simple and solid edifice of which it is difficult to know the duration.

355. (E) Footnote 3 elaborates on the image of the dropping leaves of autumn. The footnote mentions that this image is peculiar to Homer (an allusion) and describes this image as natural and melancholy.

356. (A) In this context, "propagated" most nearly means "spread." In discussing the destruction of fire, the writer says that the mischief of fire can be kindled (or started) and propagated (or spread).

357. (B) The date of November 15, A.D. 64 refers to the persecution of the Christians, not to the major fire of Nero's reign.

358. (D) The title of the work cited in footnote 5 is *Annal. Histoire Critique de la République des Lettres* is the work cited in footnote 4.

359. (D) The speaker can best be described as learned with his range of details and references throughout the passage.

360. (C) The primary purpose of the passage is analyzing the four principal causes of the ruin of Rome. This passage is analyzing in detail the cause of injuries of time and nature.

Passage 8b

361. (A) The first sentence of the passage can best be described as the writer's thesis because it makes the major claim about the Grateful Dead's position as the most unique popular American musical phenomenon of the 20th century. What follows this first sentence is support for its major claim.

362. (C) "Singularly" is another way to say "very," which is unnecessary when calling something unique. "Unique" expresses singularity, so placing these terms together is redundant.

363. (D) Since the writer is classifying the Grateful Dead as a "phenomenon" and not just a "band," it is helpful to define what a typical band is or does. The writer should leave the underlined portion in so as to make the argument that the Grateful Dead is more than a band.

364. (B) "In fact" is the best transition as it supports and amplifies what came before it. Sentence 2 defines the Grateful Dead as a "phenomenon," and sentence 3 goes on to define their fanbase as a "family," both of which support the Grateful Dead's uniqueness.

365. (A) The added information should be included because it provides more than a date. It gives helpful context to readers and helps the writer express the longevity of the Grateful Dead's presence as a touring band and its consequent impact.

366. (A) "Elevated" is the best option because it communicates that the classification is one of privilege, rewarding bands that carry on the spirit of the Grateful Dead. "Relegated" means to put in a lower position, and the other options are either neutral or too physical.

367. (D) The description of the "Stealie" is helpful information for all readers. While readers can imagine the Dancing Bears, the term "Stealie" may not conjure up any images in their minds.

368. (B) The opening of the sentence provides examples of Grateful Dead artwork and how it continues, and this second portion of the sentence should be included because it communicates the significance of this enjoyment, which helps support the major claim of the passage.

369. (D) Disc golf is brought up as an example to show how far-reaching the influence of the Grateful Dead is, but a full explanation is not necessary to understand this paragraph or the passage as a whole.

370. (A) Choice A provides a concluding sentence that returns to the major claim of the passage, which argues that the Grateful Dead is a unique musical phenomenon. The other sentences provide more supporting details but do not conclude the passage by returning to the thesis.

Passage 8c

371. (D) The mode of composition of paragraph one is definition. The paragraph is defining "freedom," "natural liberty," "freedom of men under government," and "freedom of nature." While the term "legislative authority" is in the paragraph, the speaker does not explore what it is and is not, as he does with the other terms.

372. (D) The evidence used in the paragraph is a direct quotation from Robert Filmer. The italicized text is a direct quote, which is cited. The title of the work and the page from which the quotation are taken are provided: *Observations*, A. 55.

373. (C) The evidence, or direct quotation, provided in paragraph one is being used as counterargument. This can be seen because the writer says, "Freedom then is not what Sir Robert Filmer tells us." He provides the quotation, which is a definition, but disagrees with it and goes on to argue against it, making it counterargument.

374. (A) To mirror the overwhelming will of another man on a man, the writer uses asyndeton, meaning that he omits conjunctions between the adjectives that modify "will." The list of so many adjectives without any breaks to describe the will of another man seems overwhelming in its overloading of words without any pauses.

375. (B) In context, "arbitrary" means "determined by impulse or chance." This meaning is clear from the other words used in the list that show the random nature of the will of another man.

376. (D) In the second and third uses of the word "arbitrary," it most nearly means "not limited by law or despotic." It is used as a close synonym for "absolute" and is used to modify "power."

377. (A) The irony is in the first claim because one would think that a man without power is someone who could easily become a slave, which is a state of powerlessness. The claim that a man without power cannot enslave himself is an example of situational irony because it is the opposite of what we would expect.

378. (A) The first sentence of the paragraph offers a definition of slavery, which is "the state of war continued, between a lawful conqueror and a captive." Although other parts of the paragraph are italicized, only "slavery" is defined.

379. (C) The purpose of the passage is to explore the meanings and states of freedom and slavery. Locke is ultimately building a treatise on government by thoroughly exploring all of these separate issues.

380. (C) The author is both forceful and confident in his tone. He defines with authority and points out the errors in another's definition and reasoning.

Passage 8d

381. (B) Option B introduces the specific quiche that will be explored in this recipe. It also describes the dish as easy to make, delicious, and healthy, which will engage the reader in wanting to continue reading the recipe. The other options provide interesting information about quiche but are less relevant to this passage.

382. (A) The writer should remove "to have" after "you need" because it is redundant. When the writer states that the reader needs the subsequent list of ingredients, there is no need to include both of the phrases quoted above because they both serve the same purpose.

383. (D) Sentence 5 should not be removed because it helps the writer and reader transition from the preparation phase to the cooking phase of the recipe. A recipe is designed to be followed, so clear directions are useful to readers.

384. (E) This type of passage calls for clear sequencing transitions to follow the steps of a process. The last sentence told the reader that it is time to begin, so this sentence should be the first step of the cooking process, hence "first" is the best option.

385. (A) The writer should use the proposed new sentence for sentence 9. The writer has been using "you" throughout the passage to guide readers through the recipe, and the switch to "I" for this sentence is unnecessary and inconsistent.

386. (C) Choice C, which uses the coordinating conjunction "and" to combine the two sentences, is the best choice because sentence 11 continues the process by adding another step after sentence 10. The other options don't reflect the relationship between sentences 10 and 11.

387. (D) Choice D combines sentences 12 and 13 most effectively to remove any redundancy. This sentence is able to express the idea in the simplest, shortest, and clearest way.

388. (B) Since the writer takes up three sentences to ultimately say using either the 6-ounce or 8-ounce bags of cheese is fine, it seems like it could be cut without any loss of meaning or clarity to the recipe as a whole.

389. (D) "For example" would be the best transition to open sentence 18, because the details in this sentence serve as examples of the statement made in sentence 17 that you could add other fillings.

390. (E) The writer should not remove the sentence because recipes often discuss their origins or have family stories to engage readers. This sentence also has the added benefit of making the claim that this recipe is easily adaptable for various preferences.

Passage 8e

391. (B) The stated occasion of the passage is a letter written from a man in the country that thinks that the writer of the passage needs to define the terms that he uses in his writing.

392. (A) The intended audience for the passage is country readers, because the writer of the letter is a person from the country and he is asking for definitions of terms used by the writer in his narratives.

393. (A) "Appellations" most nearly means "identifying names." All of the other terms are too limited. The titles presented are not only careers, nor do they only apply to men.

394. (B) According to the second paragraph, the most important thing is being inoffensive to the people around the gentleman. It is a product of good breeding, but the breeding is not the important characteristic.

395. (B) Sophronius is provided as an example of a gentleman. He is a skilled conversationalist and he never appears to be cunning.

396. (C) "Office" most nearly means "a function or duty assumed by someone." In this statement, Sophronius is described as doing a good job in handling all types of conversation—that is, he is skilled in doing all functions or duties in conversations.

397. (B) Jack Dimple is provided as an example of a Pretty Fellow, which is a poor substitute for a Gentleman. Jack Dimple is an artificial imitation.

398. (B) The Gentleman is referred to as a man of conversation, a master of his companion, a man of superior understanding, and an agreeable being. The man of pleasure is not the gentleman, but he is one whom the gentleman entertains.

399. (D) The passage is primarily using the mode of definition, as the writer is defining what a gentleman is. While some of the other points are made throughout, the introduction to the piece makes it clear that defining the gentleman is the primary purpose.

400. (E) The speaker's tone is playful and informative as he defines the gentleman with information to enhance his readers' understanding, but he is also playful and lighthearted at times in his delivery.

Chapter 9

Passage 9a

401. (D) The passage's primary purpose is to define poetry, the poet, and imagination. The rhetorical questions in the first paragraph help make this clear.

402. (A) "Subordination" is "the treatment of something as less valuable or important." In this context, the poet brings the soul of man into activity, and each faculty is ranked below another according to their worth.

403. (C) "Its" refers to the whole soul of man, which can be traced back to line 8.

404. (E) The poet is described as first bringing the soul of man into activity (bringing to life), then subordinating (separating and ordering) the different faculties (abilities), and then joining them (blending or fusing). Paradoxically, it is the poet's job to both separate and join. The process creates imagination.

405. (C) The writer says that he would "exclusively appropriate the name of Imagination" (i.e., he would call Imagination) "that synthetic and magical power."

406. (E) "Novelty" and "freshness" are synonymous in the pairings and are set up in opposition with "old and familiar objects." Both "novelty" and "freshness" are about being new, which is in opposition with what is old.

407. (B) From the list, only nature is seen as superior to its counterpart, art. The manner is seen as less than the matter. This can be seen from the construction that begins this list of three pairs. It states, "still subordinates art to nature" (i.e., art is placed under nature in importance or value). Admiration of the poet and the soul are not included in these pairs.

408. (B) The writer of the passage includes the poem, which is about the soul, to characterize the Imagination. Before providing the poem, the writer says, "and his words may with slight alteration be applied, and even more appropriately, to the poetic Imagination." In other words, the poem can be used to describe the Imagination.

409. (A) The final paragraph relies on personification of poetic genius as a body and uses metaphor throughout to figuratively describe Fancy, Motion, and Imagination. This reliance on figurative language is an appropriate way to conclude his points on poetry.

410. (E) The speaker regards poetry with awe at its powers. In defining poetry, he also celebrates its vast abilities.

Passage 9b

411. (C) Describing lemon chicken as "widely enjoyed" and "easy to make" is the best opening sentence for this recipe. It engages readers by persuading them why they should make lemon chicken and introducing them to the ease of the recipe.

412. (A) "Some" should be removed because it does not provide any pertinent information to the list of ingredients. Because it isn't useful information, it would be better to remove it from sentence 1.

413. (B) The writer should add this underlined phrase to sentence 3 because it serves to clarify the phrase "large Ziploc bag," which may be clear enough for some but too vague for others. This phrase could be helpful.

414. (D) Choice D is the best combination of sentences 3 and 4 because it cuts out any unnecessary words. Sentence 4 is not an additional step; it is a description of what was done in sentence 3.

415. (A) Sentence 5 provides a step in the process of making the lemon chicken, and as a result, a sequencing transition is the best choice to begin the sentence. "Next" is a perfect transition to move readers into the next step in the recipe process.

416. (A) The writer should remove the underlined phrase "begin to" before the word "sauté" because it doesn't serve a purpose. Telling readers to "begin to sauté" and "sauté" are the same directive.

417. (D) Choice D is the best combination of sentences 8 and 9 because it cuts out any unnecessary words. Sentence 9 does not need to repeat "to the chicken" because it is understood that you would be adding the pepper to the chicken.

418. (D) All of the options are sequencing transitions, and are appropriate in type, but this step is not the first, second, third, or last step of the recipe. As a result, "then" is the best option for a transition at the beginning of this sentence.

419. (B) Sentence 14 is too close to sentence 13, not offering any new directions or information. Sentence 14 is repetitive and redundant and should be removed.

420. (C) While these options are all suitable for concluding sentences, only choice C comments on the recipe's versatility by telling readers that it can be served at several meals and to small or large groups.

Passage 9c

421. (B) Including both the time and the place, the first sentence of the passage simply presents the setting of the passage, which is elaborated upon in the rest of the paragraph.

422. (D) In context, "outfits" here means "sets of equipment or articles for a specific purpose," which is, in this case, traveling to Santa Fe. It's not a shipment because it is traveling with them in their wagons.

423. (A) "One of these" is a steamboat. The one being presented is called the *Radnor*. The sentence before states that "almost every day steamboats were leaving."

424. (C) The boat is personified as a woman starting with the sentence "The boat was loaded until the water broke alternately over her guards." This gives the boat life, which matches the activity of the passengers and the amount of freight.

425. (D) The statement appeals to the reader's sense of adventure in discussing the long and arduous journey and it flatters the reader by praising his persevering nature.

426. (C) The writer enumerates all of the many things and people carried on the *Radnor*; the writer provides many details of the freight and the passengers on board.

427. (B) The fourth paragraph relies on description, a description of the Missouri River.

428. (A) The paragraph, with its vivid depictions of the Missouri, has a tone of awe as it impresses upon the reader the power of the river.

429. **(B)** In context, "treacherous" most nearly means "marked by hidden dangers" because the shallows are described as having secrets (something is hidden) and the next sentence discusses the frightful results (hence the danger).

430. **(A)** The tone is informative and enthusiastic, as she provides lots of accurate information about the boat and the river, while having an enthusiastic regard for all she sees.

Passage 9d

431. **(C)** While all other options provide interesting background information on the course being introduced, only choice C serves to provide a warm and inviting greeting for readers as they begin to learn about the course.

432. **(D)** While not grammatically necessary to the sentence, the underlined portion helps to amplify, or clarify, what it means to read and write as writers. The underlined portion of the sentence should not be removed because it provides helpful information.

433. **(A)** The underlined portion should be removed because it is an unnecessary phrase that does not add any meaning to the sentence.

434. **(B)** Choice B is the best combination of the two sentences because it is the shortest and simplest version. It removes all unnecessary words while leaving the meaning intact.

435. **(D)** "For example" is the best transition to begin sentence 7 because it provides three illustrations of the texts described in sentence 6. The other options suggest that sentence 7 is providing conclusions or a change in direction from sentence 6.

436. **(A)** Readers of this type of text expect this sort of information and would be interested in more examples of texts, even if they are only possibilities.

437. **(C)** Choice C is the best combination of sentences 8 and 9 because, although connected, sentence 9 is an additional thought. It is not a result of sentence 8, nor is it a change in direction, which some of the other options communicate.

438. **(D)** Although writers normally seek consistency in pronoun use, the choice of pronoun has to make sense for the content, and "we" would not work in sentence 10.

439. **(A)** The phrase "due to lateness" should not be revised because it maintains both the objectiveness and the formality that have been used throughout the passage and that are appropriate for this type of text. Choices B through E are all too informal, negative, or conversational.

440. **(C)** While all of the options provided could be used as follow-up statements after sentence 13, only choice C provides the excitement and enthusiasm the writer is hoping to communicate as the concluding remark for this passage.

Passage 9e

441. (C) The speaker opens with a series of simple sentences that lend the passage a directness from the shortness of the statements, which is coupled with a depth, or profundity, based on the heavy topic and the sentiments expressed.

442. (B) The dominant impression of sorrow, based on the first paragraph, is that it slows down the passage of time. The speaker explains this concept in several ways, including the claim that each day feels just like the last.

443. (B) Primarily, the writer is describing sorrow and his particular experience of sorrow in his prison cell. This is seen through his use of imagery.

444. (C) The first two paragraphs define, describe, and discuss sorrow as a concept, but line 22 brings the readers into the speaker's personal experiences of being a prisoner and losing his mother.

445. (C) The writer is using "it" to refer to his family's name, which he feels he has disgraced through the behavior that has led to his being imprisoned.

446. (E) The writer is a husband, writer, son, and prisoner. He refers to his wife, calls himself a former "lord of language," and mentions the calendar outside his door that has his (prison) sentence written on it. He also discusses losing his mother, but never speaks of having his own children.

447. (A) In context, "tremulous" most nearly means "exceedingly sensitive," because the writer is saying that a leaf of the most sensitive gold would register direction, probably due to the wind, that the eye cannot see, but it is less sensitive than sorrow, which is the most delicate and sensitive of all things. "Having little substance" is a close meaning, but it ignores the sensitivity that the writer is describing.

448. (C) The final paragraph uses the mode of composition of definition as it defines sorrow. This can be seen in the construction "sorrow is the most sensitive of all created things," which defines what sorrow is amongst other things. This is accomplished through language that is both descriptive (the leaf of gold) and figurative (the bleeding wound).

449. (C) While this line refers to the specific sympathy provided to the writer, overall the passage is a musing on sorrow, especially on its ability to stop time and to be more powerful than anything else. This line does not describe nor define sorrow, and defining and describing sorrow is the major purpose of this letter.

450. (A) The tone can best be described as plaintive, as the writer is sad, mournful, melancholy, etc. He discusses his never-ending sorrow, his shame at disgracing his family's name, and his grief upon losing his mother.

Chapter 10

Passage 10a

451. (A) Above all else, the writer values works that are simple. She disparages detailed works in this context as just "lively pieces of reporting" and equates all of the other qualities with writing that is successful in the moment but ultimately fleeting.

452. (D) The journalistic successes serve as counter-examples to the definition of good writing that is explored throughout the passage, which values simplicity. The journalistic successes value novelty.

453. (A) "Novelty" most nearly means "newness" in the context in which it is used. This is most clearly seen in the construction "now that the novelty upon which they counted so much is gone," which means that the newness inevitability wears off.

454. (C) "They" refers to "the dazzling journalistic successes," which is also renamed as "stories that surprised and delighted by their photographic detail."

455. (C) The author twice uses the dash in order to set apart her conclusions. One example is "novelty—never a very important thing in art," and the other is "They . . . —taught us to multiply our ideas instead of to condense them."

456. (B) The tone is ironically disparaging because the beginning of the sentence seems to be praising the merits of a good reportorial story, but ultimately the sentence is saying that these stories are useless after their one relevant moment in time.

457. (E) According to the speaker, revision should remove that which is not essential. The line "Art, it seems to me, should simplify" expresses that art should express the spirit of the whole in a form that is the tightest and most universal.

458. (D) Millet's *The Sower* is provided as an example of simplicity in composition, as the painter had hundreds of sketches but finally edited his work down to one picture that was simple.

459. (C) In the portion of the paragraph that discusses writing, not the writer, the primary mode of composition is classification, as the writer separates writing into the two categories of business and art.

460. (C) The primary mode for the whole passage is argument with the major claim of "Art, it seems to me, should simplify." The problem posed is: what are the difficulties facing young writers? Then the author of the passage offers her opinionated response, which is an argument.

Passage 10b

461. **(A)** The first sentence of the passage provides the major claim of the passage, or the thesis, that it is the writer's goal to teach students to think. What follows this statement are further elaborations and reflections on that one major idea.

462. **(B)** To use the word "critically" in place of the underlined phrase and in place of the other proposed alternatives is the best choice, because "critically" is the simplest choice and retains the parallelism of the sentence due to the use of the adverbs to modify the verbs in the other parts of the sentence.

463. **(E)** For this type of passage, background on the writer's initial thoughts on teaching and the subsequent shift in outlook are appropriate and helpful for the readers' understanding of the writer's current educational philosophy. As such, the writer should not remove sentence 3.

464. **(D)** The underlined portion of the statement should not be removed because it serves as a useful illustration of how students can refine their questions and helps to support the writer's major claim about teaching students how to think.

465. **(A)** The writer should add the underlined phrase into sentence 7 because it offers a helpful elaboration on what the writer means by "step out of the center of the classroom." Literally, the writer will not be standing in the center of the classroom, and figuratively, the writer will give students more voice and agency in the class.

466. **(C)** This sentence should be included because it serves as a useful transition between the paragraphs (expanding upon "this type of instruction") while also serving as a topic sentence that helps prepare the reader for the subsequent sentences of paragraph 3.

467. **(B)** The best combination of these two sentences uses the coordinating conjunction "but" because the second sentence changes direction from the first. Sentence 9 discusses the positive environment in which students feel safe, but sentence 10 reminds readers that this work can be messy.

468. **(D)** While all of the phrases provide details of John Dewey's life, only option D provides a general overview that is relevant to the passage and useful as an introduction to those who may not know of him.

469. **(E)** John Dewey's quotation is used to support the claim that thinking can be unpredictable and what will emerge in the classroom may be surprising. While the other sentences support other claims in the passage, this quotation most clearly supports the claim that "thinking is not predictable."

470. **(D)** The writer should not remove the sentence because it serves as a conclusion for the paragraph and the passage. The writer is using this sentence to summarize the role of the educator as defined throughout.

Passage 10c

471. (C) The first paragraph serves the purpose of classification, as the writer classifies the subjects of feminine literature into cooking, children, clothing, and moral instruction.

472. (D) The second paragraph, which is quoted to be in the voice of someone other than the writer, presents counterargument. The counterargument is that there is no men's literature because men are people and women are distinguished as the opposite sex.

473. (C) The tone of the second paragraph can best be described as "exasperated," which can be defined as irritated or provoked. This can be seen through the use of exclamations.

474. (C) "Generally speaking" qualifies the statement that women had only recently been taught to read, meaning that the original claim is a generalization and the author qualifies, or modifies, the original statement by acknowledging that it is a generalization and that there are exceptions to the rule.

475. (A) The writer puts the two terms in quotation marks to distance herself from speaking them, as an indication that she does not agree with these categorizations.

476. (E) In context, "construed" most nearly means "understood." In this sense, the sentence means that men are not put into a strictly understood category of what it means to be a man; however, women are put in such a category.

477. (C) The reference to women as "the sex" means that they are the only gendered sex. In other words, men are just people and women are women.

478. (E) The portion of the sentence in parentheses is an allusion to the Bible. It alludes to the fact that Eve was made from the rib of Adam—that is, she is a "side-issue." This allusion helps make the claim that men are considered the dominant sex, or to be more human, while women are considered "the sex," or the gendered sex.

479. (B) The phrase "vertical reach" is used make a claim about the uses of literature through time. The "lateral spread" is about reaching a lot of people and the "vertical reach" is about spanning time with the permanence of written literature.

480. (C) The final paragraph introduces the examples of masculine literature that will be discussed in the next paragraphs. The writer will begin with the examples of history and fiction.

Passage 10d

481. (D) The writer should not remove the underlined portion of sentence 4 because it offers information on past and potential future guests based on the hotel's location. It is not meant to be exclusive, and it just serves to offer pertinent information.

482. (D) Choice D is the only one that describes the building's style, which is what the writer is hoping to communicate. The other options all add information about Kevin Roche.

483. (A) "All" should be removed because it is unnecessary and misleading. It is not the many destinations that are making this a perfect location, but rather, it is the fact that the hotel is within walking distance of them.

484. (E) By using the word "guests" and saying that they "may want to," the writer can create an inviting tone for readers to exercise if they wish. The other options are more forceful and declarative rather than inviting.

485. (D) The writer should not remove sentence 9 because it is an appropriate and useful sentence to be included in a travel blog, which offers helpful tips to readers about when to stay, what to do, why to visit, and so on.

486. (C) "For example" is the best transition between sentences 10 and 11 because sentence 10 claims that there are many dining options on the property, and sentence 11 provides the first of several examples of those dining options.

487. (B) Sentence 12 is the second example of a dining option in this paragraph so "Second," is the most fitting transition to begin this sentence. Although the first example in sentence 11 did not use the transition "First," that sentence still provided the first dining option example.

488. (D) As sentence 13 provides another example of a dining option on the hotel property, "In addition" is the most fitting transition for this sentence. The other options express a relationship of contrast, comparison, or conclusion between sentences 12 and 13 that does not fit the writer's needs.

489. (C) For the fourth and final dining option, "Finally" is the best transition to begin sentence 14. Choices A and B are too formal for this sentence and passage, and choices D and E both express that a conclusion is forthcoming, which is not fitting for sentence 14.

490. (C) Choice C effectively concludes the passage by returning to the opening claims and highlighting all of the hotel's offerings, not just focusing on smaller, minor claims.

Passage 10e

491. (B) The purpose of the passage is to narrate how women's labor has shifted according to the changes in the types of society over time. The chronological structure helps readers to see her narration.

492. (A) "Clamour" most nearly means "loud continuous noise" in context. The sentence states that beneath the clamour (continuous noise), a keynote can be heard.

493. **(C)** The tone of the sentence is insistent and forceful, as it is making a demand, which is to give women labor and training.

494. **(C)** The sentence uses anaphora as it repeats "we" in the successive clauses that display all of the many tasks that women did to serve humanity. This repetition shows the varied roles and talents of women, including artistic and domestic skill, physical strength, and intelligence.

495. **(E)** The statement is a rhetorical question, but it also relies on anaphora, with its repetition of "while" at the beginning of the successive clauses, and it shows the strength, resiliency, constancy, and capacity. It shows women's patience and reliability, not impatience.

496. **(D)** The greatest shift occurs at line 40 because that is the point in the passage in which men move into the women's spheres and take their work. The shift that happens at line 14 doesn't mark such a big transition because women still have most of their forms of labor.

497. **(D)** The purpose of the sentence is to level the different types of women, be they wives of men of status or not, and to express that all women had work to do regardless of their class distinctions.

498. **(A)** The tone can best be described as resilient as the writer discusses how women, even after all of the changes that have altered their role, continue to have work to do and how they continued doing such labor as was needed.

499. **(E)** The passage moves from the distant past into the more recent past; therefore, it's chronological in sequence. This can be seen in the time-marking transitional paragraphs, such as "Then a change came" and "Then again a change came."

500. **(A)** The primary mode of the passage is narration because, although the writer is making a claim about how women's work has changed over time, the way in which the writer expresses her points is in the form of narration. She is telling the story of woman's labor over time.

NOTES

NOTES